W9-BLI-868

THE TAROT

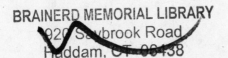
BRAINERD MEMORIAL LIBRARY
920 Saybrook Road
Haddam, CT 06438

ROBERT M. PLACE

CRIVENS MEMORIAL LIBRARY

HISTORY,

SYMBOLISM, AND

DIVINATION

JEREMY P. TARCHER/PENGUIN
a member of Penguin Group (USA) Inc.
New York

JEREMY P. TARCHER/PENGUIN
Published by the Penguin Group
Penguin Group (USA) Inc., 375 Hudson Street, New York, New York 10014, USA •
Penguin Group (Canada), 10 Alcorn Avenue, Toronto, Ontario, Canada M4V 3B2 (a division
of Pearson Penguin Canada Inc.) • Penguin Books Ltd, 80 Strand, London WC2R ORL,
England • Penguin Ireland, 25 St Stephen's Green, Dublin 2, Ireland (a division of Penguin
Books Ltd) • Penguin Group (Australia), 250 Camberwell Road, Camberwell, Victoria 3124,
Australia (a division of Pearson Australia Group Pty Ltd) • Penguin Books India Pvt Ltd,
11 Community Centre, Panchsheel Park, New Delhi–110 017, India • Penguin Group (NZ),
Cnr Airborne and Rosedale Roads, Albany, Auckland 1310, New Zealand (a division of Pearson
New Zealand Ltd) • Penguin Books (South Africa) (Pty) Ltd, 24 Sturdee Avenue,
Rosebank, Johannesburg 2196, South Africa

Penguin Books Ltd, Registered Offices: 80 Strand, London WC2R 0RL, England

Copyright © 2005 by Robert M. Place
All rights reserved. No part of this book may be reproduced, scanned, or
distributed in any printed or electronic form without permission. Please do not
participate in or encourage piracy of copyrighted materials in violation of the
author's rights. Purchase only authorized editions.
Published simultaneously in Canada

Most Tarcher/Penguin books are available at special quantity discounts for bulk purchase
for sales promotions, premiums, fund-raising, and educational needs. Special books or book
excerpts also can be created to fit specific needs. For details, write Penguin Group (USA) Inc.
Special Markets, 375 Hudson Street, New York, NY 10014.

Library of Congress Cataloging-in-Publication Data
Place, Robert Michael.
    The tarot : history, symbolism, and divination / Robert M. Place.
       p.   cm.
    Includes bibliographical references and index.
    ISBN 1-58542-349-1
    1. Tarot.   I. Title.
    BF1879.T2P56   2005   2004058065
    133.3'2424—dc22

Printed in the United States of America
10 9 8 7 6 5 4 3 2 1

Book design by Mauna Eichner

THIS BOOK IS DEDICATED TO CORMAC AND TADHG.

ACKNOWLEDGMENTS

I wish to thank my editor, Mitch Horowitz, for his enthusiasm and encouragement on this project. I want to thank historian Ronald Decker for his assistance and for answering my inquiries, and historians Michael Dummett, Robert O'Neill, and Tom Tadfor Little for also answering my inquiries and providing leads. I want to thank William M. Voelkle for making a copy of de Gébelin's text for me. I wish to thank Grazia Mirti for providing me with a copy of Fanti's *Triompho di Fortuna*. I also want to thank my wife, Rose Ann, for her encouragement and assistance. And thank you to Arthur Edward Waite for sending me the Tarot in a dream.

CONTENTS

THE TAROT

INTRODUCTION

It will be thought that I am acting strangely
in concerning myself at this day with what appears at first sight
and simply a well-known method of fortune-telling.
—A. E. WAITE, FROM HIS PREFACE TO *THE PICTORIAL KEY*
TO THE TAROT, 1910

I have been interested in the Tarot and other esoteric subjects since I was studying art in the late 1960s. My girlfriend at that time read the cards. She used the deck that was then called the Rider Waite deck but is now commonly referred to by Tarot scholars as the Waite-Smith deck. With its colorful archetypal images, this early twentieth-century deck is what will come to mind for most people when they think of Tarot.

At that time, I even began to create my own hand-drawn deck based on the Tarot of Marseilles, the traditional French deck that developed in the seventeenth century, but I finished only four cards before I lost interest in the project. Although as an artist I have always been involved in symbolism in my work, I was not directly engaged with the Tarot for many years after that.

When I did become reacquainted with the Tarot, I did not actually choose so in a conscious way. It started with a dream in the summer of 1982, a dream that startled me with its clarity and intensity. I was dreaming that I was following someone through a red brick building. Then I dreamed that a phone rang, interrupting the events of the first dream in the same way that a phone call can interrupt one's thoughts during the day. The sound of the phone startled me into lucidity and intensified the events in the dream in a way that made them impossible to forget. I remember thinking, *How can someone call you in a dream? I didn't know that could happen.* Even in the dream it was clear that this message came from a place distant from my normal consciousness. The phone was the perfect symbol for this. I picked up the dream phone and on the other end I found an international operator, who informed me that she had a person-to-person call for me from a law firm in England. I accepted the call, and a secretary from the firm came on the line. She told me that she was sending me my "ancestral inheritance." She could not tell me what it was, but only that it would come from England, it is kept in a box, and that it is sometimes called the key. She added that I would know it when I saw it. Then she ended the conversation with some precautions: this gift contained a hidden power, but before I could receive this gift, I had to accept the responsibility that came with it. I accepted without hesitation.

I awoke that morning naively expecting to find the box at the foot of my bed; but, of course, there was nothing there. As the week progressed, I eagerly anticipated receiving my "inheritance." In a few days, a friend came over with his new deck of Tarot cards. It was the Waite-Smith deck, the deck designed in England in 1909 by Pamela Colman Smith with the direction of Arthur Edward Waite, and it came with a book authored by Waite called *The Pictorial Key to the Tarot*. As my friend walked through the door, I felt my head turn in his direction as if of its own accord. My eyes also seemed to be working on their own. As they focused on what he was holding, I knew that this was my inheritance. This was not, of course, the first time that I had seen this deck, but I now saw it in a new light. After my friend left, taking his Tarot with him, I made up my mind that I would obtain a Tarot of my own.

In a few more days another friend came to visit and gave me the traditional French deck, The Tarot of Marseilles. This is the deck that evolved in southern France in the seventeenth century and came to this final form in the eighteenth century. It was the one that first drew the attention of the eighteenth- and nineteenth-century occultists, and because of that it has come to be considered the standard deck. My friend said that he just had a feeling that I needed a Tarot deck and he had an old copy of the Marseilles deck hanging around. This was the first deck that I owned, but the Waite-Smith deck remained on my mind, and soon I made a trip from the New Jersey suburbs, where I lived, into Manhattan to buy a copy.

Over the next month, I began experimenting with the cards. At first, I resolved not to read any books on the Tarot since most books that were available then on the Tarot passed on spurious histories and misinformation that stemmed from the occult fantasies of the nineteenth century. I wanted to communicate directly with the images unhindered by these preconceptions. My girlfriend had shown me the so-called Celtic cross spread in college, which involved laying out seven cards in an equal-arm cross and another four in a column to the side for further commentary. So I decided to begin with that approach combined with Jungian techniques of dream interpretation.

As I worked with the Waite-Smith cards, the images spoke to me with amazing clarity. Over the next few months, I began developing new techniques for reading, designed to clarify the communication. From the images alone, I was able to glean philosophical messages that related to my questions. The answers opened up new questions and I began to search for the best books that I could find on the Tarot, Neoplatonism, Gnosticism, alchemy, Renaissance art, ancient and Renaissance philosophy, and related subjects.

The Tarot was like a door that opened onto the Western mystical tradition. I wanted to discover who devised this series of images. I wanted to know the artists who created this deck and to understand what its original creators and users were thinking. Every table in my studio was soon covered with stacks of books reaching toward the ceiling, and I filled a large hardbound notebook with charts, lists, and notes. I was on my way to becoming a Tarot scholar and my primary guide was the Tarot itself.

Since then, I have written four books on the Tarot and created four modern decks. Each book was intended to accompany one of my decks, exploring its particular theme and relationship to Tarot tradition. This, my fifth book, is not about one of my decks. It is about the Tarot in general and how it can be one's companion on the mystical quest. Here I will focus on the imagery in the Waite-Smith deck but I will also delve into the history that lies behind these images and will share my insights on how to use the Tarot for divination.

Occultists, from the eighteenth century on, have recognized that the Tarot illustrates a mystical philosophy. To explain this, they have often resorted to creating a fanciful and exotic origin for the deck. The most popular choice has been ancient Egypt but others have suggested Morocco or even China. Occultists have also invented systems that connect the Tarot to systems such as the Kabalah, the Hebrew alphabet, and astrology. Often their misconceptions lead one away from a true understanding of the actual imagery that is in the Tarot. Historians, meanwhile, have been able to correct these factual errors but have offered little that would help one to understand the Tarot's symbolism. Some historians have gone as far as denying that the images in the Tarot have one unified message. To understand what is in the Tarot, I feel that it is essential to examine its historic origin in the Italian Renaissance, to study the iconography and symbolism of that era, and to explore the relationship of that art to the ancient mystical philosophy that was revered by Renaissance artists and writers. This method helps ground one's understanding of the Tarot in the history of its actual development, while connecting to the mystical philosophy and symbolism that underscore the deck's synchronous uses. This has been my approach in this book.

Of all the occultists, Waite was one who recognized the historical inaccuracies of his colleagues and was quick to point out their fallacies. But he also realized that the Tarot contained a timeless mystical teaching, for which he used the label coined by the philosopher Leibniz, the perennial philosophy. By making use of historical information that was not available to Waite I have been able to verify his insight and show that the Tarot does contain a mystical philosophy expressed in pictures. Its text describes how one can find divinity within, and it can be used to open a dialogue with that inner light. This book will help the reader to see the Tarot as its creators would have seen it and acquaint her or him with a mystical heritage that is at the root of our culture. The book is not only about the Tarot but about this forgotten heritage.

THE HISTORY
OF THE TAROT

We shall see in due course that the history of the Tarot cards
is largely of a negative kind, and that, when the issues are cleared by
the dissipation of reveries and gratuitous speculations expressed in
the terms of certitude, there is in fact no history prior to the
fourteenth century. The deception and the self-deception regarding
their origin in Egypt, India or China put a lying spirit into the mouths
of the first expositors, and the later occult writers have done little
more than reproduce the first false testimony in the good faith of an
intelligence unawakened to the issues of research.
—A. E. WAITE, *THE PICTORIAL KEY TO THE TAROT*

The first time I picked up a Tarot deck I was instantly fascinated with its imagery and symbolism. Who is not fascinated by this deck that is similar to an ordinary deck of playing cards but that contains a fifth suit illustrated with a sequence of twenty-two mysterious characters from another time? Some, like Death and the Wheel of Fortune, are recognizable in modern culture. Others, like the Hanged Man and the World, have grown obscure over time.

Between the fifteenth century when the Tarot was created and the present, some have attempted to explain its mysteries with fanciful theories and speculative history. Starting in the eighteenth century, Western occultists claimed that the Tarot originated as a spiritual text in ancient Egypt and that it was spread through Europe by Gypsies. Others affirmed that the trump cards—or Major Arcana, as they were labeled by occultists—contain a type of secret code in which each of their twenty-two images is related to a letter of the Hebrew alphabet. In the Kabalah, the Hebrew letters are each associated with a planet, a sign of the zodiac, or an element. Therefore, with this correlation with the alphabet, the trumps became associated with these celestial symbols as well. None of these assertions are supported by historical evidence nor by a study of the iconography that appears on the cards. These unsupported correspondences have served to widen the gap in understanding between the fifteenth-century Italian artists who first illustrated the deck and its modern users. Indeed, these misperceptions have cut us off from the genuine philosophy and wisdom that is expressed in this allegorical series of cards. In this chapter, we will explore the known facts concerning the history of the Tarot and will develop a theory of its origin based on those facts. But first let us become acquainted with the nature and structure of a Tarot deck.

TAROT DEFINED

The Tarot is a deck of cards that developed in northern Italy in the early fifteenth century. Today, in English-speaking countries, the Tarot is primarily used for divination. Although there is evidence that it was used for that purpose in fifteenth-century Italy, its primary use at that time was to play a game. This game is the ancestor of the modern game of bridge. The early decks are consistent in that they have five suits. Four of these are similar to a modern poker deck with ten cards, called pips, displaying one or more repetitions of a suit symbol, and from four to six others called courts or royals, with depictions of figures of ascending rank. Besides these four suits, the Tarot possesses a fifth suit, consisting of a parade of illustrated cards each bearing a mysterious symbolic image. These cards are called trumps, but one card in the fifth suit, called the Fool, is not truly a trump but a "wild card" that can be played instead of a trump. The trumps together with the Fool illustrate a mystical allegory, as will be explained throughout this book. (Although the trumps and the Fool are referred to as a fifth suit in this book, some modern historians do not consider the term *suit* appropriate because the trumps do not contain a consistent suit symbol like the four minor suits.)

In most early examples of the fifth suit, the cards are unnumbered, unlabeled, and their quantity varies. Because many of the early decks that we have in collections today are fragmented and incomplete, we cannot be certain how many cards were originally included in the trumps in every deck. It appears that the largest number of trumps is contained in the sixteenth-century Florentine version of the deck, called the Minchiate, which has forty trumps and a Fool. Because twenty-one trumps and a Fool became standard in later seventeenth-century decks and many of the early fragmented decks do not contain characters that would not be accounted for in these twenty-two cards, it is likely that most fifteenth-century decks also contained twenty-one trumps and a Fool in the fifth suit. From literary sources and early numbered decks, scholars have determined that there were several variations in the order of trumps as they were commonly used in Italian games and in the existing examples of individual cards we can see that the Italian artists varied in their interpretation of many of the images on the trumps.

By 1507, Marseilles, France, and the surrounding area had become a center of Tarot production outside of Italy.[1] Eventually, the manufacturers of the Marseilles trumps consistently numbered the trumps with roman numerals, labeled them with French titles, and standardized their order. Over the next two centuries, the symbolism and imagery on each trump also grew more standardized. During the seventeenth century, the iconography of the deck as we know it today had been set. Several manufacturers existed, but there was little variation in the imagery. Presently, the most well-known example of the Tarot of Marseilles is the one that was first published in 1748 by the French card manufacturer Grimaud, and which can still be purchased from that company. Over the centuries, numerous Tarots from Marseilles were exported to other countries in Europe and manufacturers of Tarots in Paris, Switzerland, northern Italy, and other locations printed "Marseilles" decks as well. Hence, the title Tarot of Marseilles now refers to a style of Tarot that may or may not be printed in Marseilles. This is the deck that came to the attention of the occultists in the eighteenth and nineteenth centuries and on which they based their theories. All modern Tarots, including the influential early twentieth-century Waite-Smith deck, designed by occultist Arthur Edward Waite and artist Pamela Coleman Smith, are based on the Tarot of Marseilles, so for that reason it will be helpful to become acquainted with its structure.

In the Tarot of Marseilles there are seventy-eight cards divided into five suits as described above. The four suits known to occultists as the Minor Arcana contain four courts and ten pips. They are somewhat like a modern poker deck but contain four instead of three courts: the jack or page, the knight, the queen, and the king. The suit symbols are the same as the ones used for playing cards with four suits in Spain and parts of Italy—staffs, swords, coins, and cups—instead of the French and English clubs, spades, diamonds, and hearts. In the Waite-Smith deck these suit symbols have been transformed into the tools of a magician: wands, swords, pentacles, and cups.

It is the addition of the fifth suit of twenty-two cards, known to occultists as the Major Arcana and consisting of an unnumbered Fool card and twenty-one trumps, that makes this deck a Tarot. These cards depict an allegorical parade of enigmatic images each one triumphing over, or trumping, its predecessor. In the Tarot of Marseilles, the Major Arcana consist of:

the Fool

I. the Bateleur or the Magician

II. the Papesse

III. the Empress

IV. the Emperor

V. the Pope

VI. the Lover

VII. the Chariot

VIII. Justice

IX. the Hermit

X. the Wheel of Fortune

XI. Force or Strength

XII. the Hanged Man

XIII. Death

XIV. Temperance

XV. the Devil

XVI. the House of God, the Tower of Destruction, or the Tower

XVII. the Star

XVIII. the Moon

XIX. the Sun

XX. Judgement*

XXI. the World

Judgement is spelled as it appears in the Tarot of Marseilles; this spelling is retained elsewhere when referencing this card.

In the modern Waite-Smith deck, the trumps fall in the same numbered order, except that the positions of Justice and Strength are reversed, making Strength number eight and Justice number eleven. Also, when he discusses them in his book, Waite places the Fool, which he numbered zero, between trumps twenty and twenty-one. Waite's names for the cards are essentially the same except that the Papesse has been renamed the High Priestess, and the Pope has been renamed the Hierophant. Waite's reasons for these changes will be explained later.

CARDS AND PAPER

In order to begin our understanding of the history of the Tarot, it is useful to explore the medium in which it exists: paper. As we will see in the next chapter, eighteenth- and nineteenth-century occultists popularized the notion that the Tarot cards were first created in Egypt. But occultists were ignoring one of the basic physical facts about cards. Cards are made of paper and the ancient Egyptians did not have this material. Some occultists tried to correct this oversight by making unsupported declarations that the first Tarot was engraved on gold or ivory or painted on walls or panels. If, however, we define cards as images that can be painted or printed on paper, then, without paper, cards do not exist. When one examines the nature of cards and their use in card games it is apparent that the invention of paper allowed the idea of a card to develop. Paper is thin and durable. It can easily be painted or printed on. It holds its edge and its integrity when cut into cards and allows the cards to be shuffled for the purpose of game playing. To find the origin of cards in general we must look to China because this is where paper was invented.

In the second century c.e., the Chinese began to make a pulp from the bark of the mulberry tree and press and dry it into thin sheets. According to legend, the credit for the invention belongs to the emperor's eunuch, Ts'ai Lun.[2] This new substance that he discovered could be made in varying thickness, retained its edge, and lay flat without crinkling. It could be painted or drawn on, and eventually it was discovered that it would accept ink from a carved block. This innovation allowed the Chinese to become the first people in the world to create printed books, paper money, and cards. For approximately five hundred years, the art of papermaking remained confined to China and then it began to spread across Asia. Paper was introduced to Egypt from Asia around the year 800, but was not manufactured there until 900. Paper was not introduced to Europe until the twelfth century. The first European paper was manufactured in 1151 in Xativa, Spain.

In China, cards were first made as a substitute for playing pieces made of ivory, wood, or bone, but these first cards were small and thick, like the pieces that they were imitating. When the full potential of the medium was realized, paper cards became wider and thinner. They took on a unique quality of their own. They provided a suitable broad surface for creating a small work of art, a depiction of a character or a scene.

Other materials have been used for cards at times, such as mica in India and Tibet and leather by the Native Americans, but these are afterthoughts that came later, created in imitation of paper cards when paper was not available. The ancient Egyptians had papyrus, a material made by pressing and gluing stems cut from a variety of marsh grass of the same name. Later, in the Hellenistic period, they developed parchment, which was made from the skin of sheep or other animals, but neither of these materials lend themselves to the creation of cards. Papyrus tends to fray at the edge and was therefore used in a long scroll. With the development of parchment, books could be made with individual pages, but separate unbound pieces of parchment tend to crinkle and bend, and cannot easily be stacked or shuffled.

THE CHINESE DECK

It is believed that for the ancient Chinese, cards and money were one and the same at first. Historians speculate that paper money was used not only as the stakes but also as the actual cards in the first card games. This connection is suggested by the similarity of design found in early examples of Chinese paper money dating from the thirteenth century and Chinese cards, from the earliest specimens of uncertain date to the most modern. The Chinese language does not distinguish between playing pieces carved from ivory, bone, or wood, and those made by printing designs on paper. Like ivory, bone, or wood playing pieces, the first paper cards were small and thick and their designs had a primitive simplicity that fit the carving technique. From the beginning, cards have been associated with gambling and money.

We find various descriptions in the accounts of Chinese games. One account describes a deck of three suits (see figure 1):[3]

1. Cakes, which was originally called money, and depicts one to nine coins on each card in the suit.

2. Strings, which was originally called strings of money, and depicts one to nine cylindrical stacks. The familiar Chinese coin has a square hole in

Figure 1. A rendering of Chinese money cards from a European collection, from left to right: cakes, strings, myriads, and a figure card. Each measures 2" by ½".

the center which allows a string to be passed through to tie the coins into a stack. Paper money had images of these stacks on bills of higher denomination.

3. Myriads, which denotes larger denominations of money, and is depicted abstractly.

Besides these suits, there are three cards with human figures called Red Flower, White Flower, and Old Thousand. At times, instead of these names, these cards bear the names of kings, princes, and heros of Chinese legend. The deck also contains five extra cards that are not always used in the game. On these we find figures representing the five virtues: luck, promotion, longevity, prosperity, and wealth. It is easy to see in this antique Chinese deck similarities with the deck that would eventually emerge in the fifteenth century in Italy. But first we will turn our attention to how cards continued their spread though the East.

THE EGYPTIAN DECK

As the art of papermaking spread through Asia toward the Middle East, new card games were developed. The cards become thinner wider, and taller. Images of gods, kings, and heros were painted or drawn on them. We can find examples of round, oval, and rectangular cards, cards for gambling, and cards used for religious instruction, ritual, and divination. New card games were invented by the Indians and the Persians and cards spread through the Islamic world. It is believed that the Islamic culture introduced cards into Europe. The deck that is thought to have been introduced is called the Mamluk deck, named after the Mamluk dynasty who ruled Egypt and Syria from 1250 to 1517. It was the Mamluks who threw the Crusaders out of Palestine.

The Crusaders first captured Jerusalem on Christmas Day in the year 1100. They maintained a hold in the area until a Mamluk army under the command of Baybars drove them out on May 18, 1291. Afterward, the Mamluks initiated an era of prosperity and relative stability in which they are likely to have created their deck. Card historian Michael Dummett believes that their deck may be based on a Persian model.

Forty-seven cards from two Mamluk decks are part of a modern collection on display in a museum in Turkey. While they date from the 1400s, a fragment of a similar card from the thirteenth or fourteenth century exists in a private collection and attests to their earlier origin. The cards are sumptuously hand painted and gilded in the Arabic style—obviously created for the wealthy ruling class. It is evident that the complete deck possessed four suits: polo sticks, cups, coins, and scimitars. There were ten pips in each suit that contain designs created out of repetitions of the suit symbol and arabesque abstractions filling in all available space. Three court cards were included in each suit, which because of the Islamic prohibition on figurative art, contain only the suit symbol and a calligraphic inscription for the rank of the card: governor, lieutenant, or second lieutenant.[4]

METHODS OF PRODUCTION

Although our examples of Mamluk cards are hand painted, we may wonder if Islamic card makers also produced less valuable printed cards. As we saw in China, printing was used for cards from an early date. The two skills needed for making printing plates—woodblock carving and metal engraving—were practiced in Western Europe during the early Middle Ages. The ingredient that was missing for creating prints before the twelfth century was paper. Woodcutters made blocks for decorating cloth, and engravers worked on armor, jewelry, and religious plaques for Bibles and altars. In the twelfth century, Islamic culture supplied the missing element, paper, and the craft of making it. In the fourteenth century paper cards were introduced to Europe, most likely in Spain or Sicily where Muslim and Christian culture intermingled for a brief period.

Because cards are ephemeral, we lack examples of European cards from the 1300s. Literary sources tell us that cards existed in Europe at that time, but all of the examples of cards that we have are from the 1440s and after. These include both hand-drawn and printed cards. It is assumed that the hand-drawn ones came first, yet both types exist side by side and we cannot say for sure. Also, it is sometimes difficult to make a sharp distinction between what is hand drawn and what is printed, because cards that are drawn may make use of production techniques such as stencils and templates. Also, on block-printed and engraved cards, the black lines, which delineate the image, are printed from a woodblock or a metal plate but the colors may be hand painted or stippled through a stencil.

In a related development, new printers' guilds began to form in the 1400s for the purpose of producing illustrated books. These guilds were structured as a hierarchy with the illustrator at the top, the cutter or engraver below them, and the workers who inked the plate on the bottom. There were also workers who added color with the help of stencils and workers of a higher status who did hand coloring. The illustrator ran the guild, drew the designs, laid out the text. It is believed that he drew and wrote directly on the plate, which the cutter then cut. The entire text for a page, sometimes with the illustrations, was carved on one plate. Some of the first European cards were manufactured by these guilds, as a sideline to the production of books.

The invention of movable type, in 1437, was the most important cultural development in Europe since the introduction of paper. With paper and this new, less expensive printing technique, books and ideas became available to a wider segment of society, particularly the literate merchant class. The printing industry expanded as never before, and all types of printing were more in demand, including pictures and cards. To meet the demand, some printers specialized in cards. They printed secular cards for games and religious cards with pictures of saints designed for pilgrims visiting shrines and cathedrals. As we will see, wealthy nobles and merchants also commissioned art workshops to create entirely hand-painted decks of cards. The patron often commissioned the same artists to paint portraits, murals, and illustrated books. Any cards that were not created in a printing guild would have been made by these artists.

EUROPEAN DECKS

We can trace the spread of cards across Europe by searching prohibitions on games of chance and noticing when card games first appeared on these lists. In the late Middle Ages, as now, there were legal restrictions on gambling but although the primary use of cards was for gambling they are conspicuously absent from any such prohibitions until 1367, when they were banned in Bern, Switzerland. We find a similar ban in Florence in 1376, in Lille, France, in 1382[5] and in Barcelona in the same year.[6] We also find cards listed in inventories and mentioned in sermons and other literature. As the evidence begins to multiply, we can see that card games have spread over most of Western Europe.

These fourteenth-century decks were not Tarots, however. They were decks with four suits, each with ten pips and three court cards. They are the ancestors of modern playing cards, but the original suit symbols were staves, cups, coins, and swords. These suit symbols appear to be modeled on the Mamluk suits of polo sticks, cups, coins, and scimitars. The polo sticks of the Mamluk deck were simply bent sticks, not like the long-handled mallets used in the modern sport. To the Europeans, who were unfamiliar with the game of polo, the sticks would have appeared as batons or staffs. The suits of cups and coins are essentially the same and, while many European decks came to depict a straight sword as the symbol of the fourth suit, the oldest decks, particularly in Italy, depicted a sword with a curved blade like a scimitar.

As cards spread through Europe, different suits were created. We have evidence of games with suits of hounds and the tools of the hunt, with suits of flowers, bears, hares, parrots, lions, deer, leaves, acorns, and wild men. There were games with round or oval cards and games with up to sixteen suits. We can find numerous decks printed in Germany in the sixteenth century with illustrations and written instruction in music, arithmetic, astronomy, and other subjects, indicating that cards were also used for education. Two Renaissance books, the *Mainz Fortune-telling Book,* published in Ulm circa 1487, and *Le Sorti,* published in Venice in 1540,[7] both provide instruction for the use of an ordinary four-suit playing-card deck for divination or fortune-telling. Primarily, however, cards were used for gambling and game playing.

As successful game playing involves a familiarity with the deck and the rank of the cards, games tend to become standardized and these standard patterns persist over time. The different areas or countries of Europe each developed a set of four standard suit symbols for use on cards, and cards with these suit symbols can still be purchased in each of these countries today. A chart of these standard symbols is illustrated in figure 2.

In this chart, we can see that both Italy and Spain maintained the suit symbols that are based on the Mamluk deck; Italy even retained the curved blade of the scimitar. These decks also contain three all-male royal cards—the European

Figure 2. A chart of standard suit symbols for the countries of Western Europe

equivalent of the Mamluk military ranks: a knave or squire, a knight, and a king. Some German decks pictured a knave or squire, a knight, a queen, and a king for the royal cards; at times, the knight was dropped. This order presents a clear hierarchy of rank. As in feudal society, the squire is the apprentice to the knight; the alternative title, knave, refers to a servant who serves the knight; the knight, in true chivalrous fashion, is pledged to serve the queen, and she, in turn, to serve the king.

THE FIRST TAROTS

All known evidence indicates that the first deck that we would call a Tarot was created in the early fifteenth century in northern Italy when a fifth suit, containing allegorical figures, was added to the already existing deck of cards. From literary evidence and observation of games played with the deck, we can determine that the main purpose of a Tarot deck was for playing a new trick-taking game in which the fifth suit acted as trumps. This game is the ancestor of the modern game of bridge but the original form of the game is still played in parts of Europe.[8] Bridge was designed to be played with a standard four-suit deck and, therefore, one of the suits has to be designated as the trump suit. In the Tarot, there is a natural trump suit. The English word *trump* is derived from the original Italian name for this suit, *trionfi,* which means "triumphs."

A triumph, as we shall see, was a type of parade popular in the Renaissance, in which each character triumphs over or trumps the one before. Renaissance artists commonly made use of the triumph as a metaphorical structure for mystical allegories in which virtues trumped vices and the final victor or triumph was an image of the highest mystical truth. The Tarot trumps would seem to be another example of this. In the Renaissance, even a game or an amusement was considered a suitable venue for illustrating a profound mystical philosophy in symbolic form.

There is disagreement on precisely when the first recognizable Tarot was designed. Tarot historians Michael Dummett and Ronald Decker believe that the Tarot was created in the 1420s.[9] Other historians widen this time to a period from 1410 to 1430. The reason for the uncertainty hinges on the work of the contemporary Italian historian Franco Pratesi. Pratesi has uncovered literary evidence of decks from this period in which a fifth suit was added to the existing four-suit deck, but the fifth suit is not closely related to what we have come to think of as the standard Tarot, i.e., twenty-one trumps and a Fool. Additionally, it is not always clear if the added cards actually constitute a fifth suit.

For example, in 1420 or earlier, an astrologer named Marziano da Tortona designed a deck for Duke Filippo Maria Visconti of Milan (1392–1447). In this deck, he included sixteen cards with images of Classical gods. Four of these were assigned to each suit, where they represented higher powers, more powerful than the royal cards. In the game played with this deck, these cards effectively acted as trumps.[10] Here we can see that the problem of dating the creation of the Tarot is connected to the question of defining what we would consider a Tarot.

Dummett identifies either Milan, Ferrara, or Bologna, all of which are in the north of Italy, as the possible birthplace of the Tarot. Each of these cities was a center for the manufacturing of cards, and can display the earliest documentary evidence of their existence.[11] Surviving cards and documents also indicate that by the end of the fifteenth century the Tarot was produced in Florence, Urbino, Venice, and other cities in Northern Italy.[12]

In the earliest literary evidence that is definitely referring to a Tarot, the deck is called *carte da trionfi,* in other words, a deck of cards with triumphs added. Around 1530, the name was changed to Tarocchi, the origin of our name Tarot. No one knows the etymology of the word Tarocchi. One guess is that it is derived from the name of the Taro River, a tributary of the Po River in northern Italy. Rivers like the Taro were a necessary source of power to turn the mill wheels in the first paper mills. The Taro River might have been the center of a paper and card-making industry. The most likely reason for the change in name is apparently that the game of triumphs was being played in Italy with an ordinary playing-card deck, and, as in bridge, the players would assign the status of trump to one of the four suits. Therefore, triumphs or trumps became an ambiguous term, and a new name was needed for the five-suited deck. There is evidence that this type of trick-taking game with a four-suited deck called Karnoffel was being played in northern Europe in the early fifteenth century, and Karnoffel or one of its relatives may have influenced Italian games.

The first definite evidence of the existence of *carte da trionfi* is a written statement in the court records in Ferrara, Italy, in 1442. Entries referring to *carte da trionfi* in the court records of Ferrara also appear in 1452, 1454, and 1461, but none appeared before 1442.[13] Historians like Michael Dummett and Ronald Decker assign an earlier date for the creation of the Tarot because they reason that the deck must have been created sometime before it would appear in an inventory and evidence suggests that the deck evolved from an earlier form.

The oldest existing Tarot cards are 271 cards from fifteen fragmented decks painted in the 1450s for the Visconti-Sforza family, the rulers of Milan.[14] We also have fragments of hand-painted fifteenth-century decks from other Italian cities including Venice and Ferrara but the ones from Milan appear to be the oldest.

Most examples that we have were saved because they are valuable works of art made for nobles. We have fewer examples of printed decks from the fifteenth century. If the original decks were less expensive prints, they were probably not considered valuable. Therefore, they would have been discarded after they were well used or were possibly lost through mishap. We also have literary references that mention cards being burned as a sacrifice in the "bonfires of the vanities" which marked the end of the bawdy festival, Carnival, and the beginning of the pious period of Lent.[15] Printed decks have always been more ephemeral. For example, historian Michael Dummett points out that of the 1 million Tarot decks believed to have been created in France in the seventeenth century we now have only three, not all of which have all of their cards.[16]

The most complete of the early decks in existence is the hand-painted Visconti-Sforza deck, also known as the Pierpont Morgan–Bergamo deck, because the majority of its cards are now in the collections of the Pierpont Morgan Library in New York and the Accademia Carrara, in Bergamo, Italy. Seventy-four cards are in existence from this hand-painted deck which is dated circa 1450. Among the seventy-four cards are a Fool and nineteen trumps. This work and the two other most complete decks created for the rulers of Milan are attributed to the artist Bonifacio Bembo, who is believed to have lived from 1420 to 1478. Bembo is known to have worked for the Sforza family creating frescoes, portraits, and book illustrations, including illustrations for the Arthurian romance *The Story of Lancelot of the Lake* written by Zuliano de Anzoli in 1446. The illustrations for *Lancelot* contain figures remarkably similar to those on some of Bembo's Tarot cards. Six of the cards in the Visconti-Sforza deck differ in style and are thought to be by another artist, possibly created years after the original cards.

The cards are painted in tempera on thick cardboard with designs impressed in gold-leaf backgrounds. The backs are solid red. Each card has a hole through the top, suggesting that at one time they were hung up by a tack or a nail. Although we do not know when they were displayed in this manner, it is unlikely that they were regularly used for card play. The thickness of the cardboard and the fragility of the paint would make them impractical to actually use in a card game. This also helps to explain why the deck is so intact for its age.

CREATIVE VERITY IN EARLY DECKS

Although we have come to think of the Tarot of Marseilles as the standard form for a Tarot we find wide variation in the structure and symbolism of the earliest decks. To understand why this is so it will be helpful to take a look at the culture that created the first decks. In the fifteenth century, Italy existed as a geographic and cultural entity but not as a unified political body. What is now Italy was divided among several prosperous, fiercely independent, and competitive city-states.

The Italian North had been part of the Holy Roman Empire since the time of Charlemagne. The power of the empire was revived again by the German monarch Otto the Great in the tenth century, and after him the German kings continued to hold the title of emperor. In the fifteenth century, however, the emperor's power outside of Germany had declined. In central Italy, the pope ruled over the Papal States. He was more influential in Italy than the emperor but his power over the northern states was in decline as well. The northern Italian states were in a central position in Europe with easy access to the sea. They controlled the lucrative trade between Europe and the East and the river valleys of the North were centers of manufacturing. The wealth, ingenuity, relative freedom, and desire for life's pleasures that characterized the cities of the Italian North were the same ingredients that helped create the Renaissance. This is the fertile environment in which the Tarot took root.

It was a time of experimentation and great achievement in the arts and sciences, an era that has been lauded for its achievements ever since. Driving these achievements was the inventive and competitive nature of Renaissance artists. This desire to excel and to compete was not confined to high art alone. Popular culture came under its influence as well. It is, therefore, not surprising that many early decks that are undisputed Tarots do not necessarily follow what we now consider the standard pattern. The Visconti-Sforza cards mentioned earlier contain a Fool and all of the familiar twenty-one modern trumps, except the Tower and the Devil. Historians often assume that they are missing. However, there is no way of determining if these two cards are missing because all of the Milanese cards are unnumbered and there is no evidence of these cards existing in any of the fifteen other known hand-painted Milanese decks. They may never have been included.

To understand another variation that we find in the allegory presented in early Tarots it is first necessary to discuss one of the common symbolic themes found in the trumps. In Medieval and Renaissance Christian culture, we find numerous literary and artistic references to a list of seven virtues that were presented as a model of spiritual excellence: temperance, strength, justice, prudence, faith, hope, and charity. The first four, temperance, strength, justice, and prudence, were adopted into Christian theology from the works of Classical philosophers like Plato and Aristotle. They are called the four cardinal virtues. The last three, faith, hope, and charity, were added to the list by Christian authors and they are called the three Christian virtues. As we have seen, the Tarot of Marseilles includes no Christian virtues and only three of the cardinal virtues in the trumps: temperance, strength, and justice. The fact that the fourth cardinal virtue, prudence, is missing has puzzled the Tarot's interpreters since the eighteenth century, and as we will see in the following chapters, it is one key that helps us to unlock the secrets of this allegory. However, early Tarot decks sometimes included more than three virtues.

Another early hand-painted deck from the royal family of Milan in the 1450s is known as the Cary-Yale Visconti Tarot. This is the second-most complete deck to survive of the Milanese decks and it is also attributed to the artist Bonifacio Bembo. In eleven trumps still existing from this deck we find the Lovers, the Chariot, Death, and other familiar allegories including the virtue strength, but we also find the three Christian virtues, faith, hope, and charity. It would seem that this deck originally contained all seven virtues, instead of only three of the cardinal virtues as we find in modern decks based on the Tarot of Marseilles. As we will see, Tarots with all seven virtues included in the trumps became popular in Italy in the sixteenth century. Perhaps the Cary-Yale Visconti Tarot was the precursor of these decks. The royal cards in the Cary-Yale Visconti deck contain more surprises. There are six royal cards in each of the four minor suits: a male and female knave, a male and female knight, and the king and queen.

There are also examples of Visconti-Sforza cards that stray even further from the standard. The Rosenthal Visconti-Sforza Tarot consists of twenty-three remaining cards from a deck made for the Visconti-Sforza family in the fifteenth century that are now in a private collection. Among the allegorical cards for this deck there is an unusual male figure holding a falcon. This card may be a variation on the Fool or possibly a unique character. Another card from this deck depicts a hexagonal baptismal font flanked by two winged boys, a type of angel called a putto. Suspended above the font is an arrow with two streams of blood arching away from it and pouring into the basin. This is an illustration of the Holy Grail of Arthurian legend, which is often depicted in Renaissance art as a hexagonal baptismal font. The arrow spouting blood represents the spear that pierced the side of Christ and was said to continually drip his blood into the Grail. This card is often assumed to be the ace of cups but in other Visconti-Sforza decks we only find putti on the World card, where they are flanking an image of a celestial city framed in a circle. The celestial city represents the New Jerusalem, God's kingdom descending to earth, which is the mystical reward described in the climax of Revelation. Likewise, the Grail is the mystical reward in Arthurian legend. The organizing principle in the trumps is the *trionfi*, a parade in which each figure is known to be more powerful than the one that comes before and leading to a final victor. Both of these images are suitable alternatives for the final and most powerful trump.

A similar Grail card can be found among the four Visconti-Sforza cards in the collection of the Victoria and Albert Museum in London, among three hand-painted Tarot cards in the London Guildhall, and in the nine so-called Goldschmidt cards, which are now housed in a German collection. The Guildhall and Goldschmidt cards are Italian hand-painted cards from the fifteenth century but are not known to be created for the rulers of Milan. The Grail cards in these two decks do not include putti but they both depict the Grail on a checkered floor that only appears on other trumps in these decks. The Goldschmidt deck also includes a serpent circling around the Grail to bite his tail. This mystical symbol, called an

ouroboros, appears in alchemical texts and represents the limits of time and mortality that the
Grail conquers with its timeless mystical truth
(see figure 3).

The only complete engraved Tarot deck
from the 1400s is the Sola-Busca deck, possibly
of Ferrarese or Venetian origin. In this deck we
find the Fool, titled Mato in Italian, and in this
one example bearing the number zero, while the
twenty-one trumps are numbered with roman
numerals. This is one of the earliest numbered
decks but the twenty-one trumps have little in
common with the mystical allegory that can be
found in various forms on the other Tarots from
this era. Other than the Fool, the cards of the
fifth suit depict famous warriors from history
and legend. Although warriors do attempt to triumph over one another, we do not find recognizable threads related to symbolism, poetry, or
prose which help to clarify the order of the triumph as we do in other decks. Perhaps this is

Figure 3. A rendering of a
fifteenth-century Goldschmidt
card depicting the Grail

why it is one of the first decks to have numbered trumps. Another unique aspect
of the Sola-Busca deck is that the minor suits contain figures on all of the cards
including the pips—significantly this is the first evidence of fully illustrated pips.

The Sola-Busca was not the only numbered deck of its era. There are examples of decks printed from woodblocks at the end of the fourteenth century. One
example is the Rosenwald Tarot housed in the National Gallery in Washington.
In this example, only the first eleven trumps are numbered and the second half
are ordered only by the hierarchy of the images. The Rosenwald Tarot is also
unique in that it combines the Magician and the Fool into one card, which leaves
just twenty-one cards in its fifth suit.

From the earliest numbered decks and from lists of trumps in sermons and
other literature, we can determine that there were several different orders of
trumps in the Renaissance. It is the nature of games to demand conformity and to
standardize the order of playing pieces. Variations occurred, however, because the
games were isolated geographically and the independent Italian city-states each
developed their own standard order. As there were three city-states that were the
primary users of the cards, it is not surprising that there are three main orders of

the trumps. In the three orders each of the trumps is assigned a different number. At first, this might seem to be disruptive to the hierarchy of the allegory. However, although the numbers changed, whole groups of cards were still kept in the same sequence and most of the changes are minor. For example, if one card from the beginning of a sequence was moved to the end, the number of each card in the sequence would change but the sequence itself would not change significantly.

As we will see, occultists in the eighteenth and nineteenth centuries seized upon a numbered pattern, which they believed was part of the Tarot from its origin. They would often project secret meanings and symbolism on the Tarot's fifth suit based solely on the number and order of the cards. But the number system that they believed was traditional was developed in France in the sixteenth and seventeenth centuries. In the earliest decks, meaning is derived primarily from the images alone.

In the early sixteenth century, a new version of the Tarot, called the Minchiate, was created in Florence. This deck was destined to become the most popular on the Italian peninsula but, until recently, it has rarely been used outside of Italy. The fifth suit in the Minchiate contains forty trumps and a Fool. In the trumps, the four temporal rulers—the Papesse, the Empress, the Emperor, and the Pope— were transformed into three rulers—the Grand Duke, the Western Emperor, and the Eastern Emperor. Cards that are equivalent to the other Tarot trumps are also found. Some have been modified, such as Judgement, which has become Fame. In Renaissance art, Fame is symbolized by an angel playing a trumpet and the Christian icons depicting the Last Judgement, which are the model for the Judgement card, also contain trumpeting angels.

The expansion in the number of trumps is due to the addition of the following symbolic figures: the three Christian virtues, Faith, Hope, and Charity, and Prudence, the missing cardinal virtue; symbolic representations of the four elements; and the animals and figures representing the twelve constellations of the zodiac. This deck suggests that Renaissance artists, unlike later occultists, did not attribute the trumps in what is now considered the standard deck to elements or astrological signs. If these alchemical and celestial symbols were already there, they would not have added them.

THE TAROT OF MARSEILLES

Regardless of Italy's pioneering influence in the creation and development of the Tarot, it is equally important to acknowledge the contributions of France. In sixteenth-, seventeenth-, and early eighteenth-century France, the allegory of the trumps developed new subtleties with the addition of alchemical and Neoplatonic symbols. The cards were consistently labeled and numbered, and, through the proliferation of decks manufactured in Marseilles, the French pattern, known as the Tarot of Marseilles, became the standard form for the Tarot outside of Italy. In the late seventeenth century, the French occultists focused on this deck and used it as the basis for the modern Tarot. It seems that the Tarot first came to the attention of the French card makers at the turn of the sixteenth century when France extended its borders to include the birthplace of the Tarot.

Making use of a rival claim to the duchy, Charles VIII of France invaded Milan in 1499. From that date until 1535 Milan was under the control of foreign rulers. Michel Dummett believes that it was during this period that the Tarot spread to France and Switzerland, and therefore it was the Milanese order of the trumps that became the model for decks outside of Italy.[17] The first evidence of the Tarot being produced in France is a record of their manufacture in Lyons, a city near Marseilles, in 1507. A port and commercial center with a thriving paper and printing industry, Marseilles became a major production center of Tarots and introduced the Tarot to other parts of France and other countries in Europe.

During the late fifteenth century and into the sixteenth century, a set of images evolved on French trump cards that is related to the allegory found on the fifteenth-century Italian decks but contains some changes in the iconography. This is the deck that is called the Tarot of Marseilles. This pattern became the most popular form for Tarots outside of Italy, and we find decks that were created in Paris, Switzerland, and northern Italy that follow the same design. All of these decks are considered examples of the Tarot of Marseilles. By the eighteenth century the design of the deck was set and there were several French and Swiss manufacturers that produced almost identical decks. Most well known is the deck printed by the French company Grimaud. Their deck was first manufactured in 1748 and the same design is still available today.

The Tarot of Marseilles was the most popular, but was not the only Tarot produced outside of Italy. The decks that developed in Belgium at the same time, known as the Belgian or Flemish Tarot, evolved their own distinctive iconography. Their most notable innovation was the replacement of the Papesse with a character known as the Spanish Captain and the Pope with Bacchus, the god of wine. Similarly a deck developed in Switzerland in the nineteenth century known as the 1JJ Swiss deck, which replaced the Papesse and the Pope with the Classical gods Juno and Jupiter.

Possibly the oldest example of the Tarot of Marseilles still in existence may be the Jean Noblet Tarot, which consists of seventy-three remaining cards from a

Figure 4. A rendering of the
Jacques Vieville World card depicting Christ; Paris, circa 1650

deck printed in Paris in the mid-seventeenth century. Another notable deck, which has retained
all of its cards, is the Jacques Vieville Tarot, which
was also printed in Paris between 1643 and 1664.
The Jacques Vieville deck contains some cards
that are similar to the Marseilles deck, and others
that are closer to the Belgian Tarot. For example,
instead of the image of lightning striking a
tower, which appears on the sixteenth trump in
the Tarot of Marseilles, the Jacques Vieville deck
has the lightning striking a tree, as it does in the
Belgian deck.

The World in the Jacques Vieville deck may
be the first to depict a nude in the center of a
wreath with a lion, a bull, an eagle, and an angel
positioned in the four corners surrounding it.
This is a variant of one of the most notable images in the Marseilles deck. In all other World
cards in the Marseilles tradition the nude is female or at least of ambiguous sex. Only in the
Jacques Vieville Tarot is the nude definitely
male. The Jacques Vieville figure appears to be Christ with a halo, a cape, and
royal scepter, as can be seen in figure 4. In Christian iconography, the figures in
the four corners are symbolic of the four Evangelists who spread the word of
Christ to the four corners of the earth, and Christ would commonly be placed in
the center of this arrangement in an icon known as Christ in Majesty. The Marseilles World card with the female nude is an unusual variant on the Christian
icon, and the Jacques Vieville World card may represent a link between Christ in
Majesty and the Marseilles World.

In the beginning of the twentieth century discarded fragments of printed
Tarot cards were found in the walls of Sforza Castle in Milan. Among these fragments were found two trumps from different decks, the Sun and the World. The
designs on both of these are similar to the Marseilles pattern. The World card re-
sembles the one on the Jacques Vieville World but the torso on the figure is dam-
aged and the sex cannot be determined. This card is possibly older than the
French examples and may suggest that there was an Italian model for the French
iconography.

TAROT AND DIVINATION

No doubt, most readers of this book know of the Tarot as a deck of cards used for divination. As we will explore in Chapter Two, this use of the Tarot was popularized by occultists in the eighteenth and nineteenth centuries. Although cards were created primarily for gaming, we have seen that there exists conclusive evidence that ordinary playing cards were used for divination in the Renaissance. Naturally, one may wonder if the Tarot was used for divination as well. As the minor suits in the Tarot are essentially the same as the common four-suit deck, there is no question that these cards in a Tarot could have been used for divination. In *Le Sorti*, 1540, which was mentioned above, the author, Francesco Marcolino da Forlì, recommended using only nine cards from the suit of coins for his method of divination. One could easily have selected these cards from a Tarot or a four-suit deck. Therefore, when we ask if the Tarot was used in divination, we are really only questioning if the fifth suit was used.

We also possess several sixteenth-century literary references to a Renaissance parlor game in which the trumps were used to describe the personalities of the participants. In this system, a card would be assigned to a person at a gathering and the other members of the group would explain why it had been attributed to that individual. While this game qualifies as a type of divination, the best evidence that the Tarot's fifth suit was used for incontestably divinatory practices in the Renaissance appears in a work published in Venice in 1527, known as the *Merlini Cocai Sonnets*. This set of five sonnets was authored by Teofilo Folengo writing under the pseudonym Merlini Cocai. The sonnets describe a scene in which trump cards are dealt and laid out then used to determine the fates of the story's main characters.[18] In the library of the University of Bologna, historian Franco Pratesi discovered a document written in 1750 that describes a related method of divination utilizing the entire Tarot that was practiced in Bologna in that century. This evidence suggests that in Italy there was an ongoing tradition of using the Tarot for divination at least from the early sixteenth century to the time that the Tarot was discovered by the occultists in the late eighteenth century.

Besides the literary evidence there exists structural evidence in the Tarot deck that suggests the Tarot is related to divination with dice. Dice were a common tool used for gambling and for divination in the Classical world, and divination with dice continued to be practiced in the Middle Ages and into the Renaissance. In divination systems that use three dice there are fifty-six possible combinations that can be thrown, the same number as the cards in the four minor suits of the Tarot, with four royal cards in each suit. In the Classical world, when four-sided knucklebones were used instead of dice for divination, the combinations of five knucklebones also added up to fifty-six. In ancient divination techniques, the fifty-six throws of the knucklebones were divided into four suits that were each listed on one of the sides of a four-sided pillar. In the minor suits, the card names ace and deuce were originally the names of the one and the two on a die. Similarly, when we throw two dice, there are twenty-one possible combinations and twenty-one divinatory answers, the same number as the trumps in the Tarot.[19]

THE MODERN TAROT

The year 1781 can be thought of as the dividing line between the early history of the Tarot and the modern era. It was on this date that the first occult interpretation of the Tarot was published by the French occultist Court de Gébelin. As we will see in the next chapter, after that date, occultists began to interpret the Tarot as an ancient book of knowledge that was created in Egypt by a group of sages possibly under the direction of Hermes Trismegistus, the mythical sage who is credited with authoring the mystical body of texts known as the Hermetica. The occultists synthesized the images in the Tarot with Hermetic, Kabalistic, and astrological associations. Many of the occult theories are historically unfounded and at times the occult interpretations of the Tarot actually contradict the iconography present in the illustrations on the cards. However, not all occult insights about the Tarot are false or without value. In this book, we will attempt to separate the occult chaff from the kernels of insight.

Today, most people who are serious about studying the Tarot are aware of its Renaissance history and realize that the Tarot's supposed Egyptian origin is a myth. Yet the occult myth of the Tarot's origin persists in subtle ways. One finds that discussions of the history of the Tarot among enthusiasts often lead to speculations as to who created the deck and what this person was thinking. It is sometimes assumed that the Tarot was created by one person, such as a sage or a magician, or by one group, such as a school of Kabalists or a mystic brotherhood. This train of thought is linked to the idea that there is one true original order for the Tarot trumps and one original set of symbols.

From the evidence that we have examined in this chapter we can see that if we could locate the first Tarot deck in its entirety, we might be disappointed. We might not even recognize it as a Tarot. The allegory and complement of recognizable figures would not be fully formed. Although some early experiments may have produced mystically inspired creations, other variations might have been unexcitingly orthodox or reflections of simple folk traditions. Moreover, it is difficult to say which deck is the *first* Tarot. We could just as easily say that there is no first Tarot. The Tarot evolved throughout the fifteenth century and many people had a hand in its development. This is how collective art evolves. It was the creativity and hard work of many individuals that helped the Gothic cathedrals evolve from wooden barns and halls to thick-walled Romanesque churches and then to tall elegant temples with walls of glass, and it was through the work of many people that the Tarot became the text of the Western mysteries that it is today.

THE MYTHICAL
HISTORY OF
THE TAROT

The fact that the wisdom of God is foolishness with men
does not create a presumption that the
foolishness of this world makes in any sense for Divine Wisdom.

—A. E. WAITE, FROM HIS PREFACE TO
THE PICTORIAL KEY TO THE TAROT

In this chapter, we will discuss the second stage of Tarot history, the occult or modern stage. The first writer to bring the Tarot to the attention of occultists was the French author Court de Gébelin (1724 or 1728–1784), who first published his theories in 1781. Therefore 1781 may be thought of as the beginning of this second stage of Tarot history. The Tarot's supposed Egyptian origin, its transmission by Gypsies, and its connection to the Egyptian sage Hermes Trismegistus, the Hebrew alphabet, and the mystical Kabalah are all ideas that were first introduced by Court de Gébelin.

We will see that, after this date, occultists would seize on one or more of the ideas introduced by de Gébelin and develop them more fully. The French occultist Etteilla (1738–1791) commissioned the design of the first modern Tarot deck, designed to enhance the Tarot's connection to Hermeticism and to be used primarily for divination. The French Kabalist Eliphas Levi (1810–1875) made the Tarot a key element in his occult synthesis and developed the theory that the twenty-two cards in the Tarot's fifth suit correspond to the twenty-two letters of the Hebrew alphabet. The French Theosophist Papus (1865–1916) related every aspect of the Tarot's structure to the four letters of the Tetragrammaton, the name of God written in Hebrew. The French charlatan Paul Christian, (1811–1877) forged evidence connecting the Tarot to ancient Egyptian mystery cults and referred to Tarot cards as arcana, secrets. After Christian's introduction of this term, occultists would refer to the Tarot's fifth suit as the Major Arcana and to the other four suits, composed of court and pip cards, as the Minor Arcana. Finally, the Swiss occultist Oswald Wirth (1860–1943) designed a second modern Tarot based on Levi's teachings. The work of all of these men influenced the teachings of the famous English occult society the Golden Dawn, founded in 1888 by Dr. William Wynn Westcott (1848–1925) and Samuel MacGregor Mathers (1854–1918).

The creators of the Waite-Smith Tarot, Arthur Edward Waite (1857–1942) and Pamela Colman Smith (1878–1951), were both members of the Golden Dawn and were therefore familiar with the theories that will be presented in this chapter. No matter if these ideas were accepted or rejected by Waite and Smith, they were certainly of influence, and one must be familiar with these theories if one is to understand the symbolism presented in the Waite-Smith Tarot.

Western occult ideas are founded on the mystical Hermetic tradition that developed in Alexandria, Egypt, near the end of the Hellenistic period, the second and third centuries C.E. These teachings were collected in books on philosophy, alchemy, and astrology that were attributed to the mythical sage Hermes Trismegistus, who was said to be an ancient Egyptian who lived before the time of Moses. When de Gébelin theorized that the Tarot was Egyptian, it was because he believed that he recognized Hermetic symbols in the cards. Although de Gébelin's assertion of an Egyptian origin for the Tarot is false, there are symbols in the Tarot that can be traced to the mystical schools of Alexandria. To understand the occult theories fully and to understand the mystical aspects of the Tarot it is necessary to delve into the history of Hermeticism. Hermetic mysticism is the root from which mystical and occult ideas sprouted in Judaism, Christianity, and Islam. These mystical teachings in Judaism are referred to as the Kabalah and we will see that many of the occult theories about the Tarot are based on Kabalistic ideas of correspondences. In this chapter, we will discuss Hermeticism and Kabalah as well as the eighteenth- and nineteenth-century occultists and their theories.

OCCULTISTS DISCOVER THE TAROT

I respect him (Court de Gébelin) also for having had,
out of previous expectation, a vision concerning the Tarot,
but as he did not marry his vision to any facts on this earth,
I think he has only begotten a phantom son of the fancy.

—A. E. WAITE, FROM HIS INTRODUCTION TO THE REVISED THIRD
EDITION OF *THE TAROT OF THE BOHEMIANS* BY *PAPUS*

As stated above, all of the occult theories about the Tarot can be traced to the work of one man, Antoine Court de Gébelin. He was born in Switzerland of French Protestant parents. After being ordained as a pastor in 1754 he moved to France and eventually established residence in Paris, where he became a Freemason, reaching the highest degree in Les Amis Réunis Loge and becoming a member of the Nef Soeurs Loge, a famous Parisian lodge that included Voltaire and Benjamin Franklin as members. He also threw himself into the study of the occult.[1]

In 1772, Court de Gébelin sent out an invitation for subscriptions to his principal work, a nine-volume encyclopedia of his observations, entitled *Monde Primitif* (*Primitive World*). He received more than a thousand subscriptions, including one hundred for the royal family of France. He worked on *Monde Primitif* until the end of his life. If he had lived longer, no doubt, the work would have contained more volumes. The word *primitive* in his title is meant to convey the image of an initial or original world, not a savage or an uncivilized one. The work is based on his belief that before modern civilizations came into existence there was a golden age, a time when one civilization ruled the world with one language and one religion based on true understanding of the nature of the universe. De Gébelin believed that all modern philosophy and religion flowed from this original religion and that one can get a glimpse of this ancient knowledge by observing the profound similarities found in all of the worlds' great wisdom traditions. This is what Waite would call the perennial philosophy in its simplest form.

De Gébelin's views are similar to the archetypal myth of the golden age, which takes place in the beginning time, a time when all of the arts and knowledge were taught to mankind. Variations of this myth can be found in the myths of most cultures. For example, in Egypt it was believed that the god Amon Re was the first pharaoh who lived in an ancient golden age, and after four intervening divine rulers, his scribe, Thoth, became pharaoh and taught mankind all of the arts and sciences. The Greeks identified Thoth with Hermes, their god of writing and wisdom, and the Egyptian myth of Thoth influenced the mystical Hermetic text. This, in turn, is likely to have influenced de Gébelin. However, he attempted to prove that this myth was a historic reality.

In his encyclopedia, Court de Gébelin tried to discover the language and beliefs of this first culture by analyzing the myths and language of modern cultures and finding the common patterns. A large part of the work was devoted to his intuitive approach to etymology. Although on the surface his methods appear sound, and as the famous psychologist Carl Jung discovered, common patterns or archetypes can be found between cultures, de Gébelin tended not to distinguish myth from history, and relied on intuitive guesswork more than scholarship, freely making up facts to fit his theories. As a result, most of what he has written has been disproved, and his entire work would have been forgotten were it not for two short essays on the Tarot that only appeared in volume eight starting on page 365, toward the back of the volume. De Gébelin wrote the first essay, and the second was written by a mysterious friend called the comte de M., believed to be the comte de Mellet, a French cavalry officer of noble birth who became the governor of Maine and Perche and who was one of de Gébelin's subscribers.

THE EGYPTIAN TAROT

Court de Gébelin maintained that the Tarot was of Egyptian origin. He said that he stumbled upon this fact by accident while calling upon an unnamed countess. He visited her at her home, and found her playing a game with Tarot cards. From his description and the illustrations that he included we can see that the cards in use were similar to the ones in the Tarot of Marseilles. At that time, the Tarot was not used in Paris and, although de Gébelin had known them in his native Switzerland, the deck would have seemed novel to the women who were present. When the countess laid out the World card, Court de Gébelin said, he immediately recognized the allegory and went on to explain the significance of every trump to her and her guests. Then he declared that the Tarot is "an Egyptian Book escaped from barbarism, from the ravages of time, from accidental and deliberate conflagrations, and from what is even more disastrous, ignorance."[2]

This was not actually de Gébelin's first mention of the Tarot. He did mention it briefly in volume five of his encyclopedia, published in 1778, in his etymological dictionary of the French language, which was contained in that volume. In his dictionary de Gébelin said that the word Tarot is derived from "two Oriental (Egyptian) words, Tar and Rha or Rho, which means 'royal road.'"[3] Of course, he was writing this before anyone in modern Europe had any accurate knowledge of the ancient Egyptian language. In 1799, the Rosetta Stone was discovered which contained an identical text written in Greek and Egyptian. After the French scholar Champollion made use of the stone to decipher Egyptian hiero-glyphs, de Gébelin's Egyptian source for the word *Tarot* could be proved false, but before that discovery it would not have been possible. The French name, Tarot, or as it was originally spelled, Tarraux, is actually derived from the older Italian name for the deck, Tarocchi.

In his later essay in volume eight, de Gébelin repeated this etymology and bolstered his theory of an Egyptian origin with new observations. He stated that the number seven was sacred to the Egyptians and demonstrated that the Tarot was entirely based on this number. Although the Fool is originally unnumbered, de Gébelin assigned the Fool a zero, which he pointed out has no value; therefore, he reasoned, there are seventy-seven cards in the deck with value, which is eleven times seven. The numbered trumps are twenty-one, or three times seven, and the other four minor suits contain 14 cards in each suit, or two times seven. He also stated that the four minor suits represented the four estates of Egyptian society:

The sword represented the sovereigns and all the military nobility.
The stick or club of Hercules represented agriculture.
The cup represented the sacerdotal rank, clergy or priesthood.
The denier (coin) represented commerce of which money is the sign.[4]

He said that the trumps told the story of the creation of the world as taught by the ancient mystagogue Hermes Trismegistus, starting with trump twenty-one and working backward through the suit. He also made a connection between the twenty-two cards in the fifth suit and the letters of the Hebrew alphabet. He stated that "The set of 21 or 22 atouts [his name for the trumps], the 22 letters of the Egyptian alphabet common to the Hebrews and Orientals, which also served as numerals, are necessary in order to keep count . . ."[5]

De Gébelin's observation that the number seven is prominent in the Tarot's structure is accurate. He is right that the number seven is important in ancient Egyptian symbolism. For example, in the Egyptian texts it states that the king-dom of the dead, ruled by Osiris, has seven mansions with seven doorkeepers by whom the deceased must pass and this is accomplished with the help of seven magical names.[6] In the Hermetic texts these doorkeepers become the gods of the seven planets that were known to ancient astronomers. However, this sevenfold pattern is also significant in Hebrew and Christian symbolism, particularly in the biblical account of the seven days of creation, and significant sevenfold symbols are common in European culture, such as the seven days of the week, the seven liberal arts, the seven sacraments, the seven virtues, and the seven vices. Also, although de Gébelin's association of the four minor suits with four classes of society is plausible, his description of the four classes of Egyptian society is more applicable to European culture. It is well known that the Egyptians used hieroglyphs instead of an alphabet. Therefore, one may wonder why de Gébelin assigned them an alphabet related to Hebrew.

De Gébelin believed that the Tarot, a book of wisdom from the ancient masters, was in the possession of the Egyptians and to preserve this valuable text the wise Egyptian priests disguised it as a pack of playing cards. They realized that disguised as a trivial game this book would evade the attention of those who would intentionally destroy it and would be faithfully copied for the purpose of amusement. In this form, it was brought to ancient Rome and, in the fourteenth century when the papacy was brought to Avignon, in southern France, the Tarot was introduced to this area. It was also introduced to de Gébelin's native Switzerland and to Germany, from where the unnamed countess brought it to Paris. Over the centuries, it had continued to exist unrecognized and ignored by scholars as something not worthy of study until de Gébelin, in eighteenth-century Paris, in a flash of insight, recognized its true worth. Alternatively, he suggests that it may have been the Gypsies who introduced the Tarot to Europe. At that time, it was believed that these nomadic tribes originally came from Egypt—hence their name in English. Historians in the next century would trace the roots of the Gypsies to India instead and show that they arrived in the West too late to have introduced cards.

Here again, de Gébelin has patterned his theory on an alchemical Hermetic myth. The alchemists, the hermeticists who combined their spiritual quest with experiments with physical matter, attempted to create a substance that they called the philosopher's stone. This substance was considered the most valuable substance in the world, capable of turning lead into gold and a common man into a spiritually evolved master. To begin the work of creating the philosopher's stone, an alchemist must first find the prime substance and transform it through the magnum opus (the great work). The prime substance is often described as something that is very common and of unrecognized value—the stone rejected by the builder and trodden underfoot, yet more valuable than gold. In modern myth, the prime material is like the comic-book hero Superman disguised as the mild-mannered Clark Kent. Here, de Gébelin has substituted the Tarot for the prime material. The implication is that now that we know the worth of this previously undervalued text we will be able to use it to progress to spiritual gold.

DE GÉBELIN'S ILLUSTRATIONS

To accompany his text, de Gébelin commissioned an artist, identified as Mademoiselle Linote, to make engravings of the trumps as he felt they should be represented. We can see these illustrations as they appeared in volume eight of *Monde Primitif* in figures 5 through 10.[7]

Allowing for the individuality of the artist's style, these images are essentially the same as the trumps in the Tarot of Marseilles, but, because de Gébelin wanted to group the cards based on what he perceived as their thematic similarities, he chose not to present them in the same order as they are presented in the Tarot of Marseilles. For example, he paired the Papesse, II, next to the Pope, V, on plate IV (figure 6); he grouped the virtues together on plate V (figure 7); and he placed cards with images of the harsh realities of life such as Death, XIII, and the Tower, XVI, together with the Devil, XV, and Fortuna's irrational Wheel, X, on plate VII (figure 9). In the last plate, VIII (figure 10), we find the last two trumps, Judgement, XX, and the World, XXI, grouped together with four aces, representing the four minor suits. Here we can see a relationship being drawn between the four creatures on the World card, which de Gébelin equated to the four seasons, and the four minor suits in the Tarot. In spit of the change in the order, the numbers on each trump are the same as in the Marseilles order, except that Temperance, usually number XIV, and Death, number XIII, are both given number XIII— obviously a mistake.

Another difference is that almost all of the figures have been reversed. This is especially obvious when we notice that the numbers, when shown in order, read from right to left—although the numbers themselves are not backward and were most likely added to the print separately. The reversal is especially obvious in the Pope, V (figure 6), who is making the sign of benediction with his left hand instead of his right as is customary. Curiously, there are three images that are not reversed: the Wheel of Fortune, X; Death, XIII (both in figure 9); and the Hanged Man, XII (figure 7).

However, unlike his image in the Tarot of Marseilles, the Hanged Man has been turned right side up and is depicted standing on one foot. This is because, realizing that there are traditionally four cardinal virtues in Classical philosophy— temperance, strength, justice, and prudence—and that only three of the four are depicted in the trumps—Temperance, XIV; Strength, XI; and Justice, VIII—de

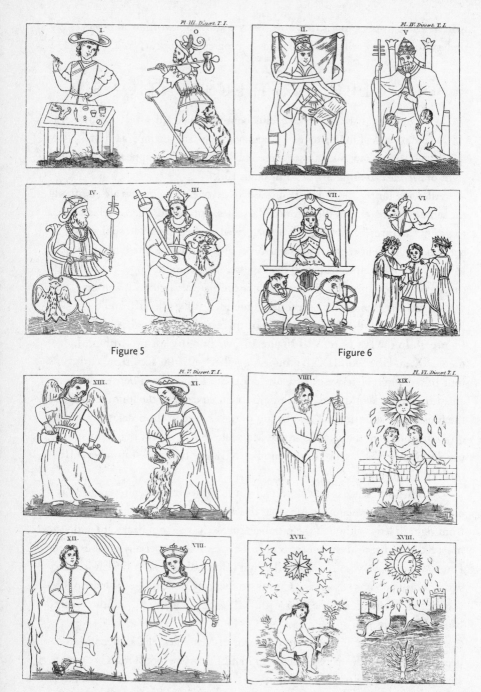

Figure 5

Figure 6

Figure 7

Figure 8

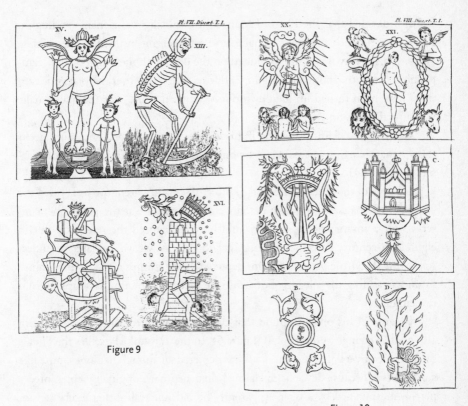

Figure 9

Figure 10

Figure 5. Court de Gébelin's trumps, left to right from the top: the Bateleur or Cup Player (the Magician), the Fool, the Emperor, and the Empress.

Figure 6. Court de Gébelin's trumps, left to right from the top: the High Priestess (the Papesse), the Hierophant (the Pope), Osiris Triumphant (the Chariot), and Marriage (the Lovers).

Figure 7. Court de Gébelin's trumps, left to right from the top: Temperance (misnumbered as XIII instead of XIV), Force (Strength), Prudence (the Hanged Man), and Justice

Figure 8. Court de Gébelin's trumps, left to right from the top: the Sage (the Hermit), the Sun, the Dog Star (the Star), and the Moon

Figure 9. Court de Gébelin's trumps, left to right from the top: Typhon (the Devil), Death, the Wheel of Fortune, the House of God or the House of Pluto (the Tower).

Figure 10. Court de Gébelin's trumps and aces, left to right from the top: the Last Judgement, Time or the World, Ace of Swords, Ace of Cups, Ace of Coins, Ace of Clubs

Gébelin decided that the Hanged Man, XII, originally was a man standing on one foot, prudently avoiding a snake, and representing prudence, the missing virtue. This is why this card is included on the page with the other virtues, Temperance, Strength, and Justice (figure 7). He reasoned that over the years this card must have been turned upside down out of ignorance and that the man's snake was turned into a rope.

Again, de Gébelin was wrong in his historical assumption. The oldest decks show a man hanging upside down by one foot just as he is in the Tarot of Marseilles (figure 11).

In some of the oldest decks and in fifteenth-century literature he is titled the Traitor. In Renaissance Italy, to be hanged by the foot was the punishment reserved for a traitor and everyone would have recognized the reference, but in eighteenth-century Paris the meaning was obscure. As we will see later, to understand why the virtue prudence is not depicted in the trumps is of key importance in understanding the allegory, but Court de Gébelin's solution is simplistic and inaccurate.

Because of his preconception that the Tarot came from Egypt, de Gébelin also made a change in the Fool, 0 (figure 5). In the Tarot of Marseilles the Fool is being chased by a dog. Here the artist has depicted an animal that looks more like a cat. This is because de Gébelin claimed that the image originally represented a man being pursued by a tiger. Apparently he did not realize that tigers are not found in Egypt. On other cards, de Gébelin changed the names when listing them in his essay to make them more Egyptian. The Charioteer, VII (figure 6), became the Egyptian god Osiris, and the Devil, XV (figure 9), became Typhon, a Greek name for Set, who in Egyptian mythology is the enemy of the god Osiris. The Star, XVII (figure 8), became the Dog Star and he said that the seven smaller stars surrounding the larger one in the center of the card represented the seven planets of ancient astronomy: the Moon, Mercury, Venus, the Sun, Mars, Jupiter, Saturn. De Gébelin particularly wanted to explain away any Christian images and therefore changed the name of the Papesse, II, to the High Priestess, and the Pope, V, to the High Priest or Hierophant. This is the origin of the titles of these cards as they appear in the Waite-Smith deck.

COMTE DE MELLET'S ESSAY

Although the two writers do not agree on details of the Tarot's history, Court de Gébelin published the second essay by his friend comte de Mellet next to his. From this we may surmise that Court de Gébelin did not think that his the-

Figure 11. A rendering of the Hanged Man in the tradition of the Tarot of Marseilles

ory was the final word and to give a more complete picture of the possibilities he published the alternative scenario of his friend alongside his own. For example, de Mellet says that the derivation of the word *Tarot* is the Egyptian "ta-rosh," which he believed meant the doctrine or science of Thoth—the Book of Thoth. He was equating the Egyptian god Thoth with the legendary author of the Hermetica, Hermes Trismegistus. We will discuss the Book of Thoth more thoroughly in the next section. Of course, de Mellet's guess on the etymology of Tarot is just as inaccurate as de Gébelin's.

De Mellet also considered seven a sacred number. To support this he stated that it was sacred in the Kabalah and in the ancient Greek mysticism of Pythagoras. He noticed that the twenty-one trumps can be divided into three groups of seven. He assigned each of these groups to one of the three ages of the history of man found in Classical mythology: the age of gold, the age of silver, and the age of iron. As we will see in the next two chapters, this division of the trumps into three sections does help one to understand the Tarot's allegory, and De Mellet's association of the Tarot with Classical symbolism is not far off.

De Mellet claimed that the first group of trumps, introduced with the World card, XXI (figure 10), illustrated the creation of the world and the golden age.

The Judgement card, XX (figure 10), he interpreted as the creation of man and woman, with the people on the card arising from the earth instead of the grave. This was followed by cards depicting the creation of the Sun, XIX (figure 8), with the union of man and woman on the lower half; the Moon, XVIII (figure 8), also showing the creation of animals; and the Stars, XVII (figure 8), showing the creation of sea life on the bottom. The Tower, XVI (figure 9), depicts the fall of man, and the Devil, XV (figure 9), leads us out of this golden age. The second age, the age of silver, dominated by images of time—the Hermit, IX (figure 8), and Death, XIII (figure 9)—was the stage when death and suffering are introduced, but it also contains the cardinal virtues, Temperance, XIV; Strength, XI; Justice, VIII; and the Hanged Man, XII, as Prudence (all in figure 7). In the iron age, the last stage, the Chariot of War, VII (figure 6), leads followed by sexual desire (the Lovers, VI, figure 6); the temporal rulers, the Emperor, IV and Empress, III (both in figure 5), surrounded by Jupiter and Juno (his name for the Pope, V, and the Papesse, II, figure 6); the Magician, I (figure 5), a deceptive trickster; and now, at the end, man has descended to the present fallen state represented by an additional card, the Fool, 0 (figure 5). Here he assigns the Hebrew letter tau, the last letter of the Hebrew alphabet, to this card.

With this one assignment, de Mellet introduces the idea that each of the twenty-two Major Arcana should be assigned to one of the letters of the Hebrew alphabet. As he started with the World, XXI, he worked backward toward the Fool, 0, to whom he gave the last letter. It is logical to assume that he would have assigned the first letter, aleph, to the World, and proceeded through the alphabet assigning the letters in that reverse direction. Later when he describes the use of the Tarot in divination he simultaneously describes the trumps as hieroglyphs and as letters. His object in divination is to use the cards as hieroglyphs in a communication with the divine.

De Mellet's story is well founded in Hermetic philosophy. What is implied in his comments but left unsaid is that if the trumps outline the descent of humans into a state of ignorance, when we read them in the forward direction, from one to twenty-one, they describe the mystical process back to the initial state of spiritual oneness. Like the Hermetica, the principal texts of the Hermetic philosophy, they are a textbook for experiencing gnosis, the ancient Greek word for enlightenment.

SEPARATING THE KERNELS
FROM THE CHAFF

Although Court de Gébelin's and de Mellet's theories are filled with historical errors and the Tarot is not from Egypt, there are kernels of truth in their intuitive guesswork. Egypt is the birthplace of some of the philosophical ideas expressed in the Tarot. The Tarot trumps do contain a mystical allegory that stems from the ancient world, but to find out why, we do not have to invent an exotic origin. As we will see in the next chapter, the Renaissance, the era when the Tarot was actually developed, was a time when ancient mystical philosophies were being rediscovered and expressed in the arts.

The facts do not bear out Court de Gébelin's history, But, as we will see, they do give support to some of his and de Mellet's philosophical insights. In particular, de Mellet's division of the trumps into three sections, each of which relate to one of the ages of man, is not far from the Renaissance view, and de Gébelin's correlation between the four minor suits and the four classes of society is probably how these suits would have been viewed in the Renaissance.

The story of this common deck of cards that secretly contained the most sacred ancient wisdom had an enormous romantic appeal and became quite popular. Thanks to this myth the Tarot has become a valued tool for divination and for mystical contemplation. Fortune-tellers and occultists continued to reiterate the story of the Tarot's Egyptian origin and one can find examples in bookstores even today of authors who continue to repeat these unfounded theories as plausible histories.

HERMES TRISMEGISTUS

As regards the Tarot claims, it should be remembered that some considerable part of the imputed Secret Doctrine has been presented in the pictorial emblems of Alchemy, so that the imputed *Book of Thoth* is in no sense a solitary device of this emblematic kind.
—A. E. WAITE, *THE PICTORIAL KEY TO THE TAROT*

As we have seen, Court de Gébelin's and comte de Mellet's theories were heavily influenced by alchemy and Hermeticism. As we proceed with this modern history of the Tarot, we will find that this is true of the theories of other occultists as well, and when we come to the discussion of the Waite-Smith Tarot

we will see that Hermetic symbolism was incorporated into the deck. This is because alchemy and Hermeticism are the roots from which the Western occult tradition sprouted. To understand the occult theories about the Tarot it is necessary
to explain what is meant by the terms *alchemy* and *Hermeticism*.

The term *Hermeticism* refers to a group of ancient writings on mystical philosophy, alchemy, magic, and astrology that were written in or around ancient
Alexandria from the first century B.C.E. to fourth century C.E. The ancient Christian scholar Clement of Alexandria (ca. 150–ca. 216 C.E.) cites forty-two such
works.[8] Within this broad group, there is a collection of nineteen works on mystical philosophy, written in the second and third centuries C.E., that eloquently
express the Hermetic view and that have received the most attention from scholars. This group of nineteen texts is referred to as the Hermetica or as the Corpus
Hermeticum. The names Hermetica and Hermeticum and the term *Hermetic* are
derived from the fact that all forty-two of these texts are said to be authored by
the mythical sage Hermes Trismegistus. Actually they were written by a group of
pagan Hellenistic-Egyptian authors. The term also applies to the oral teachings
that led to these texts being written and to the school of thought that grew out of
these texts and particularly to later texts on alchemy. We will describe alchemy in
more detail below.

Hermeticism is not one unified philosophy but a collection of related mystical-
magical beliefs that synthesize Greek philosophy with mystical religious beliefs
that were prevalent in Egypt and the Middle East. This type of synthesis was possible because of the cosmopolitan atmosphere that characterized the Hellenistic
world and that was most prevalent in Alexandria.

ALEXANDRIA

When he was the prince of Macedonia, Alexander the Great (356–323
B.C.E.) was a student of the philosopher Aristotle. In 336 he became king
of a Macedonian and Greek empire, and in the year 334 with the larger army that
was now at his disposal he waged a military campaign against Persia, the historic
rival of the Greeks. From 332 to the end of his life in 323, Alexander created an
empire that stretched eastward from Greece to include all of Persia and the Pun-
jab in India. Besides Macedonia, Greece, Persia, what is now Afghanistan and
Pakistan, and parts of India, Alexander's empire included Egypt.

Everywhere Alexander went he brought the Greek language, a respect for learning, and the Greek philosophic tradition. Through his influence, the Greek or Hellenic (derived from the Greeks' name for themselves) culture and language became

common throughout the empire and an era of international trade and communication was initiated that lasted from Alexander's lifetime up to the fourth century C.E. Because the prevalence of Hellenic culture was what characterized and unified this era, it is referred to as the Hellenistic period. The Hellenistic period was cosmopolitan and multicultural, and through the use of Greek as a common language it allowed for the free exchange and the synthesis of ideas and religious philosophies. At the center of this exchange was the city of Alexandria. This was the birthplace of the mystical philosophy that was expounded by de Gébelin and de Mellet.

Egypt was one of the areas that the Persian Empire had taken over before Alexander's campaign. When Alexander conquered Persia in 332 B.C.E., Egypt came with it and Alexander was welcomed in Egypt as a liberator. The Egyptian priests declared him the pharaoh, the king of Egypt, and as one of his first royal acts he moved the capital from Thebes, on the Nile River in the center of Egypt, to a new location near the mouth of the Nile, which would be more advantageous for trade with other Mediterranean cultures. He named the new capital Alexandria, after himself. After Alexander's death in 323, the rulership of Egypt was taken over by Alexander's general Ptolemy. The Ptolemaic dynasty continued to rule from Alexandria until Cleopatra, the last of the Ptolemies, lost her battle with Rome in 31 B.C.E. and Egypt became part of the Roman Empire.

Under Ptolemaic rule Alexandria became the largest, most prosperous city in the ancient world and remained so until it lost its position to Rome in the beginning of the Common era. It was the world center of commerce and learning and the home of one of the first great public libraries. Here Egyptian and Greek culture merged to become the model for Hellenistic culture and Hellenism in turn influenced Jewish, Roman, and later Christian culture. The mystical Egyptian god Thoth, who was said to have been the scribe of the gods and, in the ancient golden age, to have taught mankind the use of hieroglyphs and the wisdom that they contained, was amalgamated in this Hellenistic culture with the Greek Hermes, the god of communication, magic, and wisdom.

THE BOOK OF THOTH

The Egyptian god Thoth, who was depicted as a man with the head of an ibis or sometimes as a baboon, was the moon god and the scribe of the gods. The Egyptians believed that the earliest pharaohs were gods who ruled during an ancient golden age. The fourth pharaoh was the god Osiris. After Osiris, his son Horus, the sky god, ruled. Thoth was the vizier to both gods and, when Horus retired to the heavens, Thoth became pharaoh. Thoth was said to have ruled for

3,226 years and during this period to have taught his subjects all of the arts, sciences, and religious truths. To pass on his knowledge to future generations, Thoth invented the Egyptian picture-writing called hieroglyphs. Some of the oldest hieroglyphic texts claim Thoth as their author, including the famous Egyptian Book of the Dead. The priests of Thoth claimed to have secret texts authored by Thoth that contained magic instructions. With these texts it was said that one could command the gods and have unlimited power. This is the origin of the legend of the Book of Thoth, and the Book of Thoth is what de Gébelin and de Mellet believed they had found in the Tarot.

In the Egyptian texts, the name Thoth was customarily graced with a triple honorific, Great, Great, Great. The repetition of the epithet *Great* three times was intended to suggest that Thoth's greatness was endless. In the Hellenistic period, the Egyptians wrote in Greek, and Thoth's name was translated as Hermes, but to show that the Egyptian Hermes was being referred to, his epithet was appended in a shortened form, Trismegistus, or "Thrice Great."

In Alexandria during the Hellenistic period there were schools of philosophy and possibly religious communities based on ancient wisdom that was believed to derive from the teachings of the god Thoth/Hermes. Although there was a high level of literacy in Alexandria by ancient standards, this was almost entirely in Greek or Coptic. Only the secretive Egyptian priests and scribes could read hieroglyphs. Others could only learn through oral teachings that derived from the priests or simply imagine what wisdom was contained in hieroglyphic texts. By the first century B.C.E., it seems that the followers of Thoth/Hermes began to believe that when they wrote in an inspired state, the words came from their god. We might say that they were channeling Hermes. Or perhaps when they wrote they felt that they were only transmitting oral teaching that originally came from Thoth/Hermes. In either case, in recognition of the fact that Thoth/Hermes was the source of their wisdom, they signed their written works with his name. These Hermetic texts include works on alchemy, magic, and astrology, which are referred to by scholars as popular Hermeticism, and works on philosophy, which are referred to as learned Hermeticism.

The philosophic writings of this school consist of seventeen to nineteen texts (depending on how one numbers them), which were called the Hermetica. These were written in the second and third centuries after Christ. Like the hieroglyphic texts, these texts purported to be an older work written by an ancient sage, named Hermes. In these texts, Hermes is presented as a man who lived long ago in the golden age when the god Ammon was the pharaoh. Ammon is a creator god who was associated with the sun god Re, the first pharaoh. Through mystical practices, Hermes attained a mystical wisdom or enlightenment, called gnosis in Greek, and became a god.

Gnosis is a Greek word for "knowledge," but it is a type of experiential transformative knowledge that does not include book learning. Gnosis is gained through spiritual experience and one who attains it is transformed or enlightened. In the ancient polytheistic religions, one who was enlightened was considered a god. Christians would refer to these enlightened ones as saints, and Buddhists as Buddhas. Through the attainment of gnosis, the Hermeticists believed that it was possible to join the ranks of the immortals, and the Hermetica was a textbook that taught this procedure—a guidebook to gnosis or immortality. This victory over death was considered the ultimate magical power, and effectively the Hermetica was a Greek version of the magical Book of Thoth. Translations of the Hermetica were available in Europe after 1471 and occultists who wished to prove that the Tarot was the Book of Thoth would have to be familiar with the Hermetica. The first book in the Hermetica collection is called The Poimandres. This is the book that has received the most attention, and when the Hermetica was first translated into Latin, in 1471, the entire Hermetica was mistakenly given the name Poimandres. In this book, Poimandres, which means "divine mind" and is equated with an internal light, comes to Hermes while Hermes is in a trance, and describes the creation of the world in erotic terms. As we will see in the next chapter, the fact that the creation is seen as an erotic event influenced the poets and philosophers of the late Middle Ages and Renaissance and this is one aspect of Hermeticism that found its way into the Tarot.

Poimandres starts by describing how light emanating into the four elements from the one ultimate God formed the world. This God is the ultimate unity or Oneness beyond all duality and therefore is both masculine and feminine. The world is personified as Nature and is feminine. From fire and water God gives birth to a male creative being, the demiurge (craftsman), who fashions the seven governors who encircle the world. These seven governors are the seven known planets of the ancients, which in the ancient cosmology were believed to circle Earth. They include the Moon, Mercury, Venus, the Sun, Mars, Jupiter, and Saturn, and these seven celestial bodies are at the root of the mystical associations with the number seven that we find captured in the structure of the Tarot.

Next, this ultimate God creates Man in his and her own image, which would make Man both male and female. God falls in love with his and her beauty reflected in Man but Man is allowed to descend into the realm of the seven governors who also love this hermaphroditic being. Nature, as well, when she first sees Man, falls in love. To obtain the object of her desire, nature reflects Man's image in the waters of Earth. When Man sees his and her image, Man is also smitten, and descends to earth. "And Nature when she had got him, with whom she was in love, wrapped him in her clasp, and they were mingled in one; for they were in love with one another."[9]

Nature gives Man a body and from the seven governors seven qualities, which are presented as seven vices: the force of increase, cunning, lust, arrogance, audacity, greed, and falsehood. These vices are a negative interpretation of the influences of the seven ancient planets. As we said, the first Man was bisexed, but now to bind him to Earth, Man is split into two separate sexes and peoples the world through sexual procreation. Now these men and women, the descendants of Man, have fallen under the domain of Destiny, and are doomed to suffer death although the soul of each individual is eternal. "And that is why Man . . . is twofold. He is mortal by reason of his body; he is immortal by reason of the Man of eternal substance."[10]

This is the same philosophical problem that we find in all mysticism; humans are seen to possess an immortal soul that is trapped or housed in a mortal body. We find this duality expressed throughout the Hermetic literature. We can see it in the following quote from the Hermetic text known as the Asclepius. These lines were often quoted in the Renaissance at the time when the Tarot was developing and, even today, part of it is commonly repeated to express the Renaissance view of man:

> Oh Asclepius, what a great miracle is man, a being worthy of reverence and honor. For he goes into the nature of God, as though he were himself a god; he is familiar with the race of demons, knowing that he is issued from the same origin; he despises that part of his nature which is only human, for he has put his hope in the divinity in the other part.[11]

The fear of death and this longing for a return to divinity is the cause of human suffering, and the mystic must offer a cure to this suffering or a way back to wholeness and immortality. Without the cure the soul will reincarnate and continue to experience suffering and death in life after life. This is essentially the same philosophical problem that confronted Buddha. Poimandres describes the cure as an ascent back to the One, the Source. "If then, being made of Life and Light, you learn to know that you are made of them, you will go back into Life and Light."[12] The Poimandres advice on how one may ascend back to the "Light" is similar to Buddha's—first purify the soul throughout life by the practice of virtue, and second, practice turning away from the senses, a description of meditation.

When a purified soul is separated from his or her body at the moment of death, the soul may ascend the ladder of the planets and at each level let go of the vice associated with each governor. Beyond is the sphere of the fixed stars, which encircles the spheres of the planets. He or she will penetrate this sphere, ascend further, and return to the light that is God. As we will see in the next chapter, this is the same message that was expressed symbolically in the Tarot's trumps, particularly in the Star with its depiction of the seven celestial governors. In the spiritual practices of the ancient world, mystics would attempt to take this journey up the ladder of the planets while they were in a trance, the way Hermes experienced it in The Poimandres, and experience gnosis in life instead of after death.

As stated above, another branch of Hermetic writing was concerned with alchemy. As the oldest alchemical texts are signed Hermes Trismegistus, alchemists came to think of Hermes as the first alchemist. In their practice they synthesized the ladder of the planets and the mystical practice described in The Poimandres with their physical experiments.

ALCHEMY

Alchemy is the precursor of chemistry, but unlike modern chemists, alchemists married their physical experiments to a spiritual quest. Alchemists did make many practical chemical discoveries in their work, but their primary concern was the creation of the "philosopher's stone," a spiritual substance that is a universal medicine and a catalyst that provokes transformation. It was believed that the philosopher's stone would transform any substance into its highest form. As the universal medicine it could cure any illness and prolong life indefinitely, but its greatest cure was for the suffering of the soul, and the true immortality that it offered was mystical knowledge that all is one and death is an illusion. Like other Hermeticists, the alchemists attempted to achieve gnosis and immortality but their methods combined chemical experimentation with the meditative practices described above.

The creation of the stone was the "magnum opus," or great work, of the alchemists. The opus was divided into three sections designated by color and by level of refinement, from the grossest to the most pure: the nigredo (black), the albedo (white), and the rubedo (red). In later alchemy, a fourth yellow stage was added before the rubedo. The stone itself was composed of an immaterial substance that the third-century alchemist Zosimus called pneuma. Later alchemists identified it with Plato's World Soul and symbolized it as a beautiful feminine form or as the god Eros or Hermes. Some Christian alchemists identified it with Christ. As we will see, all of these alchemical deities have found their way onto the Word cards in various Tarot decks. The alchemists believed that this World

Soul, or Anima Mundi, was contained in all matter, and that it was their job to bring this spiritual essence to the fore. To the alchemists not just man but the entire physical world contained soul. Alchemy is an optimistic philosophy that sees the world as a living organism.

Influenced by the Hermetic ladder of the planets, alchemists grouped the chemical processes of their work into seven main procedures that formed a ladder of ascent toward their ultimate goal, the formation of the philosopher's stone. The process of making the philosopher's stone itself was a transformative meditation, and as stated above, once created it was believed to act as a catalyst to further transformation. Through the Hermetic belief in correspondences between what is celestial and what is earthly, alchemists also related the mystical ladder of the planets to a ladder of seven metals.

Alchemists believed that all metals were of one substance but changed their nature due to impurities. They believed that as base metals were cleansed of their impurities in nature they gradually transformed into gold, the purest form of metal. In their laboratories alchemists believed that they could speed up this natural process with the help of the philosopher's stone. In an earthly parallel to the ladder of the planets they attempted to transform lead, the most "impure" metal, associated with Saturn, into iron (Mars), tin (Jupiter), copper (Venus), mercury (Mercury), silver (Luna), and finally into gold, the purest form of metal, associated with the Sun and enlightenment.

During the early Middle Ages, alchemy was practiced in Islamic countries and ancient Greek texts were translated into Arabic. In the twelfth century, in Islamic Spain, the Arabs introduced alchemy to Western Europe. One of the first of what was to become many alchemical texts was translated into Latin by Robert of Chester in 1144. This made alchemy available to Western scholars for whom Latin was the language of literature and scholarship. It was during this period that the most famous Arabic work on alchemy, the Emerald Tablet of Hermes Trismegistus, which succinctly expresses the alchemical magnum opus in thirteen lines, was translated into Latin and became available to European scholars.

The oldest copy in existence of the Emerald Tablet is contained in a larger Arabic work, the Secret of Creation, which is credited to the Islamic alchemist ar-Razi and believed to have been written between 813–833 c.e. But some scholars believe that the Emerald Tablet may have originally been authored by the Hellenistic pagan author Apollonius Tyana in the first century c.e. Other scholars believe that it may be still older, perhaps even the oldest Hermetic text. In alchemical legend, it was said to have been inscribed on an emerald by Hermes Trismegistus before the time of Moses and discovered in a tomb later by alchemists.

It is in the Emerald Tablet that we find for the first time the Hermetic axiom "as above so below," which eloquently expresses the doctrine of correspondences that connects the seven planets with seven metals. Many occultists believed that the pose of the Magician on the Tarot's first trump with one of his arms pointing at the sky and one at the earth is a hieroglyphic representation of this axiom. However, although the story in the trumps does relate well to the alchemical magnum opus, this is probably because both alchemy and the Tarot are related to Hermetic mysticism. The rest of the images in the trumps do not relate as well to the other twelve lines in the Emerald Tablet. In the fourteenth century alchemy was widely and openly practiced in northern Italy. By the early fifteenth century, when the Tarot was born, alchemy had become an accepted part of the culture and alchemical terms and images were part of the common vocabulary. Alchemy was one of the avenues by which Hermetic mysticism influenced the arts in the Renaissance and part of the synthesis that was expressed in the Tarot.

RENAISSANCE AND MODERN HERMETICISM

By 1471 the Hermetica was also translated into Latin by the Renaissance mystic Marsilio Ficino (1433–1499). Before this time, only one of the texts, the Asclepius, was available in Latin. Ficino and other Renaissance philosophers took the proposed age of the text at face value and believed that Hermes was the name of an ancient sage who lived at the time of Moses. One of the aims of Renaissance mystics was to further synthesize the mystical teachings of Plato with Christianity and in Hermes Ficino believed he had found a common source for the teachings of Plato and Christ. Because of the work of Ficino, The Hermetica was held in high esteem in the Renaissance, and we even find a portrait of Hermes Trismegistus carved in the center of the floor of the Siena Cathedral in 1488.

In 1614, Isaac Casaubon published a work in which he used internal evidence found in the Hermetica to prove that the texts were written after the time of Christ. This greatly reduced the standing of these mystical teachings among scholars. In the seventeenth century, because of numerous charlatans and frauds claiming to be able to make gold from base metal, alchemy also fell into disrepute.

In the eighteenth century, alchemy received the death blow from the scientists Antoine Lavoisier and Robert Boyle, who discovered smaller particles within the Classical four elements of air, earth, fire, and water. They changed the definition of the term *element* to mean one of these irreducible components instead and went on to develop modern chemical terminology. From then on, alchemy was viewed as a pseudoscience. However, Hermeticism survived within the symbolism of the eighteenth-century Masonic fraternities and secret societies like the Rosicrucians. It became a permanent part of Western esotericism, but only ardent romantics clung to a belief in the proposed antiquity of the Hermetic doctrine.

SIX QUALITIES OF HERMETICISM

The following list of six qualities that define the esoteric or occult view is adapted from the work of the modern French scholar of esotericism, Antoine Faivre.[13] These qualities apply equally to Hermeticism.

1. **The world is a living being:** To the Hermeticist, all of the world, including rocks and streams, is alive and possesses a soul. In alchemy, the physical world is believed to be made of four physical elements: earth, air, fire, and water. Through four shared qualities, hot, cold, moist, and dry, they can be transformed from one into another, keeping the world in a constant state of flux. However, the elements would scatter and the entire world would fall apart if they were not held together by the mysterious fifth element, the World Soul, or Anima Mundi, also known as the Quinta Essentia, the origin of the word *quintessence* or *quintessential.*

   Regardless of the fact that modern chemists have disproved the theory of the four elements, the Anima Mundi remains as a loving intelligence that permeates all matter and all souls are part of it. Often the Anima Mundi is perceived as a spiritual energy or astral light that one can increase awareness of through meditation but in alchemy she was primarily depicted as a beautiful goddess. We will see in the next two chapters that the alchemical image of the World Soul as a goddess depicted in the midst of the four elements is the model for the image of the nude found on the World card in the Tarot of Marseilles.

2. **The value of imagination:** In scientific reasoning, the imagination is a contaminant to be weeded out of one's experiment. It takes one out of reality. To the esotericist, the imagination is valuable. It is the door for entering the reality of the soul or the unconscious mind. Without imagination the soul is not perceptible. The imagination is encountered in dreams and visions and disciplined through the practice of meditation. We may consider divination as one form of meditation, and divination with the Tarot certainly makes use of imagination as a way of communicating with the soul.

3. **The idea of correspondence:** This is the Hermetic view that there is more than a symbolic connection between celestial and terrestrial objects or the macrocosm and microcosm. It is what is expressed in the axiom "as above, so below." To the Hermiticist the planets are gods or angels and they are also alive in animals, minerals, and plants as well as in the heavens. This view is dependent on the first two points.

The modern esotericist conceives of the gods as archetypes within one's psyche and the ancient cosmology is now seen as an internal structure. Also, it is recognized that there is no separation between internal and external reality. Jung refers to this connection between psyche and matter as synchronicity and the principle of synchronicity is what we experience when we use the Tarot for divination.

At times, occultists have applied the idea of correspondences to the Tarot in a simplistic way. For example, they have forced a connection between the Tarot's fifth suit and the Hebrew letters of the alphabet based solely on the fact that they contain the same number of items, not on a symbolic or thematic connection.

4. **The belief in transmutation:** The world is alive and the goal of all life is to grow and change, to become a new and better being. Lead can be turned into gold and a common man into a sage. Of course, modern physicists have proven that lead can be changed into gold through the manipulation of the metal's atomic structure but they do not necessarily view gold as an improvement on lead. The esotericist embraces the reality of personal value or meaning. They are concerned with feelings as well as ideas.

Ultimately, the goal of life and the greatest good is gnosis or enlightenment, a mystical transformation that awakens one to the truth of spiritual oneness and removes the psychic barriers that separate an individual from the entire creation. Historians refer to the ancient mystics, who used the term *gnosis* to describe their goal, as Gnostics. In the broadest definition of the term there are three types: Hermeticists, Jewish Gnostics, and Christian Gnostics. All of these groups used the term *gnosis* but there are other ancient mystics such as Orphics or Pythagoreans who described the mystic experience in other terms. No matter what term is used, it is the view of this book that the story illustrated in the Tarot's trumps describes the quest for the mystic experience.

5. **The perennial philosophy:** This is the belief that all cultures and religions share common traits or patterns and the same yearning for the mystical experi-

ence. In its simplest, most naive form, it is the belief that all cultures stem from one culture, which existed in an ancient golden age. This is the belief that Court de Gébelin tried to prove with his encyclopedia. In its most sophisticated form, it is the Jungian observation of archetypal patterns in all cultures. As the Jungian scholar Joseph Campbell observed, one of the most common myths found in all cultures is the spiritual quest for enlightenment, a quest that he labeled the hero's journey.

As we will see, the Tarot embodies this archetypal quest. The universality of the myth found in the Tarot is demonstrated by the fact that the Tarot can be adapted to illustrate this myth as it exists in cultures outside of the Renaissance Christian culture that created the Tarot, such as in Buddhist or Native American culture.

6. **Spiritual truth is gained through transmission or initiation:** This idea stems from the ancient mystery tradition in which one received gnosis by undergoing a secret ritual initiation. It is the reasoning behind the structure and purpose of the eighteenth-century occult fraternities and secret lodges. It is also the reason that the occultists claimed that their insights were part of a secret oral tradition and why they wanted an ancient pedigree for the Tarot.

Initiation is accomplished by a reenactment of the myth of the hero's journey. Through this reenactment the hero's myth becomes a personal experience. In modern practice, one may be initiated by one's inner guide, and if one truly believes in the perennial philosophy, ancient pedigrees are not necessary. It is the view of this book that the Tarot trumps contain the archetypal myth of the hero and that they can serve as one's guide in initiation.

THE FIRST MODERN TAROT DECK

When in the course of time he (Etteilla) produced a reformed Tarot,
even those who think of him tenderly had to admit that he
spoiled its symbolism; and in the respect of antiquities he had only
Court de Gébelin as his universal authority.
—A. E. WAITE, *THE PICTORIAL KEY TO THE TAROT*

Although de Gébelin's and de Mellet's essays are the fountainheads from which all occult theories about the Tarot flow, the Tarot would not be the popular subject of occult study that it is today without the addition of the inspired work of the Parisian occultist Jean-Baptiste Alliette (1738–1791), who after 1767 wrote under the name Etteilla. From an early age, Alliette was interested in divination with cards. From the ages of nineteen to twenty-seven, by his own account, he studied traditional Italian card divination including Tarot divination with an older man from the Piedmont area in northwestern Italy. As we saw in Chapter One, historian Franco Pratesi has verified the existence of an active eighteenth-century Tarot divination tradition in Bologna, in northwestern Italy, which he believes is connected to Renaissance tradition.

Etteilla was the first professional Tarot card reader and the first Tarot teacher. He is credited with coining the word *cartomancy* for card divination.[14] He was the first person to commission the creation of a Tarot that was designed to be used primarily for divination, complete with illustrations on the pips designed to enhance their role in divination. Also, his was the first deck that modified the illustrations to incorporate modern occult ideas into the Tarot.

Perhaps as an attempt to deny the debt that they owed him, later occult authors almost unanimously scorned him. Historian Ron Decker has pointed out that Waite's interpretations of the cards for the Tarot's four minor suits are almost entirely derived from Etteilla. Yet, like the other occult authors, Waite belittled Etteilla's role. In the quote above, we can see that Waite also underestimated Etteilla's depth of knowledge and his access to sources other than de Gébelin.

In 1760, Jean-Baptiste Alliette married Jeanne Vattier and tried to lead a middle-class life selling grains and seeds. Later occult authors have mistakenly assigned to him the occupation of hairdresser or wig maker and used this as a point of ridicule. After his separation from his wife in 1767, Alliette set out to make his living as a cartomancer, an astrologer, and an alchemist. To complete his magical transformation, he changed his name to Etteilla, the reverse spelling of his last name. In 1770, Etteilla wrote his first book, *Etteilla, or a Method of Entertaining Oneself with a Pack of Cards,* in which he described his methods of divination making use of a common four-suited deck of cards. However, he also briefly mentions the Tarot in a list of tools for divination included in this book. As this book predates volume eight of *Monde Primitif,* it demonstrates that divination with the Tarot was known in Paris before de Gébelin discovered the Tarot.

After volume eight of *Monde Primitif* was published, Etteilla seized on the myth of the Tarot's Egyptian origin for his own. He announced that he had been studying the Egyptian mysteries for years and that he was aware of the Egyptian origin of the Tarot long before de Gébelin published his revelation. However, in 1782, when he submitted his first manuscript on the Tarot to the royal censors, as was required at that time, he was denied publication and accused of plagiarism. Historians Decker, Depaulis, and Dummett speculate that de Gébelin may have been the royal censor or had influence with him and that de Gébelin had been trying to block competition. By 1785 this obstacle was no longer present and Etteilla successfully published his major work on the Tarot, *A Way to Entertain Oneself with a Pack of Cards Called Tarots.*

Etteilla's Tarot book came out in four sections, each of which had a frontispiece with an engraving of one of the four cardinal virtues: temperance, justice, prudence, and strength. Etteilla claimed that the Tarot was a series of Egyptian hieroglyphs describing the creation of the world and the secret of the universal medicine, essentially, the Book of Thoth. However, in its eighteenth-century form, he reasoned, it had been distorted. Without supplying supporting evidence, he claimed that it had originally been engraved on leaves of gold under the supervision of seventeen magi presided over by Hermes Trismegistus. He calculated this event as having happened 3,953 years before his publication. He maintained that the hieroglyphs were originally placed in a fire temple near Memphis and he gave details about their placement. It seems that he grafted some of the legends connected with the Book of Thoth onto the Tarot. In 1788, when he began to teach his theories on the Tarot, he called his study group the Society of the Interpreters of the Book of Thoth.

Besides writing about the Tarot, Etteilla wrote and published a book on astrology and several other occult subjects including one on alchemy. Historians consider Etteilla's book on alchemy, *The Seven Grades of the Philosophic-Hermetic Work: Followed by a Treatise on Metal Perfecting,* from 1786,[15] the last work on alchemy from the classical period.

THE GRAND ETTEILLA TAROT

Besides practicing divination and teaching, Etteilla made his living as a dealer in art prints. The engravings that he commissioned for his frontispieces were of a high quality, demonstrating a professional standard of draftsmanship, and showing that he had access to artists who met his high standard. As he maintained that the Tarot had been distorted over time and considering his connection to the art world, it is understandable that his next step was to commission the creation of a new Tarot deck that rectified its ancient symbolism. In 1789, Etteilla published his new deck, which is now called the Grand Etteilla but it seems that Etteilla originally referred to it as the Book of Thoth.

The Grand Etteilla is the first Tarot deck made primarily for divination and to embody the views of a modern occultist. We might say that it is the first modern Tarot. In keeping with the Egyptian theme, Etteilla intended the trumps in his deck to appear to be Egyptian designs. To the modern viewer, however, the images are obviously depicting an eighteenth-century romantic view of Egypt. The temples and obelisks are neoclassical and the figures are dressed in a style that owes more to European history. Etteilla believed that the trumps illustrated the Hermetic texts, particularly the Poimandres. To improve the correlation, he rearranged the trumps to fit the Poimandres as far as it went and then he made use of other Hermetic texts to fit the rest of the trumps. He also transformed the four temporal rulers, Papesse, Empress, Emperor, and Pope, into abstract aspects of the creation and moved the Fool to the end of the deck. On the first twelve trumps, he introduced the innovation of equating them with the signs of the zodiac by including astrological symbols for the signs on the cards, placed in astrological order, one to each card.

Perhaps the most charming innovation in Etteilla's trumps is the design that he had drawn for Prudence (see figure 12). Following de Gébelin's lead, Etteilla transformed the Hanged Man into an upright figure avoiding a snake and representing Prudence. In keeping with the other virtues, the figure is female. Instead of standing on one foot, she is lifting her skirt to observe her feet and avoid stepping on the snake lying in front of her. In her left hand is a large letter *T,* perhaps a symbol of the Tarot. Two snakes intertwine on the elongated upright of the *T,* transforming it into a caduceus, a symbol of Hermes. In keeping with alchemical ideas, Etteilla has combined Hermes with the female Anima Mundi, or World Soul, and equated this Hermetic spirit to Prudence, or wisdom. By transforming her caduceus, a symbol for the universal medicine, into the initial of the Tarot, he has declared the Tarot to be the universal medicine and has made wisdom its guardian spirit. Although the Hanged Man was not meant to be Prudence, Etteilla has created a profound symbol that does resonate with the mystical allegory contained in the Tarot.

Etteilla's deck is the first to clearly relate the four minor suits to the four elements and to contain additional illustrations that were designed to aid in divination on the pip cards. In the four minor suits the pips of the Grand Etteilla contain the suit symbols arranged in geometric patterns. The bottom third of each card is a separate panel colored golden yellow. On the bottom of the suit of staffs these panels contain arrangements of black nail-like forms that Etteilla intended to be his recreation of Egyptian numbers (see the figure on the lower section of the Two of Staffs in figure 13). On the bottom of each card in the suit of coins we find a figure representing one of the seven planetary gods assigned to that card. On the eight, nine, and ten there are images representing the two lunar nodes and another astrological point. The coins themselves are circles with astro-

Figure 12. A rendering of Prudence from the Grand Etteilla

logical glyphs enclosed. These are meant to represent magic talismans—another influence of de Gébelin, who suggested that the coins may be talismans in *Monde Primitif.* This innovation is probably the source of inspiration for the substitution of magical pentacles for coins in the Waite-Smith deck.

On the two of each suit the paired suit symbols are seen suspended in front of a landscape dominated by one of the elements (figure 13). On the Two of Cups an alchemical vessel is added. Here Etteilla introduced, for the first time, a correlation between the four elements of the alchemists and the four minor suits: He correlates coins to fire, swords to air, cups to water, and staffs to earth. In figure 13 we can see the present author's renderings of the Two of Staffs and the Two of Coins from the Grand Etteilla. In both, we can see that the interlocked suit symbols are suspended in front of a landscape depicting the element associated with the suit, earth for staffs and fire for coins. On the bottom of the Two of Staffs two nails form an angle, which represents one of Etteilla's fanciful Egyptian numbers. The coins on the Two of Coins are talismans formed of circles with an astrological glyph for the planet Mercury in the center. On the bottom the planetary god Mercury is depicted.

Etteilla's royal cards contain well-drawn figures in medieval European dress.

Figure 13. A rendering of two pips from the Grand Etteilla Tarot, from left to right,
the Two of Staffs and the Two of Coins

They are meant to represent various combinations of emotional temperament
and physical coloring. Tarot historian Ronald Decker feels that the symbolism is
based on the theory of the four humors: blood, phlegm, black bile, and yellow
bile, an alchemical relationship between the four elements, four bodily fluids,
and human characteristics that dominated medieval and Renaissance medicine.[16]

The Grand Etteilla was successful in its time and remains in print in France
today. In the nineteenth century three versions were available, each expressed in a
different artistic style, neoclassical, Egyptian, and Medieval. A Russian version
that is not well known today was the first deck to include full scenes with mythological figures interacting with the suit symbols and designed to be interpreted in
divination on the pip cards. At the time, this innovation did not catch on outside
of Russia. It is because the Waite-Smith deck introduced this idea again in 1909
that it became common in modern decks.

Etteilla saw himself as an alchemist and a Hermeticist and, as we have seen, all
of his theories about the Tarot and the changes that he made when he had a deck
designed were intended to strengthen the connections between the Tarot and Hermeticism. After Etteilla, most occultists did not stress the Hermetic connections as
strongly as he did. More often, they chose to weave connections between the Tarot
and the Hebrew and Christian mystical teachings called the Kabalah.

THE KABALAH

It is time otherwise to say that the connection with Kabalism may be
in some respects like the Egyptian connection; as the later is arbitrary
and apart from evidence in history, so the other is also factitious and
apart from final warrant in the highest world of symbolism.
—A. E. WAITE, FROM HIS INTRODUCTION TO *THE TAROT*
OF THE BOHEMIANS BY PAPUS

Along with the unfounded story of the Tarot's Egyptian origin, a great deal of
modern Tarot literature equates the Tarot with the Jewish and Christian
mystical tradition called the Kabalah. Although this idea has no history before
the few speculations that we find written by de Mellet in *Monde Primitif* in 1781,
it was destined to be developed more fully in the nineteenth century. Again we
find one man who is instrumental in directing the occult Tarot in this direction.
He is the French occultist Eliphas Levi (1810–1875). But before we delve into his
story it will be useful to explain what we mean by Kabalah.

The Kabalah is Jewish mysticism. The name means "received" or "oral tradition" in Hebrew. It can be transliterated as Kabala, Kabalah, Kabbala or the same
three combinations beginning with the letter *Q* or the letter *C* instead of a *K*. The
spelling used in this book is the one preferred by Levi, Papus, and Waite. Most
scholars define Kabalah as a mystical Jewish tradition that developed in Spain and
southern France in the twelfth century. The Kabalistic ideas that are familiar today were developed in full at this time and The Sepher La-Bahir, the Book of
Brilliance, written in the twelfth century, and the Sepher ha-Zohar, the Book of
Splendor, written in the thirteenth century, are considered the two seminal
works. Like the Hermetica, these works claim an older authorship for themselves
to give their message a more ancient heritage. The Kabalah does, in fact, stem
from an older oral heritage and its theories are built on the foundation presented
in the Sepher Yetzirah, the Book of Creation, written between the second and the
seventh centuries in Palestine.

Tarot historian Robert O'Neill rightly points out in his *Tarot Symbolism* that
the first Kabalistic text is the Bible itself, and Judaism has been mystical from the
beginning.[17] It is only after the Roman army destroyed the Second Temple of
Jerusalem in 70 C.E. and the Jewish religion became a religion in exile, scattered
over the Roman world and having to redefine itself to continue its existence, that
the other mystical texts and oral tradition that became the Kabalah began to develop. At this time the survival of Judaism depended on maintaining an unchang-

ing written heritage. If the Jews could not count on the security of a temple and a homeland, they could count on an unchanging, written heritage. The Bible was closed to further revelation. Yet the creative mystical spirit of the Jewish people was not closed and new revelations needed a place to exist. This place was the oral tradition, and the sacred texts that were outside of the Bible, called the Apocrypha, in turn became the Kabalah.

This period of dispersal in the last centuries before the birth of Christ and in the early Christian era was also a time when Judaism was strongly influenced by Hellenistic culture. More Jews lived in Alexandra than in Palestine and many primarily spoke Greek. At this time the Greek translation of the Bible, called the Septuagint, was created in Alexandria for the Greek-speaking Jewish population. Much of the sacred literature in the Apocrypha is also written in Greek or at least partially in Greek. We find Greek names for angels and the secret names of God. The invocations written for the purpose of communing with angels are also in Greek. It seems that Greek was the celestial language. The Septuagint influenced the Hermetic texts and later was adopted by the early Christians as the preferred form of the Old Testament.[18] Jewish mysticism, in turn, was influenced by the Hermetica and Pythagorean and Platonic ideas and this synthesis became the oral tradition. Because the Kabalah synthesized various mystical teachings with Platonic philosophy, historians include it with Hermeticism and other ancient mystical traditions under the heading Neoplatonism.

ANCIENT ROOTS OF THE KABALAH

In Chapter Five of Genesis, we find a list of the descendants of Adam. Each lives what is, by modern standards, a tremendously long life and has many offspring, of which one male descendant is mentioned for the record. After a life span of 930 years Adam dies. His son Seth lived 912 years, then he too died. Each son enjoys a long life filled with procreation and then he dies, except Adam's seventh-generation descendant, Enoch, the father of Methuselah. "And all the days of Enoch were three hundred sixty and five years: And Enoch walked with God: and he was not; for God took him" *(Genesis 5:23–24)*.

Although Enoch is only mentioned briefly in this list, the Bible states that he did not die; God took him to Heaven while he was alive. This is the fulfillment of the mystical quest, the conquering of death. Therefore it is not surprising that Enoch captured the imagination of Jewish mystics or Gnostics. They wanted to hear more of his story. There exist three ancient books that fulfill this desire: The Ethiopic Book of Enoch, written in Aramaic between 200 B.C.E. and 100 C.E. The

Slavonic Book of Enoch, a translation of a first-century c.e. Greek text, and The Hebrew Enoch, written in the fifth or sixth century. The first two tell how Enoch was taken to Heaven and received a divine revelation, the wisdom of God, while standing at the throne of God. The third tells the story of Rabbi Ishmael who also ascends to Heaven while alive. There, in the seventh heaven, before the throne of God, he meets Metatron, the king of the angels. Metatron tells Ishmael that at one time he was the man named Enoch, and gives Ishmael divine instruction.

Enoch became a model and guide for Jewish mystics who, while in a trance, attempted to ascend the ladder of the seven planets and enter Heaven. In Heaven they found a similar layered structure leading up to the throne of God in Seventh Heaven. As this is similar to the Hermetic meditation on the seven planets and as Hermes was the model and guide for that ascent, it was natural that Enoch was equated with Hermes Trismegistus. The names Thoth, Hermes, Enoch, and Metatron became synonymous for the ascended master. Having been instructed by God, these ascended masters became the instructors of humans who desired the same divine revelation, and mystical texts and traditions were attributed to each of them. The divine knowledge received from these masters was called gnosis, and today the pagans, Jews, and Christians who sought gnosis are labeled Gnostics, although recently some scholars have been using the title Gnostic to primarily refer to Christian seekers.

Enoch is not the only character in the Old Testament to see the throne of God while still alive. The Book of the Prophet Ezekiel tells of how the prophet was sitting by the river Chebar when he received a vision of God on his throne. The throne is the color of sapphire and it floats above living wheels and four mysterious angels, each with four wings and four faces:

> As for the likeness of their faces, they four had the face of a man, and the face of a lion, on their right side: and they four had the face of an ox on the left side; they four also had the face of an eagle.
>
> Ezekiel 1:10

In Hebrew, the throne is called *merkabah,* which means "chariot." A branch of ancient Jewish mysticism was concerned with the recreation of this vision. In a trance, *merkabah* mystics would visualize ascending a sevenfold ladder that led to the gates of Heaven. Once they had arrived, they would concentrate on the description of the chariot from Ezekiel and recreate the same divine vision. Evidence of *merkabah* mysticism is found even in the Dead Sea Scrolls, written between the second century b.c.e. and 70 c.e.

The four living creatures are found again in the New Testament surrounding the throne of Christ on Judgment Day as described in Revelation. Christians adopted the four heads as the symbols of the four Evangelists, the authors of the four versions of the Gospel found in the New Testament. In Christian art, an icon of Christ developed in which Christ is shown sitting on a throne with a winged lion, bull, eagle, and man assigned to each corner surrounding him. As we have seen, the figure on the World card in the Tarot of Marseilles is surrounded by the same creatures assigned to the four corners in the same way. Because of this, and because one of the trumps depicts a chariot, occultists speculated that there may be a connection between the Tarot and *merkabah* mysticism.

As we can see, Gnostics searched in the Bible for clues in their quest for secret wisdom. In the story of Adam and Eve, found in Genesis, Christian Gnostics saw the Creator as a lesser god than the true God. They equated this Creator with the Demiurge mentioned in the Poimandres, a lesser being who is only the craftsman of the creation not the source of life. In their mythology the Demiurge was one of the host of fallen angels called archons, who were responsible for the fallen condition of man.

In Genesis as in the Poimandres, the first man is an androgyne until the Creator separated his feminine part from the masculine. Once separated, the Creator commanded the first man and woman not to eat from the Tree of Knowledge, and added, "for in the day that thou eatest thereof thou shalt surely die" (Genesis 2:17). But on the day that Adam and Eve ate from the tree, they did not die. If this Creator lied, Gnostics reasoned, then he is not the true God. This Creator then expelled the first couple to live a life of toil and suffering and experience death. This Creator is the master of fate who has created the existential illness that the mystic seeks to cure.

Before the Creator cast Adam and Eve into this dilemma he declared his reason. "Behold, the man is become as one of us, to know good and evil: and now, lest he put forth his hand and take also of the Tree of Life, and eat, and live forever" (Genesis 3:22). Who is the "us" to which this Creator referred? The true God is singular but the Demiurge is one of a host of archons. Would not the true God, who is goodness personified, have wanted man to eat of the Tree of Life and experience eternal life? Therefore, it is the mystic's goal to find this Tree of Life and use it to undo the plan of the Demiurge and conquer death. Jewish Gnostics must have looked at the story of Eden in a similar way because the creation of a vision of the Tree of Life also became a main concern of Jewish mystics.

THE SEPHER YETZIRAH

In the Sepher Yetzirah, which claims Abraham, the founder of Judaism, as its author but is actually believed to have been written in stages between 100 and 600 C.E., the image of the Tree of Life and the Hermetic ladder of the seven planets are combined into one diagram that is said to be the vehicle of God's creation. The diagram consists of ten energized centers, called *sephiroth,* from *sephar,* Hebrew for "number," which are arranged in a vertical pattern. In this creation, God made use of Hebrew as a sacred language. The Sepher Yetzirah delves into the magical properties of the Hebrew alphabet and works out a complex system in which the letters are associated with various aspects of the earthly microcosm and heavenly macrocosm. Each letter is assigned a celestial body or constellation, a division of time, and a part of the human body. In the twelfth century, Jewish mystics used this system, along with the numerical values attached to each letter, in their meditations on the secret names of God. They hoped to use these empowered names in their magical pursuits. As always, the magnum opus of this magical pursuit was the use of the magical names as a tool for the ascent to Heaven and the attainment of gnosis. Ten names or qualities of God were discovered. These qualities can be translated into English as: crown, wisdom, intelligence, greatness, power, beauty, endurance, majesty, foundation, and kingdom.

As the Kabalah developed, the qualities were equated with the ten sephiroth on the Tree of Life and twenty-two pathways were created between the sephiroth and each was assigned a Hebrew letter. As one meditated on each letter in this system, one progressed on a pathway up the Tree of Life and moved toward the mystical goal. Figure 14 depicts the Tree of Life with the ten sephiroth labeled and numbered 1 through 10 and the paths numbered 11 through 32. In different Kabalistic texts, several orders of numbering for the paths are found. The order illustrated is the one that influenced the Kabalistic Tarot tradition. The Tree is organized into three columns representing three pillars. On the left is the passive Pillar of Severity, on the right is the active Pillar of Mercy, and in the center is the pillar of divine grace called Equilibrium. The divine force descends the Tree in a zigzagging pattern referred to as the lightning bolt.

In the original Phoenician alphabet, the letters were actually pictures of creatures or objects that were related to the sound of the letter. They were like Egyptian hieroglyphs except that they only stood for a sound, not a word or syllable. In Hebrew, these letters became abstract signs but they retained the names and symbolism of the originals. For example, the name of the first letter, aleph, means

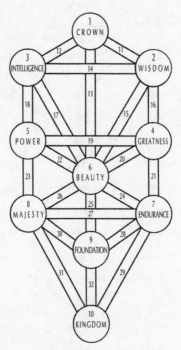

Figure 14. The Kabalistic Tree of Life

"ox" and the name of the second letter, beth, means "house." To this symbolic structure the Kabalists added the complex correspondences of the Sepher Yetzirah. The letters were divided into three divisions; three letters designated "mothers" were related to three elements, air, water, and fire; to three seasons; and to the three main divisions of the body. The seven double letters, which have both a hard and a soft pronunciation, were related to the seven planets, to the days of the week, and to the seven openings in the head. The remaining twelve letters, called singles, were related to the twelve signs of the zodiac, to the twelve months, and to twelve human organs.

In the Hebrew alphabet, there are no vowels. Only the consonants are given and the vowels are supplied from the reader's memory. Therefore, although God's name in Christian tradition is usually translated as Jehovah or Yahweh, in Hebrew, it is spelled with only four letters, yod, heh, vau, heh, which are referred to as the Tetragrammaton, the "four-lettered word." In Hebrew tradition, the true pronunciation of the Tetragrammaton was said to be known only by the high priests of ancient Israel. As the true pronunciation would give one a powerful link to God, it was believed to hold extraordinary magical power and was, therefore, a guarded se-

PATH	LETTER	MEANING	MACROCOSM	CALENDAR	MICROCOSM
11. ALEPH	א	OX	AIR	SPRING/ AUTUMN	CHEST
12. BETH	ב	HOUSE	MOON	SUNDAY	RIGHT EYE
13. GIMEL	ג	CAMEL	MARS	MONDAY	RIGHT EAR
14. DALETH	ד	DOOR	SUN	TUESDAY	RIGHT NOSTRIL
15. HE	ה	WINDOW	ARIES	NISSAN	RIGHT FOOT
16. VAU	ו	NAIL	TAURUS	IYAR	RIGHT KIDNEY
17. ZAIN	ז	SWORD	GEMINI	SIVAN	LEFT FOOT
18. HETH	ח	FENCE	CANCER	TAMMUZ	RIGHT HAND
19. TETH	ט	SERPENT	LEO	AU	LEFT KIDNEY
20. YOD	י	HAND	VIRGO	ELUL	LEFT HAND
21. KAPH	כ	PALM OF HAND	VENUS	WEDNESDAY	LEFT EYE
22. LAMED	ל	OX GOAD	LIBRA	TISHREI	GALLBLADDER
23. MEM	מ	WATER	WATER	WINTER	BELLY
24. NUN	נ	FISH	SCORPIO	CHESHVAN	INTESTINE
25. SAMEKH	ס	PROP HAND	SAGITTARIUS	KISLEV	STOMACH
26. AYIN	ע	EYE	CAPRICORN	TEVET	LIVER
27. PE	פ	MOUTH	MERCURY	THURSDAY	LEFT EAR
28. TZADDI	צ	FISHHOOK	AQUARIUS	SHEVAT	ESOPHAGUS
29. QOPH	ק	BACK OF HEAD	PISCES	ADAR	SPLEEN
30. RESH	ר	HEAD	SATURN	FRIDAY	LEFT NOSTRIL
31. SHIN	ש	TOOTH	FIRE	SUMMER	HEAD
32. TAU	ת	CROSS	JUPITER	SATURDAY	MOUTH

Chart I. The paths on the Tree of Life with the corresponding letter of the Hebrew alphabet, the meaning of its name in English, its celestial correspondence, its correspondence in the calendar, and its correspondence to the human body.

cret. The written Tetragrammaton was believed to share some of this magical power, and fourfold systems of correspondences were worked out for its four letters. The Tetragrammaton was equated with the four elements, the four fixed signs of the zodiac, the creatures of Ezekiel's vision, and four kabalistic worlds of progressively greater material reality through which God's essence emanated during the creation, Atziluth, Briah, Yetzirah, and Assiah. God's essence was said to pass through four consecutive Tree of Life patterns, one for each world.

In chart 1, the Hebrew letters are listed in order next to a number representing the corresponding path on the Tree of Life as depicted in figure 14. To the right are lists of other correspondences that are associated with each letter in the Sepher Yetzirah. There are some aspects of these sets of correspondences that suggest that they were adapted form the earlier systems designed for the Greek alphabet and known to have existed as early as the fourth century B.C.E.

Because Hebrew is a Semitic language related to Phoenician, the names of the letters have retained their meaning. In Greek the names of the letters no longer make sense in the language. For example, the first letter, aleph, which means "ox," becomes alpha in Greek, which is only the name of the first letter. It may be that because the correspondences were originally worked out in Greek, the part of the body that is associated with a letter, in most cases, has little to do with the meaning of the name of the letter even when that name is a body part. For example, ayin (path 26), which means "eye," is associated with the liver and pe (path 27), which means "mouth," is associated with the left ear.

Although the Greek alphabet is adapted from the Phoenician alphabet, just like the Hebrew alphabet, the Greeks modified their alphabet. One of the innovations that the Greeks added was seven vowels. Vowels are the most prominent full sounds found in each syllable. They are like the musical notes of speech. In fact, the Greeks used the vowels in musical notation to represent the seven musical notes in their scale. They created seven vowels to ensure that there was one for each note. In Greek mysticism, stemming from the school of Pythagoras, the notes of the scale were believed to represent the sounds made by each of the seven planets of ancient astronomy, the Moon, Mercury, Venus, the Sun, Mars, Jupiter, and Saturn, as they moved in their orbits. Therefore, through this musical connection there was a natural symbolic link between the planets and the vowels, and starting from circa 403 B.C.E. various systems were worked out with different correspondences between the letters and planets in each. Because there are no vowels in Hebrew, there is no natural place for this correspondence in the Hebrew alphabet. The authors of the Sepher Yetzirah attempted to solve this prob-

lem by equating the planets to seven letters in Hebrew that each have two pro-
nunciations. Kieren Barry, the author of *The Greek Qabalah,* points out that in
the case of resh (path 30) the suggestion that it has a double pronunciation is
"phonemically strained, indicative of a slightly forced fit."[19]

Besides the four Classical elements, earth, water, air, and fire, the Greeks believed that there was a more refined fifth element, called ether (the Quinta Essentia in Latin), that was central to the others. When the names of the five elements
are written in Greek, although there are from two to five letters in each name,
only five consonants and five vowels are used in various combinations and repetitions to form all of the names. These five consonants considered separately were
then associated with the five elements: gamma to earth, delta to water, theta to
ether, pi to fire, and rho to air.

Kieren Barry also points out that, because the Greek alphabet has twenty-
four letters, once we subtract the seven vowels and the five elemental consonants
there are twelve consonants remaining. These twelve were likely to have been associated with the twelve signs of the zodiac as they are in the Hebrew system. After assigning twelve letters to the signs of the zodiac, the authors of the Sepher
Yetzirah were handicapped in this endeavor by having only twenty-two letters to
work with. Because they had two fewer letters they dropped the elements earth
and ether and only made use of the other three—air, water, and fire—which they
fit with the so-called three mother letters, aleph (path 1), mem (path 23), and
shin (path 31).

THE CHRISTIAN KABALAH

Dr. Papus dreams stertorously when he says that Ramon Lull—who
was termed in his day the illuminated doctor of Majorca—based his
Ars Magna on the Tarot keys, and I suggest that he omitted to read
the colossal sheaf of treatises which are included under that title.
—A. E. WAITE, FROM HIS PREFACE TO *THE TAROT
OF THE BOHEMIANS* BY PAPUS

The twelfth- and thirteenth-century Spain of the Jewish Kabalists was a melt-
ing pot of Christian, Islamic, and Jewish culture. At that time, it was customary for wealthy Christian nobles to have Moorish or Jewish servants, and for
Jewish scholars to work with Christians to translate Greek, Hebrew, and Arabic
texts into Latin. The Christian nobleman Ramon Lull (1236–1315) was born

into this environment in Majorca. Lull came to admire many aspects of Islamic culture, particularly the mystical teaching of the Sufis. He taught himself Arabic so that he could study Sufi literature, extract what he felt was truthful in it, and Christianize it. Although he did not write as much about Jewish culture, many aspects of his mystical system show the influence of the Kabalah.

Both Kabalistic and Sufi traditions have their roots in the synthesis of Platonic philosophy and mystical practice that developed in the Hellenistic period. The term that historians have coined to describe this family of ancient Western mystical philosophies and the Medieval and Renaissance philosophies that have grown out of them is Neoplatonism. Lull seemed to admire this common thread in the Sufi and Kabalistic traditions. He created his own system in which he took Islam and Judaism out of this Neoplatonism and added Christ instead. He hoped to use his system to show Muslims and Jews that Christianity was the true religion. Today scholars consider him one of the greatest Medieval Neoplatonists and the originator of the Christian Kabalah. Lull was a major influence on the philosophers of the Renaissance.

In 1272, while sitting on top of a mountain, Lull had an epiphany. He saw the workings of the whole creation and how each part related to God through nine qualities: goodness, greatness, purity, power, wisdom, free will, strength, truth, and glory. He limited these qualities to nine, a tripling of the Trinity. All of these qualities can be found in Christian literature but they also show a clear relationship with the qualities of God that the Kabalists arranged on the Tree of Life. These nine qualities can be seen as related to the first nine sephiroth: crown, which is also called divine will, relates to free will; wisdom to wisdom; intelligence to truth; greatness, which is also called love or mercy, relates to goodness; power to power; endurance to strength; majesty to glory; and foundation relates to greatness. Lull did not feel the need to include kingdom. He designated one letter to represent each quality, another borrowing from the Kabalah. Lull called his system the Ars Magna. In the Ars Magna Lull used the initials representing the nine qualities to relate them to every aspect of nature, science, and art, and created a complex system of wheels and calculating devices with these letters and the names of other systems of knowledge written on them. As the wheels were turned and various combinations were created, Lull believed that the philosophical truth would be uncovered and that the Christian Trinity would be shown to be reflected in the entire creation. This was the tool for which he had been searching: one that he could use to convert the Jews and the Moors—but his technique was strongly influenced by the Kabalists' meditations on the Hebrew alphabet.

THE RENAISSANCE REVIVAL

In the Renaissance, Christian interest in the Kabalah was revived by the Neo-platonist Pico della Mirandola (1463–1494), who was associated with famous Renaissance philosopher Marsilio Ficino (1433–1495) and his Florentine Neo-platonic Academy, which he founded in 1462 with the backing of Cosimo de' Medici. With the help of a friend who had converted from Judaism to Christianity, Pico studied the Kabalah and published Kabalistic texts translated into Latin. Pico believed that the Kabbalah contained a lost divine revelation, a mystical key that lay under the teachings of the Orphics, Pythagoras, and Plato, and that demonstrated how all ancient mystical philosophy culminated in the teachings of Christ. Like Lull, della Mirandola believed that he could use this Jewish system to prove the reality of God as the Holy Trinity. Della Mirandola made the Kabalah a part of his Hermetic Christian synthesis and at the end of the fifteenth century presented it to the intellectuals of the Renaissance. His influence spread to Germany where Johannes Reuchlin published two books on the Kabalah in the early sixteenth century. The emperor Maximilian drew Kabalists to his court and it was in this environment that the famous magician Cornelius Agrippa wrote his *Occult Philosophy*, published in 1531. In *Occult Philosophy*, Agrippa made use of Kabalistic divine names in his magic invocations. After this, the name Kabalah was synonymous with magic.

In the late sixteenth century, this Christian, Hermetic, magical Kabalah was married to alchemical symbolism, and alchemy, Kabalah, and magic became interchangeable terms. Kabalah became a part of the occult philosophy of the Rosicrucian philosopher and alchemist Robert Fludd (1574–1637), the alchemist Thomas Vaughan (1622–1666) and Queen Elizabeth's astrologer John Dee (1527–1608). Dee titled one of his books that dealt with his Kabalistic efforts to contact angels *The Book of Enoch*. The Christian Kabalist Athanasius Kircher (1602–1680) attempted to divorce the Kabalah from Judaism. He claimed that Moses learned the Kabalah from the Egyptians, who were the descendants of Noah's son Ham. He felt that the Jews had corrupted the teaching and he attempted to find a new set of correspondences for the Hebrew letters which included the nine ranks of angels. By the late eighteenth century, the alchemical Kabbalah was part of the mystical occult synthesis preserved in the Masonic and Rosicrucian lodges. By the beginning of the nineteenth century, however, the scientific revolution of the Age of Enlightenment had taken its toll and interest in this occult synthesis had declined. The occult literature from earlier periods was labeled antiquated superstition and ignored.

THE KABALISTIC TAROT

Being armed at every point with such a rule of interpretation,
he (Eliphas Levi) remained an occult philosopher
for whom there was no occultism, save indeed a set of Kabalistic
theorems adapted to his metaphysical notions by a process of
wresting and a set of symbolical picture-cards—called Tarot—
into which he read that which he wanted.

—A. E. WAITE, FROM HIS PREFACE TO
TRANSCENDENTAL MAGIC BY ELIPHAS LEVI

In the early to mid nineteenth century, a time when interest in the occult was dying out, one man stepped forward and carved a career for himself as a magus. This man was born Alphonse-Louis Constant but in later life he preferred to call himself by what he felt was the Hebraic equivalent of his first two names, Eliphas Levi. Constant was born in 1810, in Paris, to a poor family. At the age of fifteen, Constant entered the junior seminary of Saint-Nicolas du Chardonnet and rose to become a deacon in 1835. However, in 1836 when he was scheduled to be ordained into the priesthood, he confessed a passion for a young female student and was refused ordination until he came to peace with his feelings. He left the seminary and never became a priest.

Constant had a talent for drawing and writing and made a living for himself as an illustrator of magazines and books, by creating paintings for churches, as an actor, a schoolmaster, and various other jobs. His spiritual striving also led him into social reform and he became a vocal advocate for women's rights and communism. His first book expressing his political views, *The Bible of Liberty,* was seized by the government and earned him eight months in prison. He continued writing and later spent another six months in prison. In 1846, Constant married Noemie Cadiot, a young woman of eighteen. They had a daughter the next year. Constant's marriage also ended badly, however. In 1853, Noemie left him and the following year their daughter died.[20]

It is at this time in his life that Constant embraced occultism. To mark the transition, he changed his name to Eliphas Levi. In 1854 Levi published his first book under his new name, *The Doctrine of High Magic.* The following year he completed a second volume entitled *The Ritual of High Magic.* They were combined together as one book and, in 1896, Waite translated the two volumes into English. It was published by Rider under the title *Transcendental Magic.*

LEVI'S MAGICAL SYNTHESIS

Levi considered high magic a mystical path to enlightenment. The goal was self-mastery and the development of one's will. To him magic was "a science which confers on man powers apparently superhuman."[21] But this science was not meant to be used for vulgar tricks; the true initiate, Levi reasoned, used his will to transform himself. Levi felt that the knowledge of this innate power was universal but hidden or occult. This is the perennial philosophy once again, but in Levi's imagination it becomes the most complete synthesis of magical doctrine yet conceived. The key ingredients in Levi's synthesis are Kabalah, Hermeticism, alchemy, Tarot, Pythagorean number symbolism, astrology, and ceremonial magic. He never wrote a book on any of these subjects alone. His works cover all of these as one interconnected doctrine, all of which was unified by his theory that all magic is accomplished by the manipulation of a universal magical energy which he called the Astral Light. Levi's theory of the Astral Light was influenced by the theory of animal magnetism developed by the famous German hypnotist Friedrich Mesmer (ca. 1733–1815). Mesmer's theory was popular in Levi's youth. However, it is true that all religions and mystical traditions recognize the existence of a subtle psychic energy. In Christian literature, it is called soul or grace; the alchemists called it the Quinta Essentia (the fifth element); in India it is called prana; in Japan chi; and it has various names in other cultures.

Levi was influenced by Court de Gébelin and Etteilla. It is known that he possessed a copy of Etteilla's Tarot. Like his predecessors, he considered the Tarot the Book of Thoth or Hermes but he also believed that the Tarot was of Jewish origin and totally based on the Hebrew Kabalah. He based his knowledge of the Kabalah on the seventeenth-century Christian Kabalistic text by Athanasius Kircher, who believed that the Kabalah was really Egyptian. Therefore, to Levi, his theory contained no contradiction.

Levi made a correlation between the four letters of the Tetragrammaton and the four minor suits of the Tarot. In the Hermetic Christian Kabalah of the seventeenth century, there already existed a correlation between the four letters of the Tetragrammaton, the four signs of the Evangelists, the four elements, and the fixed signs of the zodiac. By adding the four suits of the Tarot, the cards now fit this magical system of correspondences.

Levi said that the pips, the Ace to Ten of each suit, represented the ten sephiroth of the Tree of Life. In the Kabalah there are four trees, one for each world of the emanation, each of which is represented by a letter in the Tetragrammaton. Levi already equated the suits to those letters and it would be natural that the

SUIT SYMBOL	STAFFS	CUPS	SWORDS	COINS
EVANGELIST ANGEL	LION	MAN	EAGLE	BULL
ZODIAC FIXED SIGN	LEO	AQUARIUS	SCORPIO	TAURUS
ELEMENTS	FIRE	WATER	AIR	EARTH
ALCHEMICAL ESSENCE	SULPHUR	MERCURY	AZOTH	SALT
TETRAGRAMMATON	YOD	HE	VAU	FINAL HE
KABALISTIC WORLD	ATZILUTH	BRIAH	YETZIRAH	ASSIAH

Chart 2. Levi's correspondences for the four minor suits

Tarot would contain four corresponding trees. However, it seems that he was not sure about what to do with the four royal cards. He explains them away with the following rhyme:

> King, Queen, Knight, Esquire.
> The married pair, the youth, the child, the race;
> Thy path by these to unity trace.[22]

Levi thought of the royal cards as a family with a father, a mother, a young man, and a child, but he does not explain why they should come after the ten sephiroth. Perhaps he felt that they represent mortal life and reproduction which manifest in the tenth and final sepher, Kingdom.

The central component of Levi's synthesis was his correlation between the twenty-two cards in the Tarot's fifth suit, which he called keys, and the twenty-two letters of the Hebrew alphabet. Here Levi was influenced by de Mellet but he conducted his correlation in the opposite way, starting with trump one, the Magician or Juggler, aligned with the first letter, aleph, and proceeding in order. This is the simplest correlation one could make, except that Levi did not place the Fool before the Magician; instead he chose to align him with the letter shin, the next-to-the-last letter. This would result in the Fool coming between Judgement and the World, as he appears in Waite's book. Perhaps Levi did not want to give the Fool, a madman, a place of importance at the beginning or end of the sequence.

The two volumes of Levi's *Transcendental Magic* contain twenty-two chapters each. Each chapter is loosely linked to the symbolism of its number, to the corresponding Hebrew letter, and to a Tarot key. In each chapter, Levi discusses only the aspects he chooses to delve into and freely ignores others. For example, Chapter Seven in volume one is linked with the seventh Hebrew letter, zain, which means "sword." Appropriately, the title of the chapter is "The Fiery Sword." In this chapter, Levi links the image of the sword to the seventh trump, the Chariot, by describing the charioteer as a warrior with a fiery sword in his hand. He then proceeds to link these symbols to the seven virtues and the seven planets. In both volumes of *Transcendental Magic,* Chapter Thirteen, which is linked to the letter mem and key number thirteen, the Death trump, is titled Necromancy. Levi discusses his theory of the Astral Light and his experience with necromancy but neglects the other correlations such as the fact that mem means water. Likewise, Chapter Fourteen, which relates to Temperance pouring from one vessel to another in the Tarot keys, deals with transmutation; Chapter Fifteen, the Devil key, deals with black magic; Chapter Sixteen, the Tower key, bewitchments; Chapter Seventeen, the Star key, astrology, and so on. Levi relies more heavily on the Tarot imagery and only pulls in other symbols as he needs them. There is, nonetheless, something compelling about the spirit and totality of Levi's system. He enthusiastically places everything in one neat basket. If the Tarot keys are the Hebrew letters then meditating on them will move one up the Tree of Life and toward the mystic experience. However, the images and symbols suggested by the letters are not the images on the cards and the correlations do not naturally flow together. When facing such contradictions, Levi is sometimes ingenious in finding a way to weave them together and derive meaning. He looks at the pose of the Juggler and he sees the shape of the Hebrew letter aleph in his arms, one raised and one lowered. He also sees an illustration of the alchemical axiom "as above so below." The second letter, beth, means "house" but the second trump is the Papesse. Why would the Tarot's designers show a female Pope for the house symbol? Levi answers that the house is actually the sanctuary of the law, or the secret teaching, and that the woman is actually the embodiment of that mystery. But, as ingenious as Levi is, he seduces us away from a true understanding of the icons in the Tarot. It never occurs to him to ask what these images represented in Renaissance art. He assumes that they are secret messages from ancient Kabalists.

At times, even he cannot find a satisfactory correlation and just forces a given trump to fit a given letter. As compelling as his description is of the Juggler, he offers no explanation for the fact that aleph means ox. He equates the Wheel of

Fortune with the letter yod, which he sees as a phallus, a symbol of virility. With this correlation he moves away from the true meaning of this important icon, which is an ancient symbol of mortality and the fickleness of fate that is at the core of the Tarot's message. Because he is following Kircher's correspondences for the letters, Levi equates the planet Mercury to the Devil, Jupiter and Mars to Death, the Moon to the Tower, and the Sun to Temperance. The Moon card ends up being equated with the elements and the Sun with minerals or composites. One might ask: "Don't you think that the original designers would have preferred the Sun to relate to the Sun and the Moon to the Moon?"

Levi's theory of correspondence between the trumps and the Hebrew alphabet is based on the idea that the order of the trumps as found in the Tarot of Marseilles is the original order, but we have seen that this assumption is not true. Not only were there several orders of the trumps in the original decks but there were different quantities of trumps in some decks. Even in the Tarot of Marseilles, there are not actually twenty-two trumps but only twenty-one, which are numbered and considered to be a unified group. The Fool is an extra wild card.

In effect, Levi has created a new Tarot. Through his influence on occultists and particularly on the influential late nineteenth-century occult society, the Golden Dawn, a correlation between the Tarot and the Hebrew alphabet has become a common way of working with the Tarot, although later occultists tended to work out entirely different correlations for the cards and letters. While many people derive benefit from using this system, it moves one away from understanding the actual historic Tarot and unlocking its wisdom. At worst the collection of letters and numbers with their memorized meanings becomes more important than the pictures. Instead of letting the pictures unlock images in one's mind, they are ignored and one recites the correspondences from rote memory.

LEVI'S VIEW OF HISTORY

Levi's theory that the Tarot was created by Jewish Kabalists is unsupported by historical fact. It is highly unlikely that Jewish Kabalists would have designed a set of religious images because the Jewish religion prohibits such images out of fear of idiolatry and, if they had created it, it certainly would not have included the Christian, Egyptian, and Hindu symbols that Levi finds. As we have seen in Chapter One, the Tarot is a form of popular art created by the predominantly Christian culture of early fifteenth-century northern Italy. This was a time when artists attempted to synthesize pre-Christian pagan themes with Christian mysti-

Figure 15. Levi's illustration
demonstrating the correlation
of Christ's monogram to the
letters TARO

cism, but the Kabalah did not become a component in that synthesis until the end of the fifteenth century, and even then it had little
influence on the arts. In the earliest decks we can
see that the Tarot included common Christian
images such as the Pope and the Last Judgment
and that all of the images in the Tarot can be
found in other works of art from the same fifteenth-century culture.

However, Levi maintained that all cultures
knew of the Tarot and its secret universal doctrine. To explain why mystics in the past do not
mention this book of knowledge he asserts that
they guarded it as a great secret and only refer to
it with cryptic messages. To support his claims,
Levi leafed through history looking for hidden
clues. If a book has twenty-two chapters, such as Revelation, then he says it is a
reference to the Tarot. In *Transcendental Magic,* Levi focuses on the Christian
monogram for Christ, which is made of the first two letters of Christ's name in
Greek, chi and rho. He claims that when the chi is transformed into a Latin cross
and is placed between the first and last Greek letters, alpha and omega, as is common in its Latin form, the monogram is also a reference to the Tarot because the
letters transliterate as TARO. The chi Levi interprets as a tau, which is the letter
T, the alpha is the letter *A,* the rho is *R,* and the omega is *O.* Of course, the chi
really transliterates as a *CH* in Latin, the beginning of Christ's name. His illustration for this can be seen in figure 15.[23]

Levi also found the letters ROTA (Latin for wheel) placed around a circle in
a sixteenth-century text called *Key to Things Kept Secret from the Foundation of the
World* by the esoteric writer Postel. Because they may be read, starting with the T,
as TARO, he decided that it was the author's cryptic reference to the Tarot. Waite
points out in his footnote in his translation of Levi's book that this monogram
was not in the original edition but was created by the publisher for the 1646 edition that Levi saw.[24] This discovery, however, sparked Levi's creative speculations.
He makes a connection between rota or wheel and the Tarot and, by placing the
letters at the ends of the arms of a cross, forms a mystic wheel which he, in turn,
relates to the Tetragrammaton and fourfold alchemical symbols. This is the
source of the occult meditations on the anagrams for these letters TARO, ROTA,

TORA, ORAT, and ATOR and the source for the symbolic inscriptions found on the Wheel of Fortune card in the Waite-Smith Tarot.

LEVI'S TAROT DESIGNS

In the same way, Levi looked for hidden messages in the trumps. To him the curving edge of the wide-brimmed hats worn by the Juggler and the lady of Strength is actually the lemniscate or infinity sign (∞) suspended above their heads. The pillars on the Papesse card are actually Jakin and Boaz, the light and dark symbolic pillars of Solomon's Temple, which Levi equates to the Chinese symbols for active and passive, yang and yin. He reads hidden symbolism into a figure's crossed legs and finds the shapes of the Hebrew letters in their bodies.

Levi has the intuitive imagination of an artist and his ideas are most eloquently expressed in his illustrations. His drawings make use of creative free association of symbols and icons from different traditions, both Western and Eastern. A consistent theme of his work, one that demonstrates the most sophisticated aspect of his mystical vision, is the balancing of opposites, such as dark and light, good and evil, and masculine and feminine. This work resonates with the collective unconscious and needs no other authority to verify its timeless truth. Many of his inventions have found their way into modern Tarot decks. As he was an artist, it is surprising that he never completed his own deck—it is believed that he was working on one. In volume two of *Transcendental Magic,* however, he does provide us with his design for the Chariot card and another illustration that influenced the Waite-Smith Devil card.

In figure 16, we can see how Levi placed the Arabic number seven and the Hebrew letter zain prominently on either side of his charioteer.[25] Levi has changed the horses found in the Marseilles trump into Egyptian sphinxes and contrasted their tone to represent the polarities good and evil, and light and dark. Between them is a shield with the Tantric symbol for the union of male and female placed under the solar disk of the Egyptian god Horus. The Chariot is transformed into the cubic stone of the alchemists, a symbol of the prime material. Curiously, although he described the charioteer as carrying a flaming sword in Chapter Seven of volume one, in his illustration the charioteer only carries a mace.

In figure 17, we find Levi's illustration for what he calls the Sabbatic Goat and the Baphomet of Mendes.[26] This accompanies the Introduction to volume two of *Transcendental Magic,* which contains a discussion of Lucifer. Because Levi equated the Devil Tarot key with Mercury, he gives his figure Mercury's caduceus,

Figure 16. Levi's Chariot of Hermes,   Figure 17.
Seventh Key of the Tarot   Levi's Sabbatic Goat or Baphomet

rising like a phallus from his groin. There are parallels between this image and his Chariot. Like the charioteer, Baphomet sits on a cubic stone and we find similar pairs of opposites. One arm points up toward a light crescent and the other one down toward a dark one. The gesture is another illustration of the axiom from the Emerald Tablet. On his forearms are the alchemical opposites, dissolve and coagulate. All of these opposites are reflected in the two snakes of his caduceus, one dark and one light, and the figure itself is both male and female, and animal and human. Levi's Devil is the unconscious necessity to create balance, the trickster, who shows us the one-sidedness of our plan. In the twentieth century, Jung would label this archetype the shadow.

In the final chapter of *Transcendental Magic* Levi claimed that:

> An imprisoned person with no other book than the Tarot, if he knew how to use it, could in a few years acquire universal knowledge, and would be able to speak on all subjects with unequaled learning and inexhaustible eloquence.[27]

Although this claim may seem overstated, it demonstrates that Levi believed, like Plato, that all knowledge is within and that we actually remember it. He viewed the Tarot as a tool for remembering the truth that is within, and it was the recovery of this internal truth that allowed Plato "to speak on all subjects with unequaled learning and inexhaustible eloquence." There are nuggets of truth in Levi's theories.

In a later book on magic called *The Key to the Great Mysteries,* Levi switched from using Kircher's correspondences to using the correspondences found in the Sepher Yetzirah, as shown in chart 1 (page 64). As this was the set of correlations that was picked up by Levi's followers, particularly the French occultist Papus (1865–1916), it is the set that came to influence the Golden Dawn and the Waite-Smith deck.

LEVI'S FOLLOWERS

One of Levi's students was his neighbor Jean-Baptiste Pitois (1811–1877), who changed his name to Paul Christian. Christian developed his own system of astrology and incorporated Tarot into his unified magical theory. Decker, Depaulis, and Dummett, the authors of *A Wicked Pack of Cards,* have this to say about Christian: "As an occultist, he was that rare thing among those encountered in these pages, a wholehearted charlatan."[28] His most famous work, published in 1870, is his *The History of Magic.* In book two of this work, Christian describes an initiation ceremony for the ancient Egyptian mysteries that took place inside the Great Sphinx and Great Pyramid. At one point Christian describes how the initiate descends a seventy-eight-runged ladder into a room with twenty-two mystical paintings that contain the secret doctrine and are each related to an ancient letter and number. He never mentions the word Tarot but from his descriptions of the paintings there is no doubt that they are intended to be the Tarot keys.[29]

If this were presented as a fantasy, there would be nothing wrong with this exercise but Christian claims that he found this description in *On the Mysteries,* written by the famous fourth-century Neoplatonist Iamblichus. Needless to say, there is no such description in any work by Iamblichus. But Christian's false evidence is so persuasive that we find it mentioned in the works of numerous later authors. For example, the Swiss occultist and hypnotist Oswald Wirth (1860–1943) repeats the story in his *Essay Upon the Astrological Tarot* and the well-respected Russian Theosophist P. D. Ouspensky (1878–1947) repeats it in his *The Symbolism of the Tarot: Philosophy of Occultism in Pictures and Numbers.*

In 1889, Oswald Wirth published the first redesigned occult Tarot since the Grand Etteilla. On the trumps and Fool in his deck, Wirth followed the example of Levi's Chariot of Hermes and added the recommended Hebrew letter and Arabic numeral to each card. Following Levi, he assigned the Fool the penultimate letter shin and the number zero. Also, following Levi, he gave the Magician the four suit signs on his table and a lemniscate-shaped hat. His Chariot, with sphinxes instead of horses; his Devil, with a goat's head, breasts, and alchemical tattoos; and his Wheel of Fortune, with a sphinx on top and intertwined snakes at the base are all strongly based on Levi's illustrations.

Another influential and energetic follower of Levi's was the occultist Dr. Gerard Encausse (1865–1916), who wrote under the name Papus. Papus was only ten years old when Levi died. He never met him, but it was through Levi's books that he became a follower. Papus was a Theosophist, a Rosicrucian, and a medical doctor. In his short, life he wrote 260 books on various occult topics and on medicine but he is best known for writing *The Tarot of the Bohemians* and for designing an occult Tarot deck. The name Bohemians in the title of Papus's book is the French name for the Gypsies. It is a reference to de Gébelin's theory that the Gypsies brought the Tarot to Europe. In this text Papus picks up on Levi's mention of the letters TARO fitting into a mystic wheel that is related to the Tetragrammaton. He proceeds to create an excessively complex and mathematically flawed system of numerological and symbolic correspondences in which he equates every card in the deck with one of the letters of the Tetragrammaton and invests each letter with projected meaning. His is yet another invention that reduces the Tarot icons to signs and takes us further away from understanding the Tarot.

THE GOLDEN DAWN

In 1854, before he wrote his first volume on high magic, Levi visited London to meet with fellow occultists. While he was there, he conducted a necromantic ritual in which he attempted to summon the spirit of the first-century Neopythagorean Apollonius of Tyana. Later, he wrote about this event in Chapter Thirteen of *The Doctrine of High Magic*. By the latter half of the nineteenth century interest in the occult had continued to grow in England. Unlike Levi, who initiated himself and professed his ideas openly, the English occultists revived the practices of eighteenth-century secret fraternal societies, which included a hierarchical structure with grades of initiation and oaths of secrecy. The English occult societies valued teachings that were transmitted from an older society—the more ancient the lineage that a society could claim for its teachings, the greater the prestige of that society.

One English society, the Societies Rosicruciana in Anglia (referred to as the SRIA) founded in 1867, included Levi as an honorary member and provided lessons on alchemy and the Kabalah. One of the members of the SRIA, Frederick Holland, formed a new society in 1883 called the Society of Eight. The occult scholar and medical doctor Dr. William Wynn Westcott (1848–1925), who had also been in the SRIA, became a founding member of the Society of Eight and it is likely that his friend Samuel Liddell Mathers (1854–1918), who later changed his last name to MacGregor Mathers, was also a member. Through their connection with the Society of Eight, Westcott and MacGregor Mathers could have been introduced to Levi's teachings and his theories on the Tarot. It is known that in 1886 Westcott made ink sketches of Tarot trumps in which he demonstrated a familiarity with themes introduced by Etteilla and Levi.[30]

In 1886, Westcott obtained a mysterious document which he referred to as the Cypher MS or Cypher Manuscript. Except for some terms written in Hebrew using the Hebrew alphabet, the document was written in English but in a cipher or code with the sentences written from right to left. Westcott recognized the code as one used by an alchemist in the sixteenth century and was able to read the text. The watermark on the paper read 1809 but the content and wording of the document suggests that it was not as old as that and the paper was most likely used to suggest greater age.[31] Waite speculated that the Cypher MS was actually written by Kenneth Mackenzie, another member of the Society of Eight.[32] The Cypher MS laid out the plans for a secret Hermetic Kabalistic society that would admit both men and women. It even provided the name, the Hermetic Order of the Golden Dawn. It would have grades like a Rosicrucian lodge but they were equated to the sephiroth of the Tree of Life, so that as one progressed in the teaching of the Golden Dawn and was initiated to a higher grade, one was progressing up the Kabalistic Tree.

In 1888, Westcott joined with his friend MacGregor Mathers and founded The Hermetic Order of the Golden Dawn as described in the Cypher MS. Of course, it was necessary to expand on the lessons offered to the members, and MacGregor Mathers was an energetic writer with a gift for creating rituals and an expertise in the occult Tarot. His *The Tarot: Its Occult Signification, Use in Fortune-Telling and Methods of Play,* 1888, which was the first book devoted to the subject in England, presented a synthesis of the views of de Gébelin, Etteilla, and Levi.

Several pages in the Cypher MS also dealt with the Tarot and its attributes.

Westcott's and Mathers's expanded these lessons and included them in a Golden Dawn document which they titled Book T. In Book T, the Fool and the trumps, called the keys, receive the names that are now common in English decks. As in Levi's books, a Hebrew letter is attributed to each key. Unlike Levi, the Fool is first and aligned with aleph. With this placement, Book T had changed the letter assigned to every card from the order found in Levi except for the World card.

As in Levi's later work, Book T uses the order found in the Sepher Yetzirah as the basis for assigning celestial and elemental attributes to each letter. If the trumps are listed in the order found in the Tarot of Marseilles, this system of correspondences would result in the sign Leo, the lion, lining up with Justice, key 8, and Libra, the scales of justice, lining up with Strength, key 11, which depicts a woman with a lion. In Book T, the order of these two cards is switched so that the sign of Leo corresponds to Strength, now key 8, and Libra corresponds to Justice, now key 11 (see chart 3).[33] This is the order in which these two trumps are placed in the Waite-Smith Tarot. While Westcott and MacGregor Mathers seem to have made this change in the order of the keys to create greater harmony between the image on the card and the Kabalistic attribute, it does not seem that they were as troubled that although the sun aligns with the Sun key, the moon does not align with the Moon key.

In Book T the traditional names of the four minor suits—staffs, cups, swords, and coins—are changed to transform them into the tools of the magician: wands, cups, swords, and pentacles. Each suit is assigned an element based on Levi's correlations: wands with fire, cups with water, swords with air, and pentacles with earth. The top-ranking royal card is the Knight, also called the Lord; followed by the Queen; the King, also called the Prince; and the Knave, also called the Princess. Every pip card is assigned a planet and a sign of the zodiac.

The initial Order of the Golden Dawn flourished briefly, then after a little over ten years it split into fragments. Among the members of the Golden Dawn and the splinter groups, however, were some of the best-known occult figures of the day, such as the poet William Butler Yeats, the actress Florence Farr, the notorious magician Aleister Crowley, occult authors Dion Fortune and Israel Regardie, and Arthur Edward Waite and Pamela Colman Smith, the creators of the Waite-Smith Tarot. Therefore, it is not surprising that the Waite-Smith Tarot is influenced by the Golden Dawn's teachings on the Tarot. However, we will save the discussion of Waite's and Smith's deck for later. First, we will explore Renaissance art and philosophy and find clues that will help us interpret the Tarot as it would have been interpreted in the century when it was created.

TAROT KEY	HEBREW LETTER		ATTRIBUTE
0. Fool	ALEPH	א	AIR
1. Magician	BETH	ב	Mercury
2. High Priestess	GIMEL	ג	Moon
3. Empress	DALETH	ד	Venus
4. Emperor	HE	ה	Aries
5. Hierophant	VAU	ו	Taurus
6. Lovers	ZAIN	ז	Gemini
7. Chariot	CHETH	ח	Cancer
8. Fortitude	TETH	ט	Leo
9. Hermit	YOD	י	Virgo
10. Wheel of Fortune	KAPH	כ	Jupiter
11. Justice	LAMED	ל	Libra
12. Hanged Man	MEM	מ	WATER
13. Death	NUN	נ	Scorpio
14. Temperance	SAMEKH	ס	Sagittarius
15. Devil	AYIN	ע	Capricorn
16. Blasted Tower	PE	פ	Mars
17. The Star	TZADDI	צ	Aquarius
18. The Moon	QOPH	ק	Pisces
19. The Sun	RESH	ר	Sun
20. Judgement	SHIN	ש	FIRE
21. Universe	TAU	ת	Saturn

Chart 3. The Tarot keys with attributes from the Golden Dawn's Book T

THE SEARCH
FOR MEANING

On the hypothesis that there is or may be a deeper meaning in the
chief Tarot Symbols than attaches thereto on the surface, it becomes
necessary at this point to summarize that which can be said concerning them and to justify in this manner the fact that as a Mystic
and Ritualist I have been at great pains about them.

—A. E. WAITE, *SHADOWS OF LIFE AND THOUGHT*

In the Waite-Smith Tarot, which is the ultimate focus of this book, the fifth
suit is referred to as the Major Arcana, the greater secret, in contrast to the
other four suits, which are called the Minor Arcana. When this mysterious
fifth suit is included in a deck of cards it defines the deck as a Tarot. It is the view
of this book that Waite is correct in his belief that the Tarot's Major Arcana tells a
story that is in essence mystical, and that this was the intent of its creators.

As we have seen in the last chapter, occultists unanimously agree that the
Tarot, as they discovered it in its French form known as the Tarot of Marseilles, is
mystical. Unlike Waite, however, they have generally attempted to back their
views with unsupported claims that the Tarot was created by ancient Hermeticists or Kabalists. In Chapter One, we saw that historic evidence leads us to con-
clude that the Tarot was actually created in northern Italy in the early fifteenth
century (1410–1430) as a deck of cards primarily designed for playing a unique
game. The first decks were created by artists and printers who were part of Renaissance culture, and who created other forms of popular art as well. The story

presented in the Tarot of Marseilles trumps evolved from these early Italian cards and a relation to the Marseilles pattern can be recognized in most Italian decks created after 1450.

All of the images and symbols in the Tarot can be found in other works of popular art from the Italian Renaissance, demonstrating that the Tarot was part of popular culture and made use of a common iconography. The Tarot is mystical because the secular arts of the Renaissance commonly expressed a mystical philosophy.

Although we can find some similarities between Kabalistic mysticism and the Tarot, the Kabalah was not part of this predominantly Christian culture until the last quarter of the fifteenth century when the philosopher Pico della Mirandola made it a part of his mystical synthesis, and even then, it had no recognizable influence on popular culture or the arts. Except for one text, the Asclepius, the Hermetica was also not available as an influence in the early fifteenth century because the philosopher and mystic Marsilio Ficino did not translate it into Latin until 1471. Hermeticism in the form of alchemy, however, was popular in fourteenth-century Italy and because of its use of enigmatic imagery it did influence Renaissance art. Although the Tarot does share common themes and images with alchemical texts, it is not strictly alchemical. More accurately, the Tarot is an expression of a mystical view that parallels the Kabalah and Hermeticism and that can be classified with Hermeticism and the Kabalah under the broader heading Neoplatonism.

In this chapter, we will demonstrate that the Tarot is mystical and Neoplatonic by examining its relationship to the art and philosophy of the fifteenth-century northern Italian culture that created the deck and to the ancient mythology and philosophy that underlies Renaissance culture. In many ways, the culture of fifteenth-century Italy is foreign and unfamiliar to the modern reader. The Renaissance was a time when artists and intellectuals attempted to reclaim the philosophy and aesthetics of the Classical world, but their view of ancient culture was colored by the writers of late antiquity. It was a view that included magic and mysticism intermixed with what we now consider the foundations of modern science and logic. To understand the Tarot we will first have to familiarize ourselves with this Renaissance culture and the Neoplatonic philosophy that they prized.

NEOPLATONISM

Neoplatonism is a term coined by scholars to describe a broad group of Western philosophies that synthesize Platonic philosophy with various other mystical and philosophical systems. It is not one but a group of philosophies that are not identical but share some common traits, the most important of which is that they view Plato (428–347 B.C.E.) as a mystic. At times, it is more of a branch of religion than of philosophy. Although the first Neoplatonists were Classical pagans, their views were incorporated into the mystical teachings of Judaism, Christianity, and Islam. Therefore the term *Neoplatonism* can be used to refer to most of the Western mystical traditions. Hermeticism, Gnosticism, Kabalah, Sufi mysticism, and Christian mysticism can all be considered Neoplatonism.

Scholars view Neoplatonism as a synthesis that arose in the third century C.E. As we have seen in Chapter Two, Hermeticists and Jewish and Christian Gnostics were already synthesizing Platonic philosophy with their mystical religious beliefs before this time. Neoplatonists incorporated these earlier philosophies into their synthesis, and scholars tend to use Neoplatonism as an umbrella term to cover all of these groups. One thing that distinguishes the Neoplatonist philosophies in the modern mind is that they saw Plato not as the source but the transmitter of many of his ideas. They viewed Plato as a link in a chain that led back to Pythagoras (582–507 B.C.E.), the philosopher who founded a mystical sect in southern Italy in the sixth century B.C.E. Pythagoras taught the doctrine of reincarnation and a method of purification through contemplation, which allowed the soul to free itself from the wheel of rebirth. Because of their focus on Pythagoras, Neoplatonists may also be referred to as Neo-Pythagoreans.

There were no ancient, Medieval, or Renaissance philosophers who called themselves Neoplatonists. The term Neoplatonism was invented by nineteenth-century German scholars to distinguish the views of some Hellenistic Platonists from earlier Platonic philosophers.[1] These modern scholars believed that a new term was necessary because they thought of Plato as a champion of reason in opposition to superstitious magical, mythical thinking and believed that the later Hellenistic Platonists who viewed Plato primarily as a mystic were creating an essentially different philosophy. Plato's philosophy encompassed both aspects and almost all ancient philosophers saw Plato as a mystic as well as a rationalist. Plato did help to develop rational investigation into the nature of reality but he also created myths to illustrate his mystic vision.

The determination of who is and is not a Neoplatonist depends solely on the judgment of modern scholars and their opinions differ. Most scholars think of the Alexandrian philosopher Plotinus (205–270 C.E.) as the first Neoplatonist. Some, however, may consider his teacher Ammonius Saccas (185–250) the first. Two other important early philosophers are unanimously included: Plotinus's student Porphyry (234–305 C.E.) and Porphyry's student Iamblichus (245–325). In late antiquity, the great Christian philosopher St. Augustine (354–430) was instrumental in synthesizing Neoplatonism and Christianity. One of the most influential and prolific Medieval Neoplatonists was Ramon Lull, who infused his mystical philosophy into the Romance literature of the thirteenth and fourteenth centuries and laid the foundation for Renaissance mysticism. The Renaissance school of Neoplatonism is said to start with Marsilio Ficino and his Platonic Academy founded outside of Florence in 1462. However, Neoplatonic influences can be found in the works of the first Renaissance artists in the mid-fourteenth century and were certainly influential at the time of the Tarot's creation.

As we have said, Neoplatonism is a broad group that incorporates Hermeticism with other branches. Therefore, the six elements of Hermeticism listed in Chapter Two—the belief that the world is alive, the value of imagination, the idea of correspondences, the belief in transmutation, the belief in the perennial philosophy, and transmission through initiation—may also apply to Neoplatonists, but not necessarily to all branches. The most broadly applicable of the six qualities is, first, that the world is alive and, second, that the purpose of life is to transmutate or progress to a higher spiritual state through the experience of enlightenment or gnosis. To this list we can add that Neoplatonists describe their mystic quest in terms and images derived from Plato's philosophy and that they believe that the creation happens through a process called emanation, in which the physical world is continually emerging from an ideal spiritual reality through a series of intermediary stages. As both of these elements are essential to the philosophy expressed in the Tarot, we will describe each one separately and show how it was incorporated into the Tarot.

PLATO THE MYSTIC

From a Neoplatonic point of view, Plato's goal was to find the answer to the eternal question that all philosophy and religion tries to answer: how does one conquer death and find eternal life? Plato saw that we are beings who are in possession of a divine intelligence, capable of understanding the abstract patterns that underlie reality and capable of contemplating endless expanses of time. Yet this intelligence is housed in an impermanent physical body. To deal with impermanence and death he sought what was immortal in each human—the soul.

Plato believed that the abstract patterns and qualities perceived by human intelligence were a glimpse of the timeless reality that lies behind the impermanent physical world. He called this the world of the archetypes, and believed that the archetypes were the ideal patterns that allowed physical reality to continually recreate itself. For example, one tree will grow to maturity and die but the ideal of "treeness" is timeless and from this essence new trees will grow. At the highest level, all archetypes were part of one spiritual unity, which Plato referred to as the One. A spark of this essential oneness was housed in the soul of each living being and as long as it remained in the physical world the soul was doomed to encounter endless deaths and rebirths. The soul, however, sought to free itself from the physical and return to the timeless One. To illustrate that the One was the object of the soul's deepest desire, Plato also referred to the One as the Good and the Beautiful.

The mystical Neoplatonic view of the soul's quest was one that we find repeated in the mythology of most ancient cultures. In mythology, this quest has been expressed in stories in which a hero, mourning the loss of a loved one, longs to be reunited. The Babylonian goddess Ishtar descended into seven hells to find her lover Tammuz; the Egyptian goddess Isis wandered the land collecting the fragments of her lover Osiris; and, in Greek mythology, Psyche searched for Eros, Demeter for Persephone, and Orpheus descended into the underworld to bring back his love Eurydice but failed in the end.

Plato recreated this myth in a philosophical form and included it in *The Republic*. In his version, we are all trapped in the underworld, in a cave living an illusion, and what is missing is the sun, a symbol for the true light that emanates from the One, the Good, and the Beautiful. Plato's heroic lover is a lover of wisdom, which is the literal meaning of the word *philosopher*. Plato's hero frees himself and ascends to the mouth of the cave, drawn by his love of light and truth, symbolized by the sun. He is reunited with his missing part, but after this enlightenment he is not yet content but, like Orpheus, he enters the underworld to free others and is frustrated in his attempt. The equation of ultimate truth with light helps to explain why among the highest-ranking trumps in the Tarot we find the Star, the Moon, and the Sun—three celestial bodies of increasing radiance. In most of the earliest Italian examples, the final trump, the World, bears a depiction of the Heavenly Jerusalem, an image of the final reward from Revelations, which is described in the text as more radiant than the sun.

THE GOOD AND THE BEAUTIFUL

In his *Symposium*, Plato also relates the ultimate vision of truth to erotic desire. He makes the point that all desire, starting with the most physical aspect of sexual desire, is a desire for what is good and beautiful, and that there is no separation between this desire and the highest aspiration of the soul—the attainment of the Good and the Beautiful. He concludes that human desire for what is physical, if experienced in its deepest level in the soul, can lead us through various steps to the desire for the archetypes at the essence of physical beauty and ultimately to the highest unity of the archetypes. To illustrate the similarities and differences in these two polarities of desire, Plato crafted the image of two Aphrodites; one goddess is worldly and rules sexuality and physical beauty and the other goddess is celestial and represents Beauty itself as the principal archetype.

The image of the beautiful celestial Aphrodite held as a symbol of the highest spiritual goal seems to have captured the imagination of the Islamic Sufi sect and it was through them that this mystical Platonic image was brought to Western Europe and eventually influenced the Tarot. By the twelfth century, Sufism had developed a Neoplatonic theosophical system that freely talked of the Hermetica along with the Koran and that was well represented in Islamic Spain. Perhaps the greatest contribution that Sufis made to Islamic culture was through their poetry and songs. They became the masters of love poetry that expressed the longing of the soul for union with God, the beloved. In the poetic forms that they created, this longing was housed in the ancient mythic metaphor of a lover longing for the one he loves. Sufi poets equated eternal beauty with the image of a female beauty, who was desired by the poet but because she was a woman of a higher rank, beyond the poet's reach. Their poetry so thoroughly infiltrated Islamic culture that all Middle Eastern love poetry is influenced by it and the distinction between profane and spiritual love has become ambiguous.

In the twelfth and thirteenth centuries, these mystic poets inflamed the Christians of Spain and southern France with their passion and the troubadour tradition was born. The image of noble love that the troubadours sang of transformed European thought. The subject of their songs was always love and beauty, which they saw as a force of spiritual transformation. The songs were of noble knights who would pledge their love to a lady of higher social status, and this love would transform the lover as he tried to prove himself worthy of her love through his exploits. This was the origin of the code of chivalry, and we have seen in Chapter One how with the inclusion of a queen in the Tarot's court cards the courts came to illustrate this theme. In the original Spanish model, the king has the highest rank and the knight is below and therefore serving the king. Below the knight is the knave or squire, who serves the knight. With the inclusion of the queen in the Tarot, the knight now serves the queen in chivalrous fashion instead of the king.

ROMANCE AND THE TAROT

At the end of the fourteenth century, the troubadour ideal was fused with stories of heroic adventure and romance literature was born. Once again, at the heart of these stories was the ideal lady as the spiritual motivating factor behind a great knight's exploits. The most famous characters to come out of the romance tradition are King Arthur and his Knights of the Round Table. In Arthurian legend, we find a mixture of ancient Celtic and Christian mysticism combined with courtly love and alchemical symbolism. All of these elements converge to form the legend of the Grail, in which the ancient myth of the soul's search for its lost partner takes the form of a knight's quest for the lost chalice that Christ used at the Last Supper. At the Last Supper, Christ made a symbolic connection between the wine in the Grail and the blood that he was to spill during his Crucifixion. It is believed that he sacrificed this blood to atone for the sins of the world and thereby spiritually heal humanity. It seems that the legendary Grail was imbued with the same healing power as the blood of Christ. Like the philosopher's stone of the alchemists, once the Grail was found it was said to be a universal cure that could heal the kingdom.

As we have seen in Chapter One, the image of the Grail is depicted on the final trump of some of the earliest Tarot decks and the artist Bonifacio Bembo, the creator of the earliest existing hand-painted Tarot cards, made use of images that he created for an Arthurian romance as inspiration for some of his Tarot trumps, but the connection between the Tarot and romance is more than incidental. The message that is illustrated in the trumps is at home in romance literature and it is likely that this is its source. We can see elements of the same theme in the first romance novel.

Although romance literature was developed in northern Europe, it was crafted on the model developed by the fourteenth-century Majorcan Neoplatonist Ramon Lull, to whom we were introduced in the section on Kabalah in the last chapter. Besides creating his Neoplatonic system of correspondences, which he called Ars Magna, Lull wrote the first romance novel, titled *Blanquerna* after the name of the book's main character. *Blanquerna* is the first European novel, the first Western book to be written in the common language instead of Latin, and it was destined to be Lull's most famous and influential work.

In *Blanquerna,* although the plot is not identical to the story in the Tarot, we can see some of the same essential themes and characters that were later included in the Tarot of Marseilles. The novel relates the story of the main character, Blanquerna, who as a young man is presented with a choice between the worldly love of a young woman and the love of wisdom and virtue found in a life devoted to religion. This is the same choice that is symbolically represented on the Lovers card in the Tarot of Marseilles, where we find a young man presented with a choice between a woman with flowers in her hair, representing sensuality, and a woman with a laurel wreath in her hair, representing the path to victory achieved through the practice of wisdom and virtue. As in the story presented in the trumps, which depicts a hero on the Chariot card triumphing over love and pursuing the symbols of wisdom depicted in later cards, Blanquerna chooses the second path—the path of wisdom and virtue.

In the pursuit of his spiritual goal, Blanquerna joins a monastery, but because of his virtue and innate intelligence he finds that he is continually promoted through the ranks of the clergy until eventually he is elected pope. One might think that this would be the fulfilment of Blanquerna's spiritual goals, but he finds that the role of pope entangles him in politics instead of the spiritual devotion that he desires. The image of the pope as the highest worldly figure is exactly how he is presented in the Tarot. The Tarot's Pope is the highest ranking trump of the four temporal rulers found in the first section of the sequence: The Papesse, the Empress, the Emperor, and the Pope. All of these cards are trumped by the Lovers card, which presents the choice between what is worldly and what is spiritual, and true images of spiritual growth, such as the Hermit and the virtues Justice, Strength, and Temperance, are found in the next section.

As the pope, Blanquerna realizes that he is confronted with the same choice between the worldly and the spiritual that confronted him when he was a young man. Only now, the role of pope represents the worldly path instead of a young woman. Blanquerna longs to leave his position and devote his life to contemplation. At this point, the emperor sends Blanquerna a jester named Ramon the Fool, who arrives with a dog and a hawk, an image close to the Fool card in the Tarot of Marseilles. Ramon is like a Zen master who clarifies with riddles and cuts through misconceptions with simplicity and ease. He is a model for the wise fool that will be enshrined in the Tarot's wild card. With Ramon the Fool's help, Blanquerna sets the affairs of the Church in order, and is at last free to do what he set out to do. He resigns his office and sets out to become a hermit and seek divine illumination. As in the Tarot, the Hermit is a higher trump than the Pope.

Blanquerna's first duty as a hermit is to help his fellow hermits defeat temptation. At their request, he composes a book of meditations to give them daily guidance. This book, called *The Book of the Lover and the Beloved,* is a book within the novel and is often published as a separate piece. In the novel Blanquerna freely admits that it is inspired by Sufi poetry. *The Book of the Lover and the Beloved* consists of 365 love poems, one for each day of the year, in which the devout in contemplation is the lover and sometimes a fool, and the beloved is God. The image of the beautiful woman standing in the center of the symbols of the four Evangelists that we find on the Tarot of Marseilles World card is the visual equivalent of the romantic sentiment expressed in Lull's book of poems.

As we discussed in Chapter One, the symbols of the four Evangelists—the lion, the bull, the eagle, and the man—when assigned to each corner as they are on the World trump—represent the throne of God in Christian iconography. In the Tarot, but for the one exception illustrated in Chapter One (see figure 4, page 24), instead of finding Christ on this throne as we would in an orthodox representation, we find a beautiful woman who represents the beloved. By combining the two images the Tarot artists were expressing the same sentiment as Lull's poems. In the late fifteenth century, Plato's Symposium was admired by Ficino and his Neoplatonic Academy, and through Ficino's influence the female nude entered Western art as a symbol of Plato's celestial Venus and spiritual Beauty. It is because of this Neoplatonic influence that the "beloved" depicted on the World trump in the Tarot of Marseilles as a symbol of the highest truth is also a nude.

Although Plato presents two Aphrodites, representing his two polarities, the physical and the archetypal, as we saw in the previous description of the symposium, Plato believed that an individual needed to progress through various steps to reach the higher goal. This observation introduces the second Neoplatonic belief mentioned above, emanation. Emanation introduces a stairway that allows the archetypal to descend to the physical and the physical to ascend to the archetypal. The trumps in the Tarot act as a symbolic stairway in the same way and to understand the message in the trumps we need to delve into the nature of emanation. In the development of this idea, Plato seems to have been influenced by the teachings of his predecessor, the sixth-century B.C.E. mystic Pythagoras, and we will need to learn more about Pythagoras as well.

EMANATION

Although in modern history Pythagoras is remembered primarily as a mathematician and a philosopher, in the ancient world Pythagoras was spoken of with the reverence and awe accorded an enlightened religious leader. It is said that he had a golden thigh, that he could be in two places at one time, that he could charm animals, and that he could remember his past lives. Some ancient writers claimed that he was an incarnation of the god Apollo.

Although there are no known texts in existence written by Pythagoras, his biography and teachings are known to us through the writings of Hellenistic Neoplatonists, particularly Porphyry and Iamblichus. They tell us that Pythagoras was born on the Greek island of Samos in approximately 582 B.C.E. In adulthood he migrated to southern Italy where he founded a mystical sect, which as we have said, practiced purification rites designed to lead his followers to the experience of enlightenment and free their souls from the wheel of reincarnation. The sect outlived its founder and was influential for approximately two hundred years. Therefore we cannot be certain how much of the Pythagorean teachings originated with Pythagoras and how much was added by his followers.

Pythagoras was said to believe that all of reality could be expressed in numbers—a concept that is at the heart of Western science. He also taught, however, that numbers had qualities or symbolic aspects as well as defining quantity and sequential order. The divinatory symbolism associated with the ten pip cards in the Tarot and other decks is likely to derive from the teachings of Pythagoras. The Pythagoreans created a diagram composed of ten dots designed to illustrate the relationship of numbers to physical reality, and this diagram will be a useful tool for explaining the concept of emanation.

THE TETRACTYS

To represent the process by which the world is continually created by the numerical intelligence of the universe, the Pythagoreans constructed a triangular arraignment of ten dots with one at the top, two on the second layer, three on the third, and four at the base. This symbol was called the tetractys, and the Pythagoreans considered it sacred (see figure 18).

They were said to take an oath on this symbol: "By him that transmitted to our soul the Tetractys / The spring and root of ever-flowing nature."[2]

The tetractys was an illustration of the mystical concept of creation—emanation. In emanation, the act of creation of the physical world takes place in progressive stages that flow from an indivisible spiritual source, the One, represented by the single dot at the top of the diagram, to the diversity of the world of form, composed of four elements represented by the four dots at the base of the diagram. The Pythagoreans made use of this diagram to describe the creation in numerous ways. For example, the four visible layers of the tetractys with one to four dots describe the geometric emanation of the material world. The top depicts the point, a theoretical beginning with no dimension. The second layer has two points, which describe a line. Although a line has length it has no depth and cannot be perceived any more easily than a point. On the next layer, there are three points, which are necessary to form the first polygon, the triangle. This gives us a two-dimensional plan of reality. The base has four points, which brings us to three-dimensional reality and allows us to form the first polyhedron, the tetrahedron, which is composed of four triangular sides— like a pyramid with a triangle for a base. This is the beginning of physical reality.

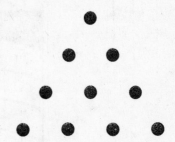

Figure 18. The Pythagorean tetractys

To the Pythagoreans, not only did the four lines of dots in the tetractys have meaning, they also found significance in the three lines of space between the lines of dots. These three immaterial layers in the tetractys symbolized the relationship between numbers represented by the dots above and below the space. These relationships are called ratios. The first ratio is between one and two, written as 1:2. Between the layers in the tetractys, we can also find the ratios 2:3 and 3:4. Pythagoras found that these ratios described the vibrations of the most important points on the musical scale: 1:2 described the whole note, 2:3 the perfect fifth, and 3:4 the perfect fourth. These three notes are harmonious realities that underlie all music in any culture, and all music scales, no matter how many notes they have, make use of these notes.

As we can see, the emanations depicted on the tetractys may be fourfold or threefold, but if we combine the three and the four there are seven emanations. The various Neoplatonic branches make use of all three of these numbers in various combinations to describe the emanations in each system. We have already seen in Chapters One and Two that the numbers three and seven are important elements in the structure of the sequence of trumps. The twenty-one trumps can easily be divided into three groups of seven cards and when divided each of the three groups of images has a common theme that is distinct. The first group is concerned with worldly power and sensuality; the second group depicts time, death, and the harsh realities of life along with the virtues; and the third group depicts a mystical ascent through celestial bodies of increasing radiance. This is our first clue that the trumps describe a ladder of emanation.

THE SEVEN-RUNGED LADDER

To complete his musical scale Pythagoras added four notes to the three essentials, and created the diatonic scale of seven notes that is still in use today. Besides completing the symbolic relationship between the musical scale and the seven layers of the tetractys, the reason that seven notes were chosen also had to do with ancient astronomy. As we mentioned in our discussion of Hermeticism in Chapter

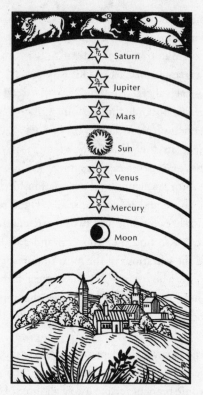

Figure 19. The ancient Greek cosmos

Two, the ancient astronomers observed that there were seven heavenly bodies that moved separately from the fixed stars in the constellations. These seven included the Sun and the Moon as well as Mercury, Venus, Mars, Jupiter, and Saturn. The ancient Greeks called these *planetes,* which meant "wanderer" in Greek. This is the origin of the English word *planet.* It appeared to ancient astronomers that the earth was in the center of the universe and that the planets and the "sphere" of the fixed stars encircled the earth. Therefore, the Sun and the Moon were planets and the earth was not. Each planet was thought to be on a separate crystal sphere, one inside the other like the layers of an onion. Eventually the planets came to be organized by the speed with which they moved around the earth. The Moon, the fastest, was on the bottom layer and Saturn, the slowest, was on the top layer, as shown in the figure 19. Pythagoras believed that each planet made a musical note as it orbited the earth and it was those seven notes that he was trying to capture with the diatonic scale.

The seven planets were believed to be gods, and these seven gods were emanations forming a cosmic ladder connecting the celestial world with the physical world. As in the Hermetic myth of the first man described in Poimandres, discussed in Chapter Two, it was believed that the soul of each individual came down this ladder into the physical world. The astrological natal chart is a map of this journey. It outlines which constellation of the zodiac was chosen as an entry and what qualities were acquired by the soul as it encountered each of the seven gods of the planets on the way down. Because the soul came down this ladder, mystics believed that at the death of the body the soul would ascend the ladder back to the spiritual realm. Until the soul reached enlightenment, however, this attainment of the spiritual height would not be permanent. At the beginning of the next incarnation the soul would descend the ladder again, and this process would continue until the soul could remember its true nature and rejoin the One.

THE WHEEL OF FORTUNE AND FATE

One of the oldest descriptions of this descent in ancient literature is found in the last chapter of Plato's masterpiece *The Republic*. This account is also valuable to us because it is likely to be the oldest depiction in literature of the Wheel of Fortune, which is the subject illustrated on the Tarot's central trump, and it will give us insight into the philosophical implications of this image. In the tenth and last book of *The Republic*, Plato ends with a description of the soul's journey after death. He tells the story of Er, a young hero who was slain in battle but returned to life after twelve days and recounted what he experienced in the afterlife. Er tells how the souls of the dead are judged and receive a reward or punishment that will last for one thousand years. When this is complete, the souls approach the physical realm where they will descend back into a body and reincarnate. As they approach, they can see that the whole of the cosmos is resting in the lap of the goddess Necessity (Ananke in Greek). The Greek goddess Necessity is the equivalent of the Latin Fortuna, the goddess depicted in the center of the Wheel of Fortune in the fifteenth-century Visconti-Sforza Tarot.

At the center of the cosmos, which is resting in Necessity's lap, there is the ball of the earth with a spindle piercing it and extending above and below to pierce eight spheres of progressively greater size, each encasing the one before it like a vessel. The eighth and largest is the rotation of the fixed stars, and on each rotation below it there is one of the seven planets known to the ancients. From the outermost down, they are: Saturn, Venus, Mars, Mercury, Jupiter, Sun, Moon. This is one of the oldest descriptions of the Classical cosmos and the order in which the planets are listed is not the order by speed of orbit that became accepted later. During the Middle Ages, the eight wheels that comprise this cosmic model were symbolically represented by one eight-spoked wheel. This icon is the Wheel of Fortune that is depicted in the Tarot.

To demonstrate that the soul's descent into this wheel of the cosmos was a descent into mortality and fate, Plato adds that Necessity's daughters, the three Fates, can be seen sitting around her. Their names are Lachesis, who sings a song of the past; Clotho, who sings of the present; and Atropos, who sings of the future. Together, they determine the quality of the thread that will become the life of each mortal and the moment that the thread will be cut, thereby ending that life. The three daughters of Necessity represent the three aspects of time—the past, the present, and the future. Further, they represent mortality and the suffering of life that the mystic is attempting to cure.

In the Visconti-Sforza Wheel of Fortune card, Fortuna stands blindfolded in the center of her wheel surrounded by four male figures. Behind each, inscribed in the gold background, is a written statement representing the sentiment expressed by each figure. The man on the left climbs the wheel. He is sprouting ass's ears, and the inscription on the ribbon issuing from his mouth can be translated as "I will reign." He is a symbol of the first part of life or the past, which is ruled by Lachesis. On top of the wheel a man sits holding a mace and an orb. He is crowned with full-grown ass's ears, and declares "I do reign." He is sitting in a precarious position, unaware that he could topple at any moment. He represents the present, which is ruled by Clotho. Descending the wheel headfirst, a man with an ass's tail but no ears bemoans, "I have reigned." He represents the future ruled by Atropos. At the bottom, a crawling man simply says, "I am without reign." This fourth figure represents the state of death, which is engendered when Atropos cuts the mortal thread.

It is evident that although the three Fates are not directly depicted on the Visconti-Sforza card, the aspects of life that they represent are. On the Tarot of Marseilles Wheel of Fortune card, Fortuna's wheel is depicted without her, and the four figures have been reduced to three monkeys: one ascending, one crowned at the top, and one descending headfirst. Although Fortuna is not present, symbolism representing the aspects of life ruled by her three daughters is depicted. Near the Wheel of Fortune card in the Marseilles order there are trumps that echo the same theme. There is the Hermit, depicted as an old man holding a lantern—in the original Italian decks instead of a lantern he holds an hourglass representing time; the Hanged Man, who represents a fall from power; and Death, who is mortality personified. We can see that one theme being expressed in this central section of the trumps is that suffering and death are part of the fate that a soul can expect to encounter once she or he has descended the ladder of emanation and entered a physical body.

Although the ladder of emanation is described as the path each soul must follow at birth, mystics believed that the emanations are an ever-present spiritual reality that could be seen while in a trance. To a mystic, this was the most important aspect of the ladder of emanation because while in a trance he or she could ascend the ladder and attempt to discover his or her true nature. Next, we will look at how different Neoplatonic branches created models of this ladder to aid them in this quest.

MYSTICAL TOOLS

We have already encountered several models of the ladder of emanation in Chapter Two in the sections on Hermeticism and the Kabalah, but let's review these systems along with some others to see what they can teach us about the nature of the trumps. In the section on Hermeticism, besides describing how the first Man, who is depicted in the Poimandres, descended the ladder of the seven planets, we discussed how he was able to free himself from the bonds of Nature and ascend back to God by climbing the ladder of the planets and letting go of the negative influences that he had received from each planet. The visualization of this process is the most common form of the meditation on the mystical ascent found in the ancient world.

Plotinus, the first Neoplatonist, developed a system with only three levels of emanation. At the top was the One; next, came the World Intelligence, visualized as a masculine force called Nous; and then the World Soul, visualized as a feminine presence called Psyche. The fourth-century Syrian Neoplatonist Iamblichus filled out this ladder of emanation from the One to the physical world by adding Plato's sphere of the fixed stars and the spheres of the seven planets between the world and the World Soul, and incorporated the mystical practice of ascending the ladder of the planets in a trance state. In the sixth century, a Syrian Christian writer known as the Pseudo Dionysus, created a synthesis of Iamblichus's system with Christianity by substituting the Christian God for the One and equating nine choirs of angels to the gods of the planets, the fixed stars, and the heaven beyond. This text was translated into Latin by the ninth-century Irish scholar Erigena and became a major component in the Christian worldview. Because the sevenfold ladder of the planets became part of Christian theology, it was familiar to artists in the early Renaissance, and this is likely to be the reason that the number seven is important to the structure of the sequence of trumps.

As we have seen in the discussion of alchemy, sevenfold systems of emanation did not have to be strictly linked to the planets. The alchemists devised a ladder of seven metals that was symbolically linked to the planets but they also organized the alchemical processes performed in their workshops into a group of seven that was not closely linked to the planets. The groups of seven trumps in the Tarot are closer to the second example. They are organized in groups of seven to demonstrate that they are emanations, but, except for the Sun and the Moon trumps, they are not symbolically linked to individual planets. The ladder of the planets is illustrated on the Marseilles Star trump, however, where the artist has depicted seven small stars arranged around a larger eighth star. This image is close to alchemical engravings depicting the ladder of the seven planets, and there can be little doubt that the Marseilles Star was based on the alchemical model.

The Kabalistic Tree of Life discussed in Chapter Two is an adaptation of the Tetractys in a new shape. As we saw in figure 14 in Chapter Two, the Tree of Life, like the Tetractys, is a diagram composed of ten dots or circles. It will be helpful to look at figure 14 again before reading the following discussion. In the Tree of Life, however, the ten dots, called sephiroth, have been rearranged so that they reside on seven levels instead of four. The kabalistic explanation of the symbolism contained in the Tree of Life, however, shows that they are symbolically linked to the four levels of the Tetractys.

In the Kabalah the ten circles, or sephiroth, were spoken of in four sections that outline the creative process. The first of the ten sephiroth, Crown, represents the supreme unity, the One. In an effort to comprehend the nature of oneness, the One is said to have contemplated himself and split into a duality of the one contemplated, and the one contemplating, or feminine and masculine. This pair became the next two sephiroth, wisdom and intelligence. The awareness that these two are aspects of one makes them a unit, with this awareness taking a third position. Through this reflection, a mirror image of the top three was created in the denser reality below. This is why the next three sephiroth, greatness, power, and beauty, form an inverted image of the three top sephiroth. This is the world of planning, and the creative momentum that built this level could not stop until it repeated itself on a lower layer. Now consciousness of this pattern again creates a separate position, this time the fourth. Therefore the bottom section has four sephiroth representing the fourfold world of the four elements, four directions, and four seasons.

In the Kabalah these four groups of sephiroth were equated to the four Kabalistic worlds that were mentioned in Chapter Two. From the top down they are: Atziluth, the archetypal world of unity and pure bliss; Briah, the creative world where concepts are born; Yetzirah, the formative world of design; and Assiah, the material world. These four worlds, which depict a progression from the immaterial to the material plane, can easily be related to the four levels of emanation that form the tetractys. Besides dividing the Tree of Life into these four levels, the Kabalists believed that the entire Tree of Life was repeated again on each level, thereby creating four Trees of increasing density as they descend. Again, the mystic could use this pattern as a meditative tool in his or her ascent to spiritual wisdom.

The Tarot's trumps seem to be a similar type of tool. Especially in the Tarot of Marseilles, the trumps can be divided into groups that form three levels with seven emanations on each. This system is similar to the Kabalistic model, but it is not Kabalistic. It makes use of seven emanations instead of ten, and three layers instead of four. Also, the theme expressed in the seven cards on each layer in the Tarot's emanations are not expressed in the Kabalistic description of the Tree of Life. The Tarot is a separate Neoplatonic system, and to understand why three layers were chosen for this system and the nature of the themes that are expressed, we will, once again, look to Plato and his mystic vision.

THE THREE PARTS OF THE SOUL

In the previous section, we determined that the number seven, which is incorporated into the structure of the sequence of trumps, is symbolic of the Neoplatonic ladder of emanation. In this section we will examine why the Tarot's creators chose to include three groups of seven cards in the trumps. As in the Kabalistic system, the trumps seem to be a system in which the ladder of emanation is represented as existing on more than one layer, each layer in the trumps being represented by one of three groups of seven cards. To unlock the meaning of this structure we will turn to Plato's theory of the three parts of the soul: the soul of appetite, the soul of will, and the soul of reason.

In Chapter Two, we read that comte de Mellet, one of the first occultists to investigate the Tarot, observed that the twenty-one Marseilles trumps can be divided into three groups of seven and that each of these groups expresses a distinct theme. De Mellet equated these three sections of the trumps to the three historical ages found in Classical mythology: the age of gold, the age of silver, and the age of iron. As we look at the sequence of trumps, it becomes obvious that, even if de Mellet's mythological explanation was not entirely correct, his observation that the allegory can be divided into three sections, each expressing a separate theme, was correct. Even historian Michael Dummett, who delves into the history of the Tarot but does not readily offer symbolic interpretation, has to admit that this is true.[3] The first section, from the Magician to the Chariot, contains a hierarchy of worldly figures; the second part, from Justice to Temperance, is darker, with images of time, suffering, and death, though the presence of virtues suggests that through the confrontation of suffering spiritual growth is nurtured; and the final section, from the Devil to the World, depicts an ascent from the trap laid by the Devil to the heavenly realms.

As we learned in Chapter One, the order of the trumps in the Tarot of Marseilles is not the only one that existed in the Renaissance. We learned that in the fifteenth century there were primarily three different patterns for organizing the trumps, and that each trump would bear a different number in each pattern. At first, this fact may seem like an insurmountable obstacle preventing us from finding meaning in the trumps. This change in numbering or order, however, is not disruptive to the threefold structure. It is not disruptive because in the different orders, the characters in each section rarely migrate to another section. The positions of the four temporal rulers changes in relation to each other but they remain as a unit in the beginning of the story. The first five cards, therefore, are either the Juggler, the Papesse, the Empress, the Emperor, and the Pope, or the Juggler, the Empress, the Emperor, the Papesse, and the Pope. The Lovers and the Chariot may change places with each other but still be placed after the temporal rulers. The last two trumps, Judgement and the World, may change places with each other but they remain at the end of the story.

The main exception to this rule is the placement of the three cardinal virtues: Justice, Strength, and Temperance. We may find them grouped together in the middle section, one after another or spread out between the Lovers and the Devil. In the third order, a virtue is assigned to each of the three sections with Justice in last place coming between Judgement and the World. This order demonstrates that there is a relationship between these three virtues and the three parts of the story. As we will see, Plato made a connection between the virtues and his theory of the triple soul, and this is a clue that confirms the Platonic nature of the story.

PLATO'S CHARIOT

Plato eloquently expresses the triple nature of the soul in his *Phaedrus*, where he crafted a myth in which the soul is compared to a chariot with a driver and two winged horses. Plato created this image in the *Phaedrus* to illustrate the immortality of the soul, but the charioteer and the chariot's two winged horses also represent the three parts of the soul. One horse is dark and moody, representing the soul of desire or appetite. This is the lowest part of the soul, that part that ties one to physical reality through its needs. The other horse is white and noble, representing the soul of will or spirit. This is the heroic soul that helps one to rise above physical limitations and to put the safety of others above one's personal needs. It can be ascetic and seeks personal glory. The driver, which is depicted as female, is the soul of reason, and she must guide the other parts. The soul of reason is the highest aspect of the soul. She is the intelligence and insight that perceives the pure world beyond the physical.

Each person is said to have a chariot existing on another plane of reality and its purpose is to carry the soul to the celestial region of the gods. The journey is said to continue over many lifetimes, for as we learned previously, Plato, like his predecessor Pythagoras, believed in reincarnation. When a person engages in unvirtuous behavior the winged horses lose feathers and cannot ascend. But the practice of virtue gives the horses new feathers and strength for the journey. In this myth, we can see the origin of Levi's illustration of the Chariot with its dark and light sphinxes that we saw in Chapter Two, but its influences can also be seen in Renaissance art and philosophy.

Plato elaborated on the theory of the triple soul throughout his dialogues. His most extensive explanation can be found in his major work, *The Republic*. This is a description of Plato's ideal society, in which the ruler is an enlightened spiritual master called the philosopher king, and in which each citizen is allowed to rise to the highest position in society that his or her spiritual development will allow. Plato believed that because the aspect of the soul that was strongest in each individual would dominate the personality, there must be three types of people. The nature of these three types is evident in the following quote from *The Republic:* "Then we may begin by assuming that there are three classes of men—lovers of wisdom, lovers of honor, lovers of gain?"[4] The lovers of wisdom are those individuals in which the soul of reason has taken control, the lovers of honor are dominated by the soul of will, and the lovers of gain are dominated by the soul of appetite.

Plato visualized his republic as having three classes, which again reflect the three aspects of the soul. Those individuals who were dominated by the soul of appetite would form the body of workers at the lowest rung of this social order; those dominated by the soul of will would form the next highest class, the warrior protectors; and at the top those dominated by the soul of reason would form the ruling class. At the head of the ruling class, one person, in whom the three parts of the soul would be working together in perfect harmony, would rise to the position of philosopher king. For the society to be properly ordered and directed, the philosopher king had to be spiritually enlightened, because, for the three parts of the republic to work together in harmony, the leader had to be an example of this harmony. To assure that this was so, the entire society would be designed to nurture the spiritual development of all citizens, and everyone, both men and women, was eligible to rise to the highest position that they were able to achieve, including philosopher king. Besides describing an ideal society, therefore, *The Republic* describes a method of advancing toward spiritual perfection through three levels of emanation, one for each aspect of the soul. As we will see, this method seems to be the model for the three levels of emanation illustrated in the trumps.

Plato's method of spiritual advancement involved the purification of each aspect of soul through the practice of the appropriate virtue. First, Plato addressed the soul of appetite, which was located in the abdomen. If the soul of appetite were allowed unchecked control of the personality the individual would fall into the excesses of lust, gluttony, and greed. To become a citizen of the Republic, therefore, one had to develop the virtue temperance, a balance of the desires in which beauty, health, and harmony are prized above excess. To achieve this appreciation of harmony, Plato recommended the study of music. The people who developed temperance became the workers who formed most of the population.

From the pool of workers, certain people would be able to purify the second soul center, the soul of will, which was associated with the desire for power and prestige but also with anger and cruelty if allowed excessive control. It was believed to be located in the heart. The soul of will would be purified through the virtue known as fortitude, strength, or courage (a word derived from the root *cor*, meaning "heart"). This virtue would be developed by the study of gymnastics, which included martial arts and developed discipline and the ability to conquer fear, besides physical strength. These men and women would rise to the level of warrior protectors. The term for the discipline of the athlete and the warrior in Greek was *askesis*, the origin of the English word "ascetic." Askesis involved self-mastery through the denial of pleasures. Later this term came to be applied to the discipline of a mystic or a philosopher as well.[5]

From this second group, some would develop the virtue prudence, or wisdom, and purify the soul of reason, which was located in the head. Prudence would be developed through the study of mathematics, which developed logic but also developed an appreciation for the abstract ideals that underlie physical reality. These men and women would become the leaders. As we can see, the leaders had to develop all three virtues, temperance, strength, and prudence, and by doing this they would have spiritually progressed through the three soul levels. Plato considered the three levels a hierarchy in which each soul level came closer to a divine model as one ascended, as in a ladder of emanation.

Education, however, did not stop once one reached the highest social level. From this elite group, one individual would develop the highest virtue, justice, and become the philosopher king. To develop justice Plato recommended the study of philosophy, which is the contemplation of the divine plan. Plato did not consider justice simply a fourth virtue, and the philosopher king was not associated with a fourth soul level. The other three virtues were all aspects of justice, and justice was achieved when temperance, strength, and prudence were working in harmony with each other, and all three souls were functioning in their proper place. Therefore, when the lower three virtues are present justice is already implied. The harmony of justice was a reflection of the divine plan and could only be accomplished when the threefold soul of the individual merged with the World Soul and the individual embodied the divine plan. Plato described one who achieved this state as "ruled by divine wisdom dwelling within him."[6]

The four virtues that Plato describes in *The Republic* are the same four that Christian philosophers and theologians later came to call the cardinal virtues. Medieval and Christian writers applied the same relationship to the cardinal virtues as Plato. They believed that there was one principal mother virtue and that the other three virtues were three parts of this one. They did, however, incorporate one change. In the Medieval Christian order the positions of justice and prudence have been reversed, making justice the third virtue and prudence the principal one. In this order temperance, strength, and justice, the same three cardinal virtues that we find in the trumps, are considered part of prudence, and prudence is associated with the Wisdom of God, which can be equated to the Tarot's World.

As we saw in the quote from *The Republic* above, Plato linked justice with the concept of wisdom. As wisdom is connected to the virtue prudence, sometimes in his writings he seemed to switch the order of justice and prudence. Later Hellenistic philosophers, particularly the Stoics, were strongly influenced by Plato's description of the virtues. Stoicism was a Hellenistic philosophic tradition founded by the Greek philosopher Zeno (335–263 B.C.E.). Zeno taught that reason should be the guiding principle behind human behavior and that human reason was a reflection of the divine order of the cosmos. Stoics adopted Plato's concept of the World Soul and the importance of the four cardinal virtues, but, because they placed importance on reason as the guiding principle of the cosmos, they preferred to have prudence depicted as the principal virtue. Stoics believed that through the practice of philosophy, reason, associated with the World Soul, would help justice to become dominant in the highest aspect of the human soul, and tranquility would be achieved. With reason as a guide, the philosopher would remain calm when faced with death and the harsh realities of life, associated with the soul of will, and when faced with the sensual temptations, associated with the soul of appetite. The Stoics believed that the World Soul and the physical world existed together on one plane and therefore they did not embrace the theory of emanation, but some of their ideas influenced the Neoplatonists and early Christians.

In ancient Rome, the Stoic order of the virtues, with prudence as the principal virtue, was adopted by the famous Roman philosopher and orator Cicero (106–143 B.C.E.). Through his influence and that of St. Augustine (354–430 C.E.) the Stoic model came to be adopted by Christian philosophers. The most complete and influential discussion of the Christian theories concerning the virtues is found in the *Summa Theologica* of St. Thomas Aquinas (1225–1274). Aquinas's text was well read in the Renaissance and his view of the virtues would have been familiar to the artists who created the Tarot. While discussing the cardinal virtues Aquinas clearly states: "Prudence is absolutely the principal of all the virtues. The others are principal, each in its own genus. That part of the soul which is rational by participation is threefold. . . ."[7] To illustrate Prudence's threefold nature, Renaissance artists sometimes depicted her as having three faces. It seems that her three aspects are also illustrated in the Tarot's trumps. We are now ready to apply what we have learned to the interpretation of the trumps.

THE TAROT AND THE THREE PARTS OF THE SOUL

We will now look at the overall pattern of the trumps and demonstrate that they contain a three-part story that is based on Plato's theory of the three parts of the soul: the soul of appetite, the soul of will, and the soul of reason. As we will see, however, the Tarot's interpretation is not directly Platonic but incorporates the views of Stoics, Neoplatonists, and Christians. We will also look into the relationship between the virtues and the triple soul and see how the Tarot's creators played with this interaction to come up with three variations on the theme. In addition, this investigation will help us to answer the question that occultists have pondered since Court de Gébelin first noticed the Tarot: where is the fourth cardinal virtue? This discussion is meant to give us an overview of the pattern that is in the trumps. We will save a detailed description of each trump for the next chapter.

We learned in Chapter One that the trumps are a hierarchical sequence of images in which each card in the sequence is more valuable than the last and therefore able to "trump" the cards below it in when playing the game. In the Renaissance, is was common to create works of art in which allegorical or symbolic figures representing various occupations, branches of learning, virtues, and celestial bodies were grouped in a hierarchical sequence from the lowest to the highest. These sets of images were created as an aid to memory, but the hierarchical ordering of the images had a spiritual message as well. These images formed a Neoplatonic ladder of emanation that could be used in meditation. These types of images influenced the popular arts in the Renaissance, and there were even parades with processions of allegorical characters that were performed every year in all of the major cities of Italy. These parades were called triumphs, and, as we learned, the Tarot originally bore the same name, but we will delve into this relationship in more detail in the next section.

For now, it is only important to realize that the trumps are related to this popular culture and that they form a Neoplatonic ladder of emanation, which is divided into three sections that relate to Plato's three parts of the soul. In the Tarot of Marseilles these three parts are neatly divided into three groups of seven cards and we will use the Marseilles order for this discussion.

The first seven cards in the Tarot of Marseilles are: the Magician, the Papesse, the Empress, the Emperor, the Pope, the Lovers, and the Chariot. The Marseilles Magician is not the ceremonial magician found in the modern Waite-Smith deck. He is depicted as a trickster or a gambler who has come to a fair for the purpose of monetary gain. He is clearly dominated by the soul of appetite. The next four trumps are the temporal or worldly rulers. At first, we might think of the rulers as belonging to a high level of soul development, but this is not Plato's ideal republic. In the Renaissance, rulers, including the pope, were considered worldly figures dominated by the soul of appetite. To make this point, all of the rulers are trumped by the Lovers card which depicts Cupid, the god of carnal love. This theme is supported by the fact that there are two male and two female rulers that are clearly mated—the Emperor has the Empress, and the Pope has the Papesse.

On the bottom of the Lovers card, a young man is given a choice between the love of a woman with flowers in her hair, representing sensuality, and a woman with laurel leaves in her hair, representing victory. The implication is that the young man must choose between allowing sensuality and the soul of appetite to rule his life or allowing the desire for victory and the soul of will to rule. The last card depicts a warrior in a chariot representing the discipline and determination of the warrior. This indicates that the soul of will has become dominant and we may move on to the next section.

In the next section of trumps, we find: Justice, the Hermit, the Wheel of Fortune, Strength, the Hanged Man, Death, and Temperance. These are images of time or asceticism (the Hermit), fate (the Wheel of Fortune and the Hanged Man), and mortality (Death), interspersed with three cardinal virtues, all of which relate to the hero's struggle with the harsh realities of life and to the soul of will. The three virtues that are included are the Platonic virtues that relate to the three parts of the soul, except that the Tarot's creators were influenced by the Stoic Roman writers and Aquinas, and have therefore replaced Plato's prudence with justice, implying that prudence is the principal virtue.

There are, however, further changes. Allowing for Justice as a replacement, the three virtues in the Marseilles deck are in the opposite order from Plato's list—Justice, Strength, and Temperance instead of Temperance, Strength, and Justice. There are two other orders that were commonly used in fifteenth- and sixteenth-century Italy. In one alternative that was popular in Italian decks, the same virtues are spread out with one virtue in each section in the proper order so that each virtue corresponds with the dominant soul of each level—Temperance with the soul of appetite in the first section, Strength with the soul of will in the second section, and Justice with the soul of reason in the third section. This is the most Platonic use of the virtues. In the other alternative order, the three virtues are placed one after the other between the Lovers (or sometimes the Chariot) and the Wheel of Fortune. This placement was used for the Florentine Minchiate, discussed in Chapter One, and, in this example, the virtues are in the correct Platonic/Stoic order. This second alternative order was also used in decks in Sicily and in Bologna, but with the virtues rearranged thus: Temperance, Justice, and Strength. Renaissance artists, apparently, allowed themselves to be creative in their use of these symbols but they consistently made use of the three cardinal virtues that form the three parts of Prudence in the Platonic/Stoic system.

The Marseilles order of the virtues, with Justice in the lead, seems like a deliberate reversal of the Platonic/Stoic order. It may be that the creators of this order were suggesting that the virtues are coming to us as a divine gift and that they are proceeding in the opposite direction as time and fate. Or perhaps they were suggesting a Stoic interpretation in which Justice, representing the soul of reason, is reaching down to the lower souls and helping them to develop the other virtues. We cannot be certain, but we can see that in the Marseilles order the virtues begin and end the second section, suggesting that, in the soul of will, while facing the truth about one's fate and mortality, one develops the three virtues that are the three parts of Prudence. With this soul development accomplished we can move into the third section, the soul of reason, and advance toward the divine unity that is Prudence.

The third section contains the trumps: the Devil, the Tower, the Star, the Moon, the Sun, Judgement, and the World. In this section, the soul of reason is dominant. We may therefore be surprised to find the Devil in the lead. The Devil is an unreasonable-looking creature that is part man and part woman, with batwings, bird's feet, and a deer's antlers. Chained to the pillar that he stands on there are two smaller minions, one female and one male. These smaller figures seem to represent the lower aspects of the soul—the female minion representing the soul of appetite and sensuality and the male minion representing the soul of will and asceticism. From the vantage point of the soul of reason, both lower souls are seen as being ruled by the demon of chaos, and this is the problem that the soul will attempt to solve.

The second card in this section depicts lightning striking a tower and toppling its crown as two figures fall from the tower. The lightning bolt suggests a divine intervention that removes the two lower aspects of the soul from power. Perhaps this has happened because the soul of reason is aligning itself with the divine will. With the soul of will firmly in command, we come to the Star. The nude depicted on the Star is pouring water from two pitchers—one is being poured on the land and one on the sea. The nude is a representation of the soul commonly found in Renaissance art. In this case she seems to represent the soul of will. The act of pouring water on what is wet and on what is dry is an alchemical symbol for the harmony of opposites. The opposites in this case are the two lower parts of the soul. The fact that the soul of reason is bringing harmony to the other parts of the soul is our first suggestion that the virtue Prudence is present. At the top of the Star the Neoplatonic ladder of the planets is depicted as seven smaller stars surrounding a larger eighth star, representing the eighth sphere of the fixed stars. The soul is now ready to climb this ladder.

After the Star we encounter the Moon and the Sun, two celestial bodies of increasing light, but in Neoplatonic symbolism they are also the archetypal masculine and feminine pair and the ultimate rulers of time. To go beyond them is to go beyond duality and time. Next we encounter Judgement, a Christian symbol for the resurrection of the dead, which was to happen at the end of time. In Neoplatonic symbolism it represents the conquering of time and death—the mystical goal.

This brings us to the final trump. Because the highest virtue was achieved as one merged one's will with the divine intelligence, in the various philosophies of the Hellenistic world the image of prudence as the highest virtue merged with the image of the World Soul. In recognition of this synthesis, the World Soul was also referred to as *sophia*—"wisdom" in Greek. To Jewish and Christian mystics, Sophia came to be regarded as the Wisdom of God, a feminine aspect of God that was active in the World. In Christian theology, Sophia was said to be the "mother" of the three Christian virtues: faith, hope, and charity, which Christian philosophers added to the four cardinal virtues to create seven emanations.

The medieval Romantics, whom we spoke of previously, seized on this image of Sophia, the feminine aspect of God, as a way of depicting God the beloved, and, in Renaissance art in the end of the fifteenth century, the image of Sophia was synthesized with the image of the celestial Aphrodite as the highest virtue and the archetypal Good and Beautiful. In Renaissance art she was depicted as the ideal nude and that is what is illustrated on the Tarot's World. The nude Sophia/Aphrodite standing on the throne of God, which is represented by the wreath surrounded by the symbols of the four Evangelists: the lion, the bull, the eagle, and the man. This image is a composite of all these themes: the World Soul, Aphrodite, Sophia, and Prudence, all in one. The fact that the trumps contain the cardinal virtues and not the Christian virtues attests to their Platonic nature. The fact that the final trump is a synthesis of Platonic, pre-Christian, and Christian images attests to its Neoplatonic nature. We will explain this synthesis in more detail in the next chapter, but, for now, we will look at how these mystical themes entered the Tarot through Renaissance art.

THE TRIUMPH

In this section we will examine how the Neoplatonic themes that we have been discussing entered Renaissance art and came to influence the artists who created the Tarot. The Tarot was a product of popular art in the Renaissance. The distinction, however, between high art and popular art was not as well drawn as it is in modern culture. One place where high and popular art merged in the Renaissance was in the street performances and processions associated with public holidays. Chief among these events in importance and impact was the parade called the triumph, and perhaps the best clue that the Tarot's creators and early users have given us to help us interpret this work of art is that they called it a triumph. First, therefore, let us examine the nature of this parade.

A triumph is a parade of ancient origin. In ancient Rome, when a conquering general would return to the city, a triumph would be arranged down Appian

Way. The parade was organized from the lowest to the highest, starting with the captives and ending with the general himself. The organizing principle in this heroic triumph was that each participant trumped the one who came before, until all of the participants are trumped by the hero in his chariot. Triumphs were also held as religious processions before games and at Roman funerals.

The oldest images that we find of a triumph in Italian art, however, are not Roman. They are Etruscan images carved into the sides of sarcophagi and funeral urns starting in the third and fourth centuries B.C.E. These images depict a man in a chariot drawn by horses in the midst of a procession. The other characters in the procession are on foot or on horseback and many are playing musical instruments.[8] These are images of the funeral procession of the deceased but, in these images, the soul of the deceased is depicted as a triumphant figure in a chariot being guided to the afterlife. Essentially, these are mystical figures designed to ensure life after death. Plato seems to have made use of this symbolic tradition connecting the image of a chariot and its driver with the soul when he created his myth of the chariot for the Phaedrus, which we have previously discussed. His predecessor, the sixth- to fifth-century B.C.E. philosopher Parmenides (the dates of his birth and death are unknown), made similar use of the chariot in the fragmented poem of unknown title for which he is famous. Parmenides's poem seems to be a firsthand description of the triumph of the deceased as it proceeds into the afterlife, and it may be that Parmenides experienced this otherworldly journey while in a trance.

These myths and the ancient funerary tradition that inspired them are all examples of the archetypal hero's journey in its simplest form. The hero's journey is always a confrontation of the central problem of life: the existence of death. The hero confronts death and searches for immortality. When the conquering general in Rome participated in a triumph he was taking the part of the hero in a ritual reenactment of the soul's journey. He was symbolically bringing immortality to the people and the republic and conquering death through his fame, his legend, which would continue to be remembered after his death.

In the thirteenth century, in southern Italy, the Holy Roman emperor Frederick II (1194–1250) combined his infatuation with Romantic literature with a desire to reclaim the glories of the Classical world. In 1237, after his victory over Milan, he played the part of the hero in a reenactment of the triumphal procession in Rome.[9] By the fourteenth century, triumphs had become a regular occurrence in the yearly festivals celebrated in every major city in Italy.

Mystery performances and religious processions were popular in all of Western Europe in the Middle Ages. In Italy, where these festivals had always been enacted on a grander scale, the triumph merged with the religious festival to become a secular parade filled with singing and dancing. The triumph reached its peak in the fifteenth century while the Tarot was developing. It was the custom that a triumph would be performed during Carnival, for weddings, and on other special occasions. It took the form of a parade with music and a procession of masked and costumed figures marching on foot and riding in chariots. To understand the excitement of the triumph we only need to think of its modern counterpart, the Mardi Gras parade. The triumph was a major focus of popular art and the greatest artists of the time worked on the setting, the costumes, the displays, and the poetic symbolic content. As in all Renaissance art, the triumph was intended to have both body and soul, visual spectacle and symbolic significance. There are accounts of Leonardo da Vinci (1452–1519) directing the triumph in Milan on at least two occasions. For one, he devised an ingenious colossal machine that represented the movements of the planets and was accompanied by singers costumed as the gods of each planet.[10]

As we have said, in the Renaissance and in the ancient world, there was not a clear distinction between high art and popular art. In the Renaissance, the popular festival attracted the talents of greats artists and the theme of the triumph was used in poetry and the visual arts from an early date. Because the triumph is a natural way to organize characters in a progression of ascent from the lowest to the highest, it became a device used by authors and artists to present a moral allegory and a way of depicting a mystical ladder of emanation.

One early example is the *Psychomachia,* "Battle of the Soul," by the fifth-century Spanish poet Aurelius Prudentius Clemens. This may be the first work to present a list of seven virtues paired with seven vices. In the *Psychomachia* the seven virtues are represented as seven women who are the servants and allies of Abraham during a war with seven vices. The poem takes the form of a progression of seven battles that lead to the final victory of the soul. In each battle, a virtue, equipped with symbolic attributes, is paired with one vice, which she vanquishes in the battle. Faith, unarmored and with disheveled hair, vanquishes Pagan Worship; Chastity, a virgin with armor, defeats Lust; Patience, wearing triple-layered armor of steel links, defeats Wrath; Hope, the friend of the lowly, defeats Pride; Sobriety, holding a cross, defeats Indulgence; Thrift, the ally of Charity, defeats Greed; and Concord is almost defeated by Discord or Heresy, disguised as a friend, but wins in the end with the help of Faith. The *Psychomachia* was popular throughout the Middle Ages in illustrated form and led to the artistic convention of depicting virtues as women with a smaller male figure, representing a vice, lying vanquished under their feet. In the Cary-Yale Visconti

Tarot, mentioned in Chapter One, we find these smaller male figures representing vice under the female representations of Faith, Hope, and Charity.

In the fourteenth century, the theme of the triumph was used by Dante (1265–1321) in the *Divine Comedy*. In the end of the second section, Dante is reunited with his love, Beatrice, who will be his guide for the third and final part of his journey. Beatrice arrives in a triumphal chariot pulled by a gryphon and accompanied by a procession with the twenty-four elders of the Apocalypse, the four beasts of the Evangelists, the four cardinal virtues, and the Apostles. However, the most influential representation of the triumph in the Renaissance, in England as well as Italy, was Petrarch's poem, which is titled *"I Trionfi,"* "The Triumphs."

"I Trionfi"

In *"I Trionfi,"* Petrarch (1304–1374) presents an allegorical procession in three parts. There are six characters each arriving separately. Therefore, most commentators speak of it as having six parts but the six characters are organized in three pairs. As in the *Psychomachia,* each vice or evil is paired with a virtue or a good. Petrarch also organizes the six into one continual triumph by having the conquering virtue, in turn, conquered by a greater evil until we reach the final triumph of good. The first pair is of Love and Chastity, in which Love is personified by Cupid and Chastity is Petrarch's ideal love Laura. Laura, in turn, is triumphed over by a greater evil, Death, the Grim Reaper, and he is trumped by Fame. Fame is trumped by the greatest evil, Time, and the final triumph is the greatest good, to which Petrarch gives the Platonic title Eternity. *"I Trionfi"* is simultaneously a triumphal procession, a purification of each of the Platonic souls, and an ascent through a ladder of emanation.

"I Trionfi" was immensely popular in the Renaissance and there are numerous illustrated versions. The illustrations were picked up as a theme in arts of every kind, particularly on marriage chests, tapestries, relief carvings, and other decorative arts. Although Petrarch does not actually supply much visual information in the poem, for example, he only mentions a chariot in the triumph of Cupid, the illustrations are rich with details that follow a prescribed set of symbols for each character. Each is shown in a chariot pulled by creatures that symbolize their driver. Love has four white horses, Laura has unicorns, Death has oxen, Fame has elephants, Time has deer, and for Eternity the illustrations show a carriage holding the Holy Trinity and pulled by the four Evangelists with their four creatures: the lion, the bull, the eagle, and the man.

It seems that the illustrations are informed by the popular symbolism of the day, possibly from the depiction of these characters in actual parades. In the same way, in modern American culture, one only has to hear the name Santa Claus to see in the mind's eye a fat, bearded man in a red suit riding in a sleigh pulled by reindeer. All of the images found in the Tarot were popular images at the time of its creation and would be as easily recognized then as an image of Santa Claus is now.

Both Dante and Petrarch are considered founders of the Humanist movement in the Renaissance. Humanism is the historian's name for the Renaissance infatuation with and desire to reclaim the greatness of the Classical past. It is this desire to revive Classicism that gave the Renaissance its name, which means "rebirth." Humanist artists illustrated Classical myths and imitated Classical figures. Humanist poets looked to the poetry of Virgil and the philosophy of Plato—as interpreted by Neoplatonists. In composing this poem, Petrarch was influence by both Dante and Plato. Each of the three parts in *"I Trionfi"* corresponds to one aspect of the Platonic soul, which we discussed in the last section: the soul of appetite, the soul of will, and the soul of reason.

The first triumph Love may not seem negative to the modern reader, but Petrarch meant it as a symbol of the lowest soul, the soul of desire or appetite, when it is overcome by the vice Lust.

> Who by short lived joys by anguish long obtain,
> And whom the pleasures of a rival pain.[11]

To symbolize this lack of control, in the illustrations Cupid is depicted as blindfolded (as he is in the earliest Lovers cards), a symbol of ignorance and self-deception that is found in Medieval images of Cupid. This triumph can be compared to the four temporal rulers and the Lovers cards in the Tarot. Next, Laura, representing Chastity, with the help of the virtues and a host of virgins, takes Cupid as her captive and brings temperance and harmony to replace Cupid's emotional turmoil.

> And there consummate Beauty shone, combined
> With all the pureness of angel-mind.

Petrarch's inclusion of Laura as a positive triumph exemplifies his romantic influence. Laura can be related to the Chariot card, which is clearly a representation of a triumphal chariot. In the earliest hand-painted Milanese decks the charioteer is a beautiful woman in a long dress. In the Visconti-Sforza deck she is given two winged

horses as in Plato's *Phaedrus* (see figure 20).
The virtues that Petrarch lists as Laura's companions include the cardinal virtues Prudence
and Temperance and others of his invention
such as Purity and Beauty. Yet, although they
are not the same virtues, the Marseilles group-
ing of the virtues, in the middle section of the
trumps, after the Chariot, may be an example
of the influence of "*I Trionfi.*"

The middle section addresses the soul of
will, which is the desire for spiritual attainment that pulls one out of the physical ap-
petites of the lower soul, but it is also a desire
for fame and reputation. This section addresses the philosophical problem that both
Plato and every philosopher and hero sought
the answer for: how can we defeat Death?
Death, pictured as a corpse armed with a
scythe and standing on a coffin, triumphs over
Chastity and takes Laura prisoner. The figure
of Death is based on images symbolizing the
plague that were developed in the fourteenth

Figure 20. A rendering of the
Visconti-Sforza Chariot trump

century. In actual life, Laura, the woman to whom the poem is dedicated, died of
the plague. This Grim Reaper is also one of the Tarot trumps.

> O blind of intellect! Of what avail
> Are your long toils in this sublunar vale?

The positive aspect of this pair is the triumph of Fame. Fame allows one's
work and reputation to outlive the body and in this way defeats death. This is the
immortality sought by ancient Greek heroes when they hoped that their achievements in battle would be recounted by poets. By writing this poem, Petrarch
hopes that his work will live on and, through his poem, Laura will continue to
live. He is also achieving the immortality of the artist through the work but, as a
philosopher and a mystic, he knows that there is a greater immortality.

> When turning around I saw the power advance
> That breaks the gloomy grave's eternal trance.

In the Minchiate of Florence we find Fame with her two trumpets substituted for the Judgement trump, which normally has a depiction of the Angel of Judgement, Gabriel, blowing his trumpet. Both angels symbolize immortality and victory over death.

The final pair begins with the triumph of Time as the negative aspect—a Saturnine old man on crutches in the illustrations. Saturn was not only the god of time but also the god of contemplation and intellectual pursuits. This triumph addresses the soul of reason. By virtue of our intellect, we can reason that although Fame can overcome death this is not true immortality. Given enough time, even our fame will die. It is our intellect that presents us with the problem of impermanence but it is through contemplation that we may find the answer.

> What is renown?—a gleam of transient light,
> That soon an envious cloud involves in night.

The card that became the Hermit in later Tarots was originally a depiction of a hunched old man with an hourglass in the Milanese decks (see figure 21). This was a personification of Time. The Wheel of Fortune trump is also an image of time and fate.

The final triumph in Petrarch's poem is a mystical Christian vision of God as the only true permanence, called Eternity. Here Petrarch sees God as the Christian equivalent of Plato's eternal Good. In this section, Petrarch envisions himself at the end of time after the resurrection of the dead and in the presence of God. Here he is reunited with Laura in eternal love, another element of Romanticism. Like all mystical heroes he has defeated death and attained immortality. Petrarch envisions immortality as a state of eternal love and bliss. This triumph relates to the final two trumps, Judgement, which represents the resurrection of the dead in preparation for the Last Judgment, and the World, which also combines the image of an ideal female beauty with the throne of God.

> Then shall I see her as I first beheld,
> But lovelier far, and by herself excelled.

In 1956, Tarot author Gertrude Moakley wrote an article making the case that the Tarot's trumps are based on Petrarch's "I Trionfi." Later, in 1966, she wrote a book, *The Tarot Cards Painted by Bonifacio Bembo,* in which she argued that the Tarot's trumps are based on the actual triumph, the parade. When she wrote these theories her ideas represented a tremendous breakthrough for scholarly research into the understanding of the origin of the images in the Tarot. Yet neither theory is exactly correct. As we saw, there is a relationship between some of the trumps and the illustrations for *"I Trionfi,"* but not all of them, and the images are not in the same order. The actual triumphs performed in the Renaissance were continually changing and it cannot be said that they present a consistent model for the particular triumph in the Tarot. It is more correct to say that the Tarot is part of the same tradition that informed the illustrations of *"I Trionfi."* And, as we have shown, Petrarch did not create many of these images. They were part of the popular culture of the time. There were numerous triumphs performed in Italy in the Renaissance, at least one in every major city each year. The triumphs were continually changing their content and symbolism in a desire for greater pageantry. In doing so, these parades no doubt made use of this same cultural vocabulary. Other artists at the time also made use of the triumph as a metaphor in

Figure 21. A rendering of the Visconti-Sforza Hermit, or Time trump

their philosophical works—as a way of depicting the soul's journey. After all, the image of the triumph represented the soul's journey from its beginning.

THE TRIUMPH OF TIME

For another example of a triumph in art, let us look at figure 22, a rendering of Pieter Brueghel's *Triumph of Time* with the background removed so that we may focus on the parade in the foreground.[12] Pieter Brueghel (1525–1569) was a Flemish painter who studied in Italy and is noted for his landscapes and images of peasant life. The original print was completed in 1574 by an engraver who worked from Brueghel's drawing. It was, therefore, completed exactly two hundred years after Petrarch completed his poem in 1374, the year of his death. At the time Brueghel's print was completed, the artist had been dead for five years. As with the ancient Etruscans, it seems that in the Renaissance this theme was connected to a desire for immortality. Brueghel, however, is more pessimistic in his creation. The

Figure 22. The foreground of Brueghel's *Triumph of Time*, engraved in 1574

title that appeared in Latin on the bottom of the print says in translation, *Time Devouring All and Each.* The background of the complete print contains a landscape in which the barren left half contains a city in flames and the right half is in bloom and prosperous. As we can see, this theme is repeated in the foreground in the central car with its half-barren tree. We can easily find similarities between this allegory and the Tarot trumps, just as we can with Petrarch's poem. There is a prominent triumphal chariot or car pulled by two horses with the sun and moon on their backs. This relates to the Chariot as a triumphal car, and the Sun and Moon cards. On the car, we find Saturn, the god of time, sitting on an hourglass similar to the original Tarot Hermit holding his hourglass. Nestled in the car is the globe of the earth, the World, surrounded by the circle of the zodiac.

As we have discussed previously, the medieval Wheel of Fortune that we find in the trumps represents, in symbolic form, the wheel of the zodiac and the ladder of the planets. Because of its connection to astrology, the zodiac was associated with fate, and, because it marked the sun's progress through the year it was also a symbol of time. As the Renaissance progressed, artists began to depict the

Wheel of Fortune as the ring of the zodiac to reclaim some of its celestial significance, and Brueghel's engraving is an example of this trend. This wheel of the zodiac, therefore, is the Wheel of Fortune. It measures time but, through its connection to astrology, it also represents one's fate.

The dark horse of the moon and the light horse of the sun, which are pulling the car, represent the daily cycle of night and day. They are also the means of measuring time. This theme is repeated by the clock perched in the fork of the tree. As if to echo this circle of the year, Saturn holds in his left hand a hieroglyph or symbol for time, the serpent biting his tail, which is called the ouroboros. The serpent, representing time, devours his tail just as Saturn devours his child and the Triumph devours the landscape. This is a pessimistic depiction of the impermanence of the physical world. The next triumphal figure is Death on a pale horse, an image derived from the description of Death as one of the Four Horsemen of the Apocalypse found in Revelation. Death is also illustrated riding his horse in some of the earliest Italian Tarots. At this point in the triumph, we may be reminded of the famous soliloquy that Shakespeare wrote for Macbeth:

Tomorrow, and tomorrow, and tomorrow,
creeps in this petty pace from day to day,
to the last syllable of recorded time;
and all our yesterdays have lighted fools
the way to dusty death.[13]

However, the final triumph, Fame, adds the one optimistic note. This is Brueghel's victory over death, his lasting reputation preserved in his work. The reality of this statement is illustrated by the fact that the print was completed after the artist's death. Notice that Fame rides an elephant just as Fame's chariot in illustrations of *"I Trionfi"* is pulled by elephants. Elephants represent the strength and endurance of Fame. As we said, Fame is depicted in the Minchiate Judgement card, but the standard Tarot is more in harmony with Petrarch's vision that takes us beyond Fame to a more mystical interpretation of immortality.

Both of these artists have made use of the triumph for symbolic statements about the nature of life, death, and transcendence. Their triumphs are similar but not identical. In the Renaissance, the image of the Wheel of Fortune was central to this theme and was a popular image in the art of the time. It is not surprising that images of Fortuna's Wheel are also commonly depicted in books on fortune-telling, which was also ruled by Fortuna. This brings us to our next example.

THE *TRIUMPHO DI FORTUNA*

Our third example is the *Triumpho di Fortuna by Fanti,* a book on divination published in Venice in 1527. Fanti's book describes a system of divination in which the querent picks a question and is directed to a series of wheels, two to each page and each with twenty-one divisions. One has the choice of using the hour in which the question was asked or another ancient technique, the throw of two dice, to find one's way through the book and find the correct answer on the appropriate wheel. The wheels have twenty-one divisions because there are only twenty-one possible combinations that can result from the throws of two dice.

As we have mentioned in Chapter One, the fact that there are also twenty-one trumps in the Tarot suggests a connection to divination with dice. It is also believed that Fanti's book influenced *Le Sorti* by Marcolino, published in Venice in 1540, a book on divination with cards that we also mentioned in Chapter One. The method described in *Le Sorti* only makes use of the pip and court cards from the suit of coins and has no connection to the trumps. The evidence of a connection to *Le Sorti,* however, suggests a connection between Fanti's book and card divination. We may, therefore, hope to find some evidence connecting the *Triumpho di Fortuna*'s wheels, each with twenty-one divisions, with the twenty-one trumps, but there are no illustrations on the divisions of Fanti's wheels to tie them with the trumps.

Throughout the book, there are woodcut illustrations above and below the wheels. There are figures from astrology and allegory. There are images of the gods of the seven planets riding in triumphal chariots. This triumph of the planets is based on common Medieval astrological illustrations called the Children of the Planets, which depict the god in his chariot in the heavens and people engaged in occupations that are ruled by that god depicted below. Other figures include the constellations of the zodiac and other constellations, and depictions of astrologers and philosophers. Some of these illustrations are similar to illustrations found on the pages of *Le Sorti,* but none of these are connected to the trumps. It is only in the frontispiece, which contains an allegory about fate and personal destiny, that we find connections with the allegory in the trumps. (See figure 23.)

In the foreground of Fanti's frontispiece there stands an athletic male nude holding a die, and a kneeling astrologer who is holding calipers and an astronomical device. The athlete is possibly Hermes, the Classical god of runners and athletes, who also ruled divination with dice or lots. Hermes is commonly depicted as an athletic nude. The astrologer is wearing Renaissance clothing and is thought to be a portrait of the author, Fanti. The astrologer is similar to the astrologers

Figure 23. Frontispiece from the *Triumpho di Fortuna by Fanti*, Venice, 1527

found on Moon cards in early hand-painted Tarots. Both of the figures in the foreground are guides who are introducing us to this allegory. They represent the two approaches to divination that we may use to find our way in Fanti's book.

Just beyond the knoll, which supports the athlete and the astrologer, a landscape dominates the lower portion of the scene. Here we see a waterway that separates the knoll from the mainland. On the mainland, there is a magnificent walled city that is entered by going through a massive clock tower with a twenty-four-hour clock. This suggests that the city is beyond time and, therefore, an eternal reward. Smaller figures in boats are rowing up the waterway toward the entrance to the city. Figures who have arrived at the entrance are on foot ascending seven stairs and moving toward the portal tower. Inside the city, there are other figures standing and walking on the city's avenues.

The most apparent significance of the city is that it represents Heaven as a final reward for the righteous. The famous Renaissance poet Dante (1265–1321) also depicted Heaven as a magnificent city in his *Divine Comedy.* Like many Renaissance artists, Dante was influenced in his choice of imagery by the Bible's description of the New Jerusalem, the heavenly city depicted as the final reward at the end of time in Revelation. Dante, however, has conveyed that he meant his creation to be interpreted on more than one level. Like most Renaissance art, it has a literal meaning and at the same time a personal mystical meaning. Revelation states that in the New Jerusalem Christ will rule, death will be abolished, and the righteous will live in peace. As the New Jerusalem is the eternal reward, beyond time and death, it is also the goal of the mystic. The waterway in Fanti's allegory can be interpreted as life's journey and people as mystics hoping to reach the city of immortality. The athlete with the die and the astrologer are there to guide them by making use of the tools of divination, which they display. The implication is that divination is more than simply a way of foretelling the future; it is a way of making informed decisions that will guide one to the best destiny—the mystical reward. This interpretation is supported by the symbolic scene on the upper portion of the frontispiece.

On the upper half of Fanti's frontispiece there is a separate allegory separated from the lower scene by a wall of clouds. It is presenting a ruling principle that governs the journey of life depicted below. In the upper scene, we see a large figure of Atlas supporting a globe on his back. Around the globe is a vertical belt with the signs of the zodiac on it and, at the central point of this wheel, there is an axle that pierces the globe and extends out to the left and right. The ends of this axle are bent to form crank handles. On our left, there is an angel, representing Bona Fortuna, "Good Fortune," turning the handle clockwise and, on our right, there is a devil, representing Mala Fortuna, "Bad Fortune," turning the handle counterclockwise. This is another Renaissance illustration that demonstrates that Fortuna's wheel was considered the wheel of the cosmos. This image is clearly concerned with determining whether one's fate is good or bad.

At the top of this Wheel of Fortune sits a Pope, as master of this world. Renaissance illustrations of the Wheel of Fortune commonly depicted a series of hats and crowns ascending the wheel by order of rank. The triple tiara of the Pope would be depicted at the top. Likewise in the Tarot the Pope trumps the other three temporal rulers: the Papesse, the Empress, and the Emperor. In Fanti's frontispiece, the artist has simply shown the Pope in the top position and omitted the lower ranks. On either side of the Pope sit one of two women with their names written in Latin above their heads. On our left is Virtue, pointing upward with

Figure 24. Recreation of the Juggler from an uncut sheet of Tarot cards, Italian, circa 1500, Museum of Fine Arts, Budapest

her right hand, and on our right, the same side as the Devil, sits Sensuality, pointing down. The Pope's fate hangs on his choice of a mate. As in the Tarot, the Pope is depicted as the master of the temporal world but whether or not he will become true master of his fate and inherit the spiritual world depends on his moral choice. Fanti is saying that fate is in the hands of each individual and depends on moral choice. If one is lazy and selfish and succumbs to luxury in excess, the Devil will take control, and if one is disciplined and virtuous, Good Fortune will come to one's aid. Fanti is also suggesting that divination can help one to make the right choice. Now let us look at how this relates to the Tarot in more detail.

The Tarot's Magician is not an astrologer or an athletic nude, yet there is a connection between him and the two figures in Fanti's foreground—particularly to the athlete with the die. One easily recognized pair of objects found on the Magician's table in the Tarot of Marseilles is a pair of dice. The dice are not always recognizable in all of the Marseilles decks but they are in many examples, including the popular Grimaud version. We can also see two dice on the Magician's table in one of the oldest printed Tarot decks from Italy. Figure 24 is the author's

Figure 25. Recreation of the World card from an uncut sheet of Italian Tarot cards, circa 1500, Metropolitan Museum, New York

rendering of this image. This card is part of an uncut sheet of Tarot woodcuts that now resides in the Museum of Fine Arts in Budapest. It is dated circa 1500 and it is possibly the oldest existing woodcut of the Magician. This card demonstrates that the dice on the Magician's table are not a late addition but something that was associated with the Magician from an early date—they are likely to have been part of his character since the fifteenth century.

As dice were used for gambling their presence could confirm that the Magician is a gambler and a rogue, but dice were also used in the Renaissance for divination, and perhaps the magician, like Fanti's athlete, is offering us a means to obtain advice about our destiny. The Magician is the first trump, and he is introducing us to the parade of trumps just as Fanti's athlete is in the foreground. Whether his dice are intended for divination or for gambling, there are two of them, and there are twenty-one possible combinations of the two when they are thrown. It would be easy to imagine the Magician making use of the throws of his dice to make connections with the twenty-one figures in the trumps. Like the figures in Fanti's foreground, it may be that the Magician is a guide offering help in finding one's way in the allegory.

The image of the heavenly city or the New Jerusalem in the frontispiece relates to the World, the highest trump in the Tarot. In the earliest Italian Tarots, the most common image depicted on the World was that of a city seen through a circular portal and being presented by one or two angels as we can see in figure 25. Figure 25 is the author's rendering of the World card from an uncut sheet of Tarot cards that now resides in the Metropolitan Museum of New York. This card is apparently from the same deck as the Magician in figure 24.

Details on the path leading into the heavenly city in Fanti's frontispiece can be related to some of the trumps leading to the World in the third section of the trumps. The massive tower relates to the Tower card at the beginning of the third section. The seven steps can be related to the ladder of seven stars on the Star. The clock on the tower has the sun in the center instead of hands. It represents time and relates to the Tarot's Sun and Moon, which are the ultimate timekeepers. In both cases, the eternal city exists in a place beyond the limits of time.

In the upper allegory in Fanti's frontispiece, the Wheel of Fortune is clearly related to the same subject in the Tarot. On the Marseilles Wheel of Fortune, three monkeys depict the past on the way up the Wheel, the present crowned at the top, and the future falling down headfirst. The Tarot's Wheel of Fortune provides the moralistic warning that whatever Fortune gives she will eventually take away, but, because the present is depicted in a fortuitous position, we can also relate this trump to the image of Bona Fortuna in Fanti. Mala Fortuna is obviously related to the Tarot's Devil.

We have already mentioned how the Pope in the Tarot is at the head of the temporal rulers and relates to Fanti's Pope, who also is sitting in the fortuitous position. Fanti, however, has had him placed between two women, Virtue and Sensuality, one of whom he must choose as a mate. In the Tarot of Marseilles the Lovers depicts a young man being given the same moral choice that faces the Pope in Fanti's frontispiece—he is given a choice between a woman representing sensuality and a woman representing virtue. This image, representing moral choice, is the strongest link between Fanti's frontispiece and the allegory in the Tarot of Marseilles. It also demonstrates the Neoplatonic nature of both allegories.

The oldest versions of the Lovers card depict only a man and a woman with a winged and blindfolded Cupid flying above. This image is based on the standard Renaissance betrothal portrait. It represents engagement or marriage. In the Tarot of Marseilles, a second female figure was added. With the addition of a second woman in the Tarot of Marseilles Lovers card, the young man like Fanti's Pope is given a choice, as can be seen in the author's rendering of the Lovers from the Jean Noblet Tarot, one of the earliest Marseilles decks, in figure 26. The woman on the Lovers card with flowers in her hair represents the woman named Sensuality in the frontispiece and the other woman, with the laurel wreath, represents Virtue. The two women seem to be fighting over the man, each one pulling the man toward her. The connection between the flowers and sensuality is obvious, but the choice of a laurel wreath, which typically represents victory, to symbolize virtue needs to be explained.

As we saw earlier in this chapter, the idea that love is the force that can bring one to the highest spiritual truth was embraced by Neoplatonists in the Middle Ages. The idea that a conscious choice is required to direct this force is an idea that

Figure 26. A rendering of the Lovers card from the Jean Noblet Tarot, one of the earliest in the Marseilles tradition, printed in Paris, circa 1650

may have its roots in the Pythagorean philosophy that Neoplatonists attempted to revive. Pythagoras taught that we are doomed to suffer and die in endless reincarnations until we can purify our spirit through the practice of virtue, purify our minds through contemplation, and thereby wake up to our true nature. He believed that it is the desire of nature to keep us tied to the wheel of rebirth, and for the mystic to break loose from this destiny he or she must consciously choose a more difficult path. To illustrate the importance of this choice Pythagoras was said to have given a lecture in which he made use of the Greek letter upsilon (which looks like a Roman *Y*) as a symbol of a fork in life's path. The text that describes this lecture is one the few that may actually be authored by Pythagoras himself. This sermon received much attention in the ancient world; we find references to it in medieval Christian writing, and it was just as popular in the Renaissance. Even Shakespeare refers to it in *Hamlet*. Figure 27 is an illustration of the Pythagorean lesson from a text by Geoffroy Tory published in 1529.[14] In the illustration, we can see that the path on our left is smooth and easy. There are steps carved in it that make the climb effortless. At the top of the left-hand path, a feast is laid out, symbolizing sensuality. A man is headed for this goal but another who already reached it is dropping headfirst, like the figure descending the Tarot's Wheel of Fortune, into a pit of fire. On the right, a man is climbing a path that is rough and natural, like a tree trunk. There are three levels to this climb, each equated to an animal—a leopard, a lion, and a fox or a dog. As in the Tarot, the man on the right is embracing the virtues and ascending through three soul levels, symbolized by the three animals. This is the path of virtue and at the top a man sits on a throne of self-mastery with the laurel wreath of the victor suspended over his head. The message is that the path of virtue leads to spiritual victory.

On the Lovers card and on Fanti's illustration, the young man and the Pope are at a place in life symbolized by the point where the two arms of the upsilon join the trunk in the Pythagorean lesson—they have to choose between two

Figure 27. The Pythagorean lesson based on the upsilon, Geoffroy Tory, 1529

paths. Instead of being illustrated as two arms of the letter upsilon, their paths are symbolized by two women, but the choice is the same—a life of sensuality that leads to suffering in the end or a life of virtue that leads to spiritual victory.

THE MYSTIC PATH

In this chapter, we have shown that the Tarot expresses a mystical Platonic philosophy labeled by scholars as Neoplatonism. Specifically, the Tarot trumps are an allegory of the soul's journey to immortality or enlightenment. This allegory is expressed in three groups of seven cards. Symbolically, the number seven is associated with the Neoplatonic ladder of seven planets that forms a stairway by which the soul may ascend to the heavens and the spiritual realm. The Tarot makes use of the symbolism of the number seven but does not contain symbolic links between individual cards and planets except for the Sun and the Moon. The three groups of seven cards allow the sevenfold ladder to be repeated on three levels of increasing spiritual awareness. These three levels are related to Plato's theory of the three aspects of the human soul.

The discussion above has shown us that the Tarot also makes use of the triumphant parade as an organizing principle and as a metaphor for the triumph of the soul. It is clear that the Tarot is one of numerous works of art, both high and popular, from the Renaissance that make use of the same metaphor to express a mystical story. It is not identical to the triumphs presented but it is another triumph with a similar message, and it makes use of some of the same symbols.

This discussion has given us insight into the overall structure and meaning of the trumps. It has shown that the philosophy expressed in the Tarot has its roots in ancient mysticism but that the Tarot makes use of the artistic vocabulary of the Italian Renaissance to illustrate that philosophy. In the next chapter we will examine each trump individually and look into the symbolism of the four minor suits.

INTERPRETING THE MAJOR AND MINOR ARCANA

It is not of Alchemy or Kabalism or Astrology or Ceremonial Magic;
but, as I have said, it is the presentation of universal types,
and it is in the combination of these types—if anywhere—
that it presents Secret Doctrine.

—A. E. WAITE, *THE PICTORIAL KEY TO THE TAROT*

We are now ready to continue our interpretation of the Tarot with a deeper look at its individual images, and later we will explore methods of creating card spreads and readings. Once again, we will be going over the Tarot of Marseilles. In many respects, the Tarot of Marseilles—while not a single deck but a closely linked family of decks emerging in late sixteenth-century France—was the fullest early expression of the disparate images that came to be regarded as the Tarot. Indeed, the Marseilles deck, in its variants, can be considered the blueprint for later eighteenth- and nineteenth-century occult decks, and, therefore, it is the blueprint for the influential twentieth-century Waite-Smith deck, which we will explore in Chapter Five.

One of the first things that can be noticed about the Major Arcana in the Tarot of Marseilles is that it is composed of twenty-one cards numbered with roman numerals, called trumps, and an unnumbered Fool. While, in rare incidents, the Fool has been assigned a zero in some decks, there is no zero or a concept of zero in roman numerals; therefore, the Fool is really unnumbered. The trumps are organized in a sequence like a parade and the Fool is not part of the sequence. As we learned in Chapter Three, this parade of trumps is modeled on the Renaissance secular parade called a triumph, in which each character in the sequence is considered more powerful than the one before. This triumphal hierarchy is used in the deck to allow each card to trump the ones that come before, and the highest trump played will win the hand when playing the game. The Fool is also called the excuse. He can be played instead of a trump but he cannot win the hand.

Because the Tarot was originally designed for playing a game, the modern reader may think that it was only intended to be a trivial pastime and that it is pointless to look for a deeper meaning in the deck. In the Renaissance, however, popular art forms such as games were considered a suitable venue for meaningful symbolic statements. As we learned in the last chapter, the actual parades that the trumps were derived from were highly symbolic and expressive, and, at times, conveyed a deep mystical message. The triumph was also used as a metaphor in mystical poetic allegories, such as the influential *"I Trionfi,"* by the celebrated fourteenth-century poet Petrarch, and illustrations designed for *"I Trionfi"* were incorporated into numerous popular works of art. In turn, the mystical message expressed in *"I Trionfi"* influenced future triumphs and popular arts based on the triumph, such as the Tarot.

The allegory in the trumps is clearly mystical. As we look at this allegory, we can see that it is in three parts or three acts. In the Tarot of Marseilles, the trumps can be neatly divided into three equal parts or acts with seven trumps in each act. The number seven is symbolic of the Neoplatonic ladder of ascent and the three acts can be equated to the three parts of the soul found in the teachings of Plato. The first act is about power, prestige, sensuality, and love, all of which relate to the soul of appetite. In the second act we find images of time and mortality but also the virtues. This represents the hero's struggle and is related to the soul of will. The last act is an ascent from the Bad, the Devil, to the Good, the World. This relates to the soul of reason and the ascent to the mystical goal.

Because of its association with the Trinity, we can find a threefold pattern in many aspects of Christian art, such as the cycle of prayers that are recited over the rosary. But even here the cycle also follows the Platonic pattern based on the three parts of the soul. In this practice, the rosary beads are used as a memory device to focus on a cycle of prayers and meditations that are divided into three groups with five mysteries in each. The first, called the Joyful Mysteries, focuses on the Nativity and Christ's physical incarnation—the soul of appetite. The second, the Sorrowful Mysteries, focuses on the Crucifixion and Christ's passion—the soul of will. The last, the Glorious Mysteries, focuses on the Resurrection and the ascent to heaven—the soul of reason. In these mysteries, we find the story of Christ clearly outlined as the three-part quest of the hero and addressing the three parts of the soul. The Tarot trumps are like a secular Neoplatonic rosary. They tell of a similar heroic journey, through three layers equated to the three parts of the soul, but the hero in the Tarot is not Christ. The hero is Everyman or Everywoman.

THE FOOL

The first card that we encounter in the Major Arcana is the outsider, called the Fool. He is not part of the allegory, but he may be thought of as the figure of Everyman that will experience the upcoming events. In the Tarot of Marseilles, for example, the Fool is facing into the series of Trumps, as if he is about to enter the story. Because of this, the story in the Tarot has often been called the Fool's Journey. In some decks, such as in the sixteenth-century Florentine Minchiate, the Fool is placed after the trumps. In the game that has traditionally been played with the Tarot since the Renaissance, the Fool had no value and cannot win a hand, but at the end of the game, when it is time to tally the score, he was one of the most valued in points. Like Ramon the Fool in Ramon Lull's fourteenth-century romance, *Blanquerna,* the Fool can appear anywhere in the Tarot story. As a character of no rank the Fool can talk with popes and common people alike and interject his wisdom.

In Italian, the Fool is called il Matto, which means madman. In the Visconti-Sforza deck (ca. 1450) il Matto is definitely a madman. He is depicted as a poor beggar with a goiter, dressed in rags, and with feathers in his hair. The feathers are a symbol of foolishness that can be found in other Renaissance works of art, such as a painting personifying Folly painted for the Arena Chapel, in Padua, by the first famous Renaissance artist Giotto (1267–1337). In another early hand-painted deck, the misnamed Gringonneur Tarot (Gringonneur was a fourteenth-century French artist and this is a fifteenth-century Venetian deck), the Fool is both a jester and a madman. The grinning figure stands wearing a festive cape, a donkey-eared hat and underpants, while smaller figures, representing boys, throw stones at him.

In the Tarot of Marseilles, the Fool is clearly a jester in festive dress with bells on his collar and his belt, as we can see in figure 28, which is the author's rendering of a Marseilles Fool published in 1672. The seat of the Fool's pants is being torn by a dog. This is meant to be comical, but it also signifies that the dog is treating him as a stranger, an assumption that is further supported by the fact that

Figure 28. A rendering of the Fool from the François Chosson Tarot, published in France in 1672

he is carrying a bag of belongings on the end of the stick resting on his shoulder. The early Franciscans, who wandered through the countryside preaching and begging, found that they were treated with suspicion at first, and, like our Fool, they had to fend off the attacks of dogs. In their wandering and preaching, the early Franciscans were following the example of the jongleur storytellers.

Jongleur is pronounced zho-'gler (the *o* is long) in French. It is the origin of the English word *juggler,* which has a similar pronunciation. Jongleurs were professional musicians, storytellers, jugglers, acrobats, and fools who traveled from one castle to another in France, Spain, and Italy in the late Middle Ages, singing for their keep. Both the Fool and the Magician or Juggler in the Tarot of Marseilles are jongleurs. In an uncut sheet of woodcut cards from the early sixteenth century called the Rosenwald Tarot, the two figures appear to have been combined into one. The Magician stands at his table, wearing a festive tunic and a fool's cap. The card bears the roman numeral one, and there is no separate Fool card.

THE MAGICIAN

Next we encounter the first trump, a card that we have titled the Magician in English. The original name, however, of the Magician card, il Bagatella, and its modern Italian name, il Bagatto, do not mean anything in Italian except the name of this card. The image in the Visconti Sforza deck—our earliest example—shows a man in a broad-brimmed hat sitting at a table with a cake, a glass, some small baked goods, and a culinary knife. The nature of these objects becomes clear when compared to other illustrations of dining painted by the same artist, Bonifacio Bembo. Bembo's Magician has been interpreted by Tarot historian Gertrude Moakley as the carnival king sitting before his meal.[1] In one of the oldest Italian woodcut decks the Magician has definitely become a street performer or trickster (see figure 24 on page 121). He has an audience of four people, and is wearing a limp pointed hat without a brim. The only objects that can clearly be identified on his table are a pair of dice. In the Marseilles deck he is given an unusual broad-brimmed hat, a knife, and a bag, but dice can still be seen on his table in most examples. In the rendering of the Marseilles Magician that was created for de Gébelin, we can see his hat and other details but the dice have been reduced to indistinct circular forms (see figure 5 on page 36).

The Marseilles Magician seems to be tempting people to gamble at dice or a shell game. But his dice, with their twenty-one combinations, may also be seen as a tool for divination or for making associations with the twenty-one trumps. Like the Fool, he is a jongleur, a storyteller and a performer. Also like the Fool, although the Magician is the lowest-ranking trump in the traditional game, he was one of the most valuable cards, in points, at the end. The Magician is the first character in the first act, which leads from the Magician to the Chariot.

The only other place in Renaissance art where one can find a similar character is in the astrological illustrations depicting the "children of the planets," the occupations ruled by each planet. These astrological woodcuts stem from the late Middle Ages and continued to be created in the Renaissance. In each illustration the god of a planet is depicted riding a triumphal chariot through the sky and the landscape below is peopled with workers engaged in all of the occupations associated with that planet. The choice of occupations associated with each planet do not entirely agree from one set of illustrations to the next. In one set of pictures, therefore, our Magician is associated with the Moon and in another with Saturn. It is clear in ancient religion, however, that the trickster was under the protection of Mercury, called Hermes in Greek, the god of gamblers, travelers, storytellers, dice, merchants, alchemists, magicians, liars, and thieves. The Magician's broad-brimmed hat is like Mercury's petasus, a traveler's hat. On his table there is a bag for keeping his belongings, which also suggests that he is a traveler. Although he is not the ceremonial magician that the occultists turned him into, the occult association of this trump with Mercury is justified.

THE PAPESSE AND THE POPE

In the Marseilles order, the Papesse resides before the Empress and the Emperor and the Pope is positioned after, but because they are symbolically a pair we will discuss them together. As we can see, the Papesse and the Pope are the first and last of the four temporal rulers, each of which trumps the ones before. The word *temporal* literally means "the world of time," in contrast to the timeless and eternal. This is a fitting name for these rulers because they are all trumped by the images of time that come in the next act—which, in turn, are trumped by the images in the third act that transcend time. The Papesse is one of the most controversial cards in the Tarot.

After the Protestant Reformation in the sixteenth century, the Papesse and the Pope were sometimes replaced with other images. For example, in the Belgian deck that developed in the seventeenth century they became the Spanish Captain and Bacchus, and in the 1JJ Swiss Tarot, which developed in Switzerland in the nineteenth century, they became Juno and Jupiter. Catholicism is extremely patriarchal and the idea that a woman could become pope was considered heretical.

In the twelfth century the Cistercian monk Joachim of Flora (1168–1202) had an epiphany in which, like St. Augustine, he saw all of history ascending through levels, each associated with one aspect of the Trinity. In the first age, the Age of the Father, the physical world was created, the law was given and the Old Testament written. In the Age of the Son, Christ was born and made his heroic sacrifice to save the world; the New Testament was written and the Church began. After this, Joachim envisioned a future age, the New Age, which would be ruled by the Holy Spirit. In the New Age, the Church would be dissolved. It will be the golden age that Christ promised when love would rule and individuals will communicate directly with God.

Although Joachim was not considered a heretic, his vision did inspire heretical groups that looked forward with hope to the New Age. One such group was called the Guglielmites, Their founder, the visionary heretic Guglielma, who had died in Milan in 1281, was believed by her followers to be an incarnation of the Holy Spirit. Guglielma had predicted that in 1300 the New Age would begin and there would be a line of female popes. When the year 1300 arrived her followers elected Sister Manfreda, a relative of the Visconti family, as the first papesse. The inquisition destroyed the sect and, although when the inquisitors found this new papesse she was already dead, they burned her body at the stake. Moakley believes that the Visconti-Sforza Papesse is a portrait of Sister Manfreda.[1] Moakley's interpretation is well supported by the details of the Visconti-Sforza illustration, which depicts the Papesse as wearing a nun's habit, as Sister Manfreda would have worn, and holding a cross, a symbol of her Christian faith.

In later decks, however, the Papesse was often called Pope Joan and the habit and cross are no longer included. The title Pope Joan is a reference to the legend of the ninth-century woman who disguised herself as a man to join the clergy and eventually rose to the rank of pope. In this story Pope Joan was found out and stoned to death. Modern researchers have uncovered evidence that suggests that Pope Joan is more than a legend. The fact that the Papesse always comes before the Pope in all of the known orders of trumps shows that she is trumped by the male Pope. In both the story of Sister Manfreda and Pope Joan the male pope triumphs, and it is plausible that the trumps are illustrating the story of either papesse. A more conservative interpretation is that the Papesse is an allegorical image of a woman wearing the Papal triple crown, which represented the Church or Faith in Renaissance art. The fact, however, that in the Tarot of Marseilles order the Empress, the Emperor, and the Pope all trump her shows the flaw in this interpretation.

A better fit with Renaissance art can be found in the mystical romance written in Venice in 1499, the *Hypnerotomachia*. The English title is usually given as *The Dream of Poliphilo.* The story recounts a dream in which Poliphilo—whose name means the lover of Polia—is led by a search for his lover, the mythical quest, into the ruins of an ancient city. He is also led out of his obsession with courtly love and alchemy back into Classical culture and erotic wisdom. Near the end of the story the lovers are united and appear before the priestess of Venus. In the woodcut, which illustrates the scene, the priestess is sitting on a throne wearing a long robe and a triple crown and bears a remarkable resemblance to the Papesse in the Tarot (see figure 29 and compare it to the Papesse in figure 6 on page 36). The woodcuts in *Poliphilo* are considered some of the most beautiful and influential illustrations produced in the early Renaissance. Although this woodcut was published in 1499 it follows the older style in Renaissance art in which Classical figures are expressed in contemporary form instead of ancient forms. Therefore, although she is a high priestess of Venus, she is dressed like her contemporary equivalent, the pope.

In Tarots other than the Visconti-Sforza (which places a cross in the hand of the Papesse) it is likely that the Papesse represents the priestess of Venus, as the image from the *Hypnerotomachia* suggests. If this is so, she represents Classical paganism and the Pope represents the triumph of Christianity over paganism, just as in the first battle of the virtues in the *Psychomachia,* Christianity or "Faith" was shown to triumph over "Pagan Worship." In the Tarot, therefore, the Empress and Emperor are seen going away from paganism and submitting themselves to the authority of the Pope. However, the next card, the Lovers, which is dominated by the Classical god Cupid, triumphs over all of them. This represents the triumph of sensuality—the theme of this first of the three parts of the trumps. Cupid is Venus' son, and, although the Pope has demoted her priestess, she has the last laugh, because even he cannot free himself from the desires that the Clas-

Figure 29. The high priestess of Venus from the *Hypnerotomachia*, 1499[2]

sical gods represent. Once again, the occultists' interpretation of the Papesse as a high priestess associated with ancient religion is not unfounded. We even find related images of Isis in Renaissance art.

The Pope card always shows the ruler of the Christian world seated on his throne with his triple tiara. This image is consistent in all Tarot decks unless the Pope has been replaced by another figure as in the 1JJ Swiss Tarot. In the Tarot of Marseilles two attendants are depicted standing in front and facing him (see figure 6 on page 36). The pope was considered the highest ruler in the temporal world. It was the pope who crowned the emperor and made him come to Rome to accept the honor. In reality, the pope's power was not uncontested by the Holy Roman emperor and history recounts their rivalries, but symbolically the pope maintained the higher rank. Furthermore, the pope was also dominant in the religious sphere during the era when the Tarot was created—the Protestant Reformation had not yet occurred, and, in the centuries before, the Vatican had ruthlessly destroyed any heretics who presented a religious alternative. As in the example of the frontispiece of the *Triumpho di Fortuna* (see figure 23 on page 119), he is sitting on top of the world. As in Lull's romance *Blanquerna,* it is not the Pope but the holy Hermit who represents true spiritual authority. The Pope is about to be challenged by Love.

The Empress and the Emperor

As the Empress and the Emperor are clearly a married couple, and, therefore, also a pair, we will again discuss them together. From the first Italian decks to the Tarot of Marseilles these figures have represented the Holy Roman emperor and his wife the empress, and they have consistently depicted the regal couple as crowned and seated on a throne.

After the fall of the Roman Empire in the West in 476, the Catholic Church, which was still centered in Rome, began to view itself as a continuation of the western Roman Empire in spiritual form. With the rise of the powerful Frankish monarch Charlemagne (742–814), the Church saw a way of reclaiming the political aspect of their empire, and on Christmas Day in the year 800, the pope crowned Charlemagne emperor. The role of emperor was strengthened by the German monarch Otto the Great (912–973) in 936, and existed in various forms for approximately one thousand years. After Otto, the emperor was effectively the ruler of what is now Germany but he did also have dominion over Italy in theory. To have actual authority, the emperor would have to take up residence in Italy as did Frederick II, who, as we learned in Chapter Three, was responsible for reinstituting the triumphal parade. Although the emperor did not have much power over northern Italy when the Tarot was developing, the political opportunists who were claiming power over the city-states often maintained claims of authority in the name of the emperor and added the imperial eagle to their coat of arms. The emperor and his symbol, therefore, were seen as a symbolic power only subject to the pope, and he and his eagle were included in the Tarot just below the Pope in the sequence of trumps.

The imperial coat of arms with the eagle was first created by Charlemagne when he was crowned in 800. To create it, Charlemagne symbolically combined the Roman eagle, which faces left, with the German or Frankish eagle, which faces right, into one two-headed eagle facing in both directions. Sometimes the German emperors preferred to use the German eagle with one head, but in the 1400s, when the Tarot was created, the two-headed eagle was in use as the official heraldic device of the emperors. In early printed cards, we can see this two-headed eagle on the Empress and Emperor cards in some decks. In the hand-painted Milanese decks and the Tarot of Marseilles and many of the decks based on it we find a single-headed eagle on each card instead (see the Emperor and Empress on the bottom row of figure 5 on page 36). Even if there was confusion about the emblem, it is common sense that the Emperor and the Empress should have the same emblem. The Visconti-Sforza Tarot gives the Roman eagle, facing left, to the Empress and the German eagle to the Emperor, and the Tarot of Marseilles does the opposite. It is typical of Renaissance symbolism to make changes in a common symbol such as the imperial eagle to embody a subtler symbolic message.

To the ancient Greeks, Delphi was the sacred center of the world. In the myth of its origin, this fact was determined by Zeus. In the myth, he sets two eagles free to fly in opposite directions around the world until they meet face-to-face in the sacred center. In ancient, Medieval, and Renaissance art two animals such as birds depicted face-to-face symbolize the sacred center, a symbol of holiness. These images in Western Christian art are influenced by Islamic designs that have an artistic lineage that links them with ancient Babylonian art.

In the Renaissance, alchemists made use of the myth of the founding of Delphi as a symbol of their quest for their mystical goal, as can be seen in an illustration in the famous alchemical text *Atalanta Fugiens,* "Atlanta Fleeing," which depicts Zeus letting the eagles fly (see figure 30). The eagles facing in opposite directions on the Empress and Emperor cards at the beginning of the Tarot trumps may be a reference to this mystical quest. This is especially relevant because, as we will see, their goal in this allegory, the World, is the sacred center. This suggests that the Emperor and Empress may be symbolically linked to the masculine and feminine opposites in the alchemical quest: the red king and the white queen. To get to their mystical goal alchemists believed that the red king and the white queen must be separated, purified, and brought back together. The story presented in the trumps follows a similar pattern in which masculine and feminine symbols are separated, purified, and reunited.

THE LOVERS

As we have seen, the four temporal rulers are presented as two mated pairs. It is fitting, therefore, that the next trump represents the triumph of Love. Originally, in the Italian decks, this card was called simply Love and the illustration was based on Renaissance betrothal portraits with a man and a woman and a blindfolded Cupid above. As we stated in Chapter Three, Cupid's blindfold symbolized his disruptive, indiscriminate nature, which needed to be safely contained by the vows of marriage. The fifteenth-century Cary-Yale Visconti Lovers even includes a small dog with the couple, a common symbol of fidelity.

In France, in the sixteenth and seventeenth centuries the tradition changed and the Marseilles deck was born. In the Tarot of Marseilles, the title was changed

Figure 30. Zeus letting two eagles fly to find the Sacred Center,
from *Atalanta Fleeing*, by Michael Maier, 1618[3]

to the Lovers and a fourth figure was added alongside the man and woman. At first, in the Jacques Vieville Tarot (ca. 1650), possibly the oldest existing Tarot in the French tradition, the fourth figure seems to be a priest performing the marriage of the lovers. In the Jean Noblet Lovers card, possibly produced slightly later than Jacques Vieville (see figure 26 on page 124), the priest has been transformed into another woman, a second choice for the central man. Now the theme became choice or temptation. The man has to choose between Virtue, represented by a woman crowned with a laurel wreath, and Sensuality, a woman crowned with flowers. In this deck, Cupid was still blindfolded but in future decks his blindfold is dropped and he represents love as a conscious choice.

As we explained in Chapter Three, the Marseilles image is thematically linked to the sermon given by Pythagoras in which the Greek letter upsilon, which forks like a *Y* (see figure 27 on page 125) is used as a symbol of two similar choices. It seems that this card may be connected to letter symbolism as Levi said, but to a Greek letter instead of a Hebrew letter. Also, upsilon is the twentieth letter in the Greek alphabet. Therefore, there can be no connection between the placement of upsilon in the Greek alphabet and the position of the Lovers, which is the sixth trump.

THE CHARIOT

As the Tarot trumps represent a triumphal parade, it is not surprising the next trump depicts a chariot, which was a prominent feature in Renaissance triumphs. In the Italian decks, this card was sometimes literally referred to as *Il Carro Triumphale,* "the Triumphal Chariot." The Milanese decks depict a chariot in profile with a beautiful young woman as the driver. In the Visconti-Sforza her two horses are winged (see figure 20 on page 113). As we mentioned in Chapter Three, this female charioteer seems to be influenced by the image of Petrarch's Laura, as the triumph of virtue in his poem *"I Trionfi,"* and possibly by the chariot of the soul from Plato's *Phaedrus,* in which the driver is also a female and the horses are winged.

In the early woodblock Tarots, the charioteer is a winged figure, possibly Cupid. In the Minchiate the figure is female but depicted as a nude Venus. Although it is redundant, these decks may represent the Chariot as a further triumph of Cupid. As an alternative interpretation, the Chariot in both of these Italian decks may represent love as a driving force that is spurring one on to a higher goal. This is reinforced by the fact that in the Minchiate the Chariot comes after the Wheel of Fortune.

In the fifteenth-century Gringonneur deck, we find perhaps the oldest depiction of the charioteer as a warrior. In this early hand-painted Italian deck the charioteer is illustrated facing the viewer, armored, and armed with a sword and halberd. He is like the figure of Mars sitting in a chariot found in the series of fifteenth-century allegorical images referred to as the Tarocchi of Mantegna. The Chariot in the Tarot of Marseilles continues in this tradition, but it depicts the charioteer as a young prince with a crown, a scepter, and Classical armor, standing in a chariot that is also facing the viewer. The chariot's two horses seem to trot directly at the viewer. In the older version, the horses' hind legs are just visible. They are like the Gringonneur horses, but the style of drawing is not as sophisticated.

Like the hero of a triumphal parade, the charioteer is trumping all of the cards that came before. He is like the lover who in the previous trump has made the decision to take the road of hardship in hopes of winning a greater reward and now he is setting out on that journey and triumphing over Cupid. He is now operating in the soul of will and ready for the challenges ahead. In various decks this triumph is interpreted differently but none of them have the flaming sword that Levi envisioned. Perhaps that is why he left it out of his illustration. However, in the oldest existing Tarot in the French tradition, the Jacques Vieville Tarot, the charioteer's beasts have human faces and lionlike bodies like Levi's sphinxes (see figure 31).

Figure 31. A rendering of the Chariot from the Jacques Vieville Tarot, Paris, circa 1650

JUSTICE

As the charioteer has embraced the path of virtue, it is fitting that the next trump in the Tarot of Marseilles is the cardinal virtue, justice. With this virtue we enter the second act and are addressing the soul of will, the heroic aspect of the soul that embraces asceticism and confronts life's challenges. As we have mentioned before, Justice is one of the four virtues praised by Plato, which Christians came to call the cardinal virtues: temperance, strength, justice, and prudence. To these four, Christian philosophers added three more virtues, which they labeled the Christian virtues: faith, hope, and charity. Except for the Cary-Yale Visconti Tarot and the Florentine Minchiate, both of which are mentioned in Chapter One, Tarot decks do not contain the three Christian virtues. The fact that they only contain the Platonic or cardinal virtues supports the theory that the nature of this allegory is Platonic.

Other evidence of the Tarot's Platonic nature is that, although it contains the cardinal virtues of justice, strength, and temperance, the forth cardinal virtue prudence, or wisdom, is not depicted directly. We have seen that in the Stoic and Christian interpretations of the Platonic virtues prudence is the final virtue, the one that leads to divine wisdom. The other three are all contained in her. Therefore, by showing the other three we already have the three divisions of prudence. When we put them together, they lead us to the wisdom that will be depicted in the final trump. The three cardinal virtues that form the parts of prudence are all contained in the second act in the Marseilles order. This choice of location seems to be influenced by Petrarch's *"I Trionfi,"* in which the virtues are the companions of Laura, the personification of Chastity, and are placed after Cupid and before Death.

In the Stoic and Christian order of the virtues, temperance should come first, then strength, and then justice. In the Marseilles order, however, justice is first and temperance is third. This is a reversal of the Stoic-Christian order. In the Marseilles order the virtues can be interpreted as going in the opposite direction. They are like divine help that is coming from the image of the Divine at the end of the series of trumps to help us get through this difficult passage. The depiction of the virtues in the Renaissance would have been heavily influenced by the views of the famous thirteenth-century theologian St. Thomas Aquinas, and the view that the virtues are coming from above is in harmony with Aquinas's views as expressed in the following quote from his *Summa Theologica*: "Infused virtue is caused in us by God without any action on our part, but not without our consent."[4]

To the ancient Greeks, justice was a divine principle of universal order, personified by the goddess Themis, who stood at the side of the Zeus, the ruler of the heavens. Themis was depicted as holding a scale, which represented order and balance, and a sword and a chain, which represented the administration of punishment for wrongdoing. Themis as the embodiment of justice is the fourth and highest virtue, as envisioned by Plato. In the Tarot's philosophical system Themis would correspond to the virtue prudence. In Greek myth, Themis and Zeus had a daughter named Dike, who was the personification of earthly justice. Dike, at times, was also associated with scales and a sword. In some accounts, Dike was included in the zodiac as the constellation Virgo and her scales were included beside her in the constellation Libra. It would seem to be Dike or her Roman counterpart, Astraea, who is depicted as Justice in the Tarot. Although Medieval Christians did not officially worship ancient goddesses, because of the influence of allegorical stories like the fifth-century *Psychomachia,* in which the virtues are described as women, the virtues were commonly personified as allegorical female figures in Christian iconography. To personify justice as a female, the Christian artists borrowed the image of Dike from Classical religion.

In the Tarot of Marseilles, Justice is depicted, like Dike, as a woman seated on a throne holding a sword and scales (see figure 7 on page 36). This image is consistent with her portrayal in earlier Italian decks except that in the hand-painted Visconti-Sforza deck a knight on horseback, who acts as her champion, has been added in the background. In the Medieval code of chivalry, knights swore an oath to uphold the virtue justice and the inclusion of a knight on this card is another example of the influence of chivalry and romanticism in the earliest decks.

The image of Justice in the Tarot as a woman holding a sword and scales is as familiar to us today as it was then, and she is still a popular subject for courthouse sculpture. The only significant difference between the modern portrayal of Justice and the one in the Tarot is that in modern images Justice is blindfolded and the Tarot's Justice is clear-sighted. The blindfold was a late sixteenth-century addition meant to symbolize her impartiality. In the fourteenth and fifteenth centuries, the blindfold would have signified that she was unfair or ignorant in her decisions, and would have been considered inappropriate. This clear-sighted version of her icon has been maintained in the Tarot.

Figure 32. A rendering of the Hermit from an uncut sheet of Italian Tarot cards, circa 1500, Metropolitan Museum, New York

THE HERMIT

As we have said, the second act in the trumps is concerned with the soul of will and embraces asceticism instead of sensuality. It is not surprising, therefore, that the next Marseilles trump depicts the Hermit, a Christian ascetic. The oldest images of the Hermit, however, found in the hand-painted Milanese decks, depict a hunched old man holding an hourglass (see figure 21 on page 115). These early representations are a symbol of Time, similar to the illustrations for the triumph of Time in *"I Trionfi."* Just as the figure of Justice was based on images of the Classical goddess Dike, the figure of Time is derived from the image of the Classical god Saturn, who was the god of time and was also depicted as a hunched old man. This personification of Time was commonly associated in Renaissance art with images of Fate and Death, and we find these same subjects depicted on other cards in this section of the trumps.

In the Italian woodcut decks from around 1500, the image changes to a holy Hermit holding a lantern instead of an hourglass (see figure 32). This change in imagery reflects a change in attitude toward the god Saturn and his astrological influences. In the early Renaissance, Saturn and time were viewed as a negative destructive force but toward the end of the fifteenth century, due to the influence of Ficino and his Neoplatonic academy, Saturn came to be seen by some in a positive light as a god of contemplation and artistic genius. By changing this trump from an embodiment of old age and deformity to a contemplative Hermit, the Tarot is reflecting the Renaissance Neoplatonic view. The Neoplatonic Hermit was also chosen for the French decks. On this card in the Tarot of Marseilles, although the Hermit is hatless, he is depicted as a similar bearded man in a robe standing with a cane and holding a lantern to light his way (see figure 8 on page 36).

Hermits were solitary Christian ascetics who patterned their practice on that of St. Anthony of Egypt (ca. 251–356). St. Anthony was a prosperous Egyptian peasant who gave his property to the poor and retired into the desert to live in contemplation. St. Anthony's example inspired emulation and there were many practicing hermits in the third and fourth centuries. Because of the austerity and dangers of solitary existence, however, the communal lifestyle of the monk eventually became a more common expression of religious devotion. In the late Middle Ages, Christian mystics, desiring a purer form of devotion than that offered by the monastery, once again began to emulate St. Anthony. As we saw in Lull's fourteenth-century romance *Blanquerna,* the title character joined a monastery to find peace of mind but found himself entangled in Church politics and eventually became pope. It is only when he resigned his papal position and became a hermit that he experienced the divine illumination that he sought.

The Marseilles Hermit is holding his lantern high, at eye level. This is a symbolic gesture that indicates that he is seeking something. This gesture is derived from descriptions of the famous pre-Christian Greek ascetic Diogenes (ca. 412–323 B.C.E.). Diogenes was a Cynic, a branch of philosophy that believed true value was only found through the rejection of the comforts and conventions of civilization. References to Diogenes were common in the Renaissance. In a Tarot deck painted in the fifteenth century for the d'Este family, the rulers of Ferrara, Diogenes is depicted on the Sun trump. The illustration depicts the famous anecdote in which Diogenes, who was living in a barrel, asked Alexander the Great to step away from the opening of his home and stop blocking the sun. Besides living in a barrel, Diogenes was said to go about the city in daylight holding a lantern high before him as a symbol of his quest for a virtuous man. The Tarot's Hermit seems to be on a similar quest for virtue.

THE WHEEL OF FORTUNE

The virtue and contemplation of the Hermit has brought him to a pinnacle of insight, and, from this hard-won perspective, he may now view the inner workings of life and learn what Fortune or Fate has planed for his future. What he sees is the suffering and mortality that is the fate of every human. As a mystic, it is his challenge to conquer Fortune and go beyond death to find the immortality of the soul. But he is not yet strong enough, and, for now, he must humbly submit to this higher trump.

In ancient Greece, there were several goddesses associated with fortune and fate. Chief among them were Tyche, the goddess of good fortune and the chance aspect of fate, and Nemesis, the goddess of divine punishment. They seem to be the models for the personifications of good fortune and bad fortune that we saw on the frontispiece of Fanti's *Triumpho di Fortuna* (see figure 23 on page 119). In ancient art, Tyche's symbols were the rudder with which she steered men's lives, the horn of plenty representing good fortune, and a globe. Each city was believed to have its individual Tyche who protected the city. Nemesis' symbols were a gryphon, a lash, scales, and a wheel. Another goddess associated with fortune was Necessity, who was also connected with the globe and the wheel of the cosmos. All of these goddesses were combined to form the Roman Fortuna.

As we saw in Plato's myth of the afterlife and soul's journey toward reincarnation that he included in *The Republic*, Necessity-Fortuna's wheel is actually the spindle of the cosmos that sits in her lap. In Chapter Three, we learned that in the ancient world it was believed that Earth was situated in the center of the cosmos, and that the seven celestial bodies that could be observed with the naked eye to travel in paths that were independent from the background of stars were believed to orbit Earth. These were the seven ancient planets: the Moon, Mercury, Venus, the Sun, Mars, Jupiter, and Saturn. Each planet was believed to move on a separate sphere, and each sphere was slightly higher above Earth than the last—forming a ladder between the heavens and Earth (see figure 19 on page 94). As the soul enters the cosmos in Plato's myth and descends the ladder of the planets to incarnation on Earth, she or he is clothed in a body and becomes subject to fate and mortality.

To stress the point that the physical world is the realm of fate and death, Plato placed Necessity's daughters, the three Fates, around her. The Fates seemed to be engaged in the craft of spinning thread, but each thread that they produced symbolized a mortal life. The first sister, Lachesis, who represents the past and the beginning of life, spins the thread; her sister Clotho, who represents the present and the span of life, draws and measures the thread; and Atropos, who represents the future and the end of life, cuts the thread.

During late antiquity and the Middle Ages, an icon of Fortuna developed in which the cosmos was symbolized as an eight-spoked wheel (although there are some examples with four or six spokes) and the goddess Fortuna was depicted standing in the center. One of the oldest references to this image can be found in *The Consolation of Philosophy* by Boethius, written in 524. In this text, Boethius attributes the following quote to Fortuna:

> I turn about my wheel with speed, and take pleasure to turn things up-side down. Ascend if thou wilt, but with this condition, that thou think-est it not an injury to descend when the course of my sport requireth.[5]

The illustrations of Fortuna's wheel included figures of four men ascending and descending the wheel as described by Boethius. Although Fortuna's daughters, the Fates, were not included in this icon, these male figures represented the aspects of life over which the Fates had dominion. This is the image that was painted on the Visconti-Sforza Wheel of Fortune card—our oldest example of this trump.

On the *Visconti-Sforza* card discussed in Chapter Three, Fortuna stands blindfolded—symbolizing her blindness to reason—in the center of her wheel surrounded by four male figures. The man on the left climbs the wheel. He is sprouting ass's ears, and an inscription on a ribbon issuing from his mouth can be translated as, "I will reign." The ascending man represents the past and the beginning of life, which is ruled by Lachesis. On top of the wheel, a man sits holding a mace and an orb. He is crowned with full-grown ass's ears, and declares, "I do reign." This man represents the present, which is ruled by Clotho. Descending the wheel headfirst, a man with an ass's tail but no ears bemoans, "I have reigned." He represents the future and the end of life, which is ruled by Atropos. Finally, at the bottom, a crawling man simply says, "I am without reign." This man represents the state of death, which is beyond life and the rule of the Fates. The inclusion of the fourth figure suggests that death is yet another phase in the movement of the wheel, and it is a short step to picturing this cycle continuing to rebirth and the process being repeated for another turn of the wheel.

As we learned in Chapter Three, reincarnation was an important part of the philosophy of Plato and the Hellenistic Neoplatonists. The views of Neoplaton-ists influenced early Christians. Some Christian Gnostics are known to have believed in reincarnation and there is controversy on whether or not other early

Christians believed in reincarnation. In the year 553, a council called by the Byzantine emperor Justinian declared the belief in reincarnation heretical. The icon of Fortuna's Wheel was retained, however, possibly because the Church identified with its moralistic message. Although the suggestion of reincarnation in the symbol seems obvious, the Medieval Church would not have thought of it as representing reincarnation, and the official interpretation of the symbol at the beginning of the fifteenth century when it was included in the Tarot would have been the same.

Yet evidence suggests that there were some who would still have recognized the reference to reincarnation in this symbol in the fifteenth century. The belief in reincarnation was reintroduced to the West by Sufis and Kabalists in Spain in the twelfth and thirteenth centuries and was also part of the beliefs of the heretical Christian sect known as Cathars in the same centuries. The Cathars were ruthlessly destroyed by the Church in the thirteenth century, but through their cultural influence some of their ideas lived on. For whatever reason, the Church found it necessary to restate that Christians did not believe in the reincarnation of the soul at the Council of Lyons in 1274 and again at the Council of Florence in 1438–1445. In the 1460s when Ficino translated Plato into Latin, many scholars came to the realization for the first time that this great ancient philosopher, who extolled the virtues and the value of the soul, also believed in reincarnation. In his writings, Ficino, at times, seems to embrace the belief in reincarnation himself, and yet, at other times, he expresses the more orthodox Christian view that there is only one incarnation of the soul.[6]

In the Italian woodcut decks from the end of the fifteenth century and the beginning of the sixteenth, Fortuna's Wheel is depicted in essentially the same manner as in the Visconti-Sforza deck except Fortune is now absent, the statements of the four men have been abbreviated, the man ascending has an ass's head and the man at the top of the wheel has been totally transformed into an ass (see figure 33). In the Marseilles Wheel of Fortune the simplification of the image and the transformation of the figures into animals has been carried further (see the drawing of the Wheel of Fortune on the lower left side of figure 9 on page 37). In the Tarot of Marseilles, the wheel supports three foolish creatures that are chasing each other's tails around the rim of a six-spoked wheel. They are three monkeys, symbols of human folly. The one on the right, wearing donkey's ears, is ascending the wheel in a foolish desire to ape the monkey on top. The one on top rules the day with his crown, his sword, and his cape flaring like a pair of wings. The third monkey demonstrates that what goes up must come down by plunging headfirst with a forlorn look on his face.

Figure 33. A rendering of the Wheel of Fortune from an uncut sheet of Italian woodcut Tarot cards, circa 1500, Metropolitan Museum, New York

These three monkeys are related to the three Fates in that they represent the past, the present, and the future, but the fourth figure representing death has been removed. Perhaps this edit was intended to remove the suggestion of reincarnation, or perhaps it was only the result of an illustrator's desire to simplify the image. Equivalent figures relating to the four men depicted on the Visconti-Sforza Wheel of Fortune are, however, included on the four trumps that depict male figures and surround the Wheel of Fortune in the Marseilles order—two figures before the Wheel of Fortune and two after. The Chariot, the first, is a young man looking forward to destiny and heading up the wheel; the Hermit has achieved the top position through his age or merit; the Hanged Man, who appears after the Wheel of Fortune, is heading down headfirst; and Death, the corpse, represents the figure that is missing from the bottom of the wheel.

With or without the suggestion of reincarnation the Wheel of Fortune is a symbol of time and mortality. It represents the foolishness of chasing after worldly riches in an impermanent world. It is a prudent vision that warns us that the only treasure that lasts is the treasure stored in the soul and this is gained by virtue not by luck. This is why the image was valued by the Church and the suggestion of reincarnation ignored.

STRENGTH

After the sobering lesson on the folly of chasing after Fortuna's rewards that was presented in the last trump, we now progress to the virtue strength, which represents the discipline and determination of a hero—the virtue Plato most identified with the soul of will. As strength is the heroic virtue, the symbols chosen in medieval and Renaissance art to illustrate this virtue are based on the stories of two famous ancient heroes who were also noted for their physical strength, Hercules and Samson.

The most popular Renaissance icon of Strength depicted a woman holding or breaking a column. This is a reference to the biblical hero Samson, who destroyed the temple of the Philistines by breaking its columns. We find the woman with a column in the Gringonneur deck, one of the earliest hand-painted Italian decks. It is also included in printed decks such as the Rosenwald deck (ca. 1500), the sixteenth-century Florentine Minchiate, and the Mitelli deck from Bologna (1664), but it is not found in most other decks.

An alternative Renaissance image of Strength depicts either a strong man or a woman with a lion. This image is a reference to the pagan hero Hercules, who slew the Nemean lion in the first of his twelve labors and wore its skin as his armor after that. Although Samson also killed a lion, the feat most indicative of his story is the destruction of the temple and the lion is more typically associated with Hercules. The hand-painted Milanese Tarot decks, which are the oldest existing examples, consistently depict a lion on the Strength card. The Visconti-Sforza deck breaks with the pattern of depicting the virtues as allegorical females—established by the other two virtues—and depicts the male hero Hercules clubbing the Nemean Lion. On the Cary-Yale Visconti Strength there is an image of a beautiful woman sitting on the back of a lion and closing the lion's mouth. In common examples of woodcut decks from the end of the fifteenth century and beginning of the sixteenth century, the illustration on the Strength card again shows a male hero wrestling a lion (see figure 34). This figure also appears to be Hercules, but the length of his hair also connects him to the legend of Samson, who believed that his strength was in his long hair. Perhaps it was intended to be a synthesis of both heros. The Tarot of Marseilles Strength card depicts a woman astride a lion in the act of closing the lion's mouth, a image that seems to be derived from the Cary-Yale Visconti Tarot (see the image in the upper right corner of figure 7 on page 36).

Hercules was popular in medieval and Renaissance art as an embodiment of heroic virtue. In his icons, just as in the Vistonti-Sforza Tarot, he was usually depicted as himself instead of as an allegorical woman, and, as we said, it was more popular to depict the female image of Strength holding a column. Perhaps this is because the images of the virtues symbolized as women were derived from the *Psychomachia,* an early Christian text, and the artists who created these allegorical female figures felt more at home depicting symbols associated with a biblical hero like Samson instead of a pagan hero like Hercules. The Cary-Yale Visconti and

Figure 34. A rendering of Strength as Hercules recreated from an uncut sheet and fragments of Tarot cards, Italian, circa 1500, Museum of Fine Arts, Budapest, and Metropolitan Museum, New York

the Marseilles images combine a pagan subject with the Christian form and also harmonize the representation of Strength with the representation of the other virtues in the Tarot.

The fact that the image of Strength in the Tarot of Marseilles extols the exploits of a pagan hero attests to the Tarot's secular and mystical nature. Unlike Samson, Hercules actually defeated death and became divine through his labors. In ancient times, the philosophers used him as an example of moral virtue and people prayed to him as a mystical guide and helper, like a Christian saint. The fourth-century B.C.E. Sophist Prodikos authored a myth called the choice of Hercules in which Hercules is faced with the Pythagorean choice of two paths. In the myth, the youthful Hercules came to a crossways where he met two women, one called Pleasure and the other Duty. Pleasure promised him a life of sensuality if he followed her, and Duty promised him a life of labor and troubles if he followed her. Hercules chose Duty, but because of that choice he became immortal. This myth expresses the same theme that is depicted on the Lovers trump, and this depiction of the Herculean virtue in this second act reinforces the idea that this section depicts the path of duty and virtue.

THE HANGED MAN

The vision on the Wheel of Fortune warned us that we could not stay seated at the top of the wheel for long. Now we have arrived at a trump depicting a man suspended headfirst like the figure descending the Wheel of Fortune. This card was originally called the Traitor, and, like the falling figure on the wheel, he symbolizes a fall from power.

The image on the Hanged Man is essentially the same from the cards in the earliest decks to the Marseilles deck and other seventeenth-century Tarots (see figure 11 on page 39). It shows a man hanged by his feet from a beam supported by two rough-cut posts. He is tied to the beam by his left foot and his right leg and his arms are folded behind him. In the early decks he was never depicted standing right side up on one foot as de Gébelin suggested. However, some later decks did mistakenly turn him right side up. In Renaissance Italy, this figure would have been easily recognized as a traitor—in the Minchiate and some early lists of the trumps this card is labeled the Traitor. In Italy, the punishment for a traitor was to be hanged by his feet or foot possibly after execution. Even in modern Italian history, the dictator Mussolini was hanged by his feet after he was executed near the end of World War II. In the Renaissance, it was also the practice to label a person a traitor by having a picture printed of them hanging by the foot, and posting it. These were called shame pictures.

Often we find money falling out of the pockets of the Hanged Man in the Tarot. This detail strengthens the sense of loss symbolized by this card. The original meaning of this card is suffering and loss. It is connected with the images of time and fate found in this section of the trumps. This is the Nemesis aspect of Fortuna. Through unvirtuous behavior or perhaps through unfair accusation the traitor has lost his position and wealth and is suffering by being hanged. In a deck from Bologna printed in 1664, we find the substitution of a man preparing to hit another man in the head with a large mallet on this card.

Modern occultists interpret this card as representing a sacrifice that is made willingly for the purpose of spiritual gain and this interpretation is not out of step with how the Hanged Man is originally presented. The Hanged Man is positioned after Hercules or a woman who symbolizes his heroic virtue. Several times in Greek mythology Hercules was found guilty of a crime and as a result was enslaved or pledged to complete a task as penance, thereby suffering an ordeal and a loss of position. The hero's journey is not without pitfalls. Instead of rewarding Socrates for his wisdom, the Athenians declared him a traitor and forced him to drink hemlock. The crucifix is a reminder to every Christian that even Christ was executed as a traitor to the state. And, as we see, Death follows the Traitor in the Tarot also.

DEATH

Although, the fourth figure is absent on the Marseilles Wheel of Fortune, the end of life and of the domain of Fate is still implied. It, therefore, should be no surprise that the Hanged Man is trumped by Death. The mystic, ultimately, seeks the secret of immortality—he wishes, in turn, to trump Death. We should therefore welcome this next trump as a sign that we are nearing our goal.

The image of Death in the Tarot has consistently been the skeletal figure known as the Grim Reaper. In the earliest cards he is standing or riding on a pale horse, a reference to death as one of the Four Horsemen of the Apocalypse found in Revelation. His weapon of choice is the scythe, though in the Visconti-Sforza deck he uses a bow and arrow. This image of death developed in the mid-thirteenth century in France and was made popular by the Dance of Death, an allegorical dance or work of art in which Death is seen to triumph over individuals of every age and class (see figure 35). Similarly, in the Tarot of Marseilles, the Grim Reaper is depicted harvesting the heads and arms of both men and women of both noble and common status (see figure 9 on page 37). Figure 35 is from a series of woodcuts illustrating *The Dance of Death* by the famous German Renaissance artist Hans Holbein the Younger (1497–1543). This woodcut illustrates the triumph of Death over a hermit—just as Death trumps the Hermit in the Tarot. Also as in the Tarot's allegory, the last image in Holbein's book is one that depicts the soul's transcendence of death.

Just as we have seen the folly in chasing after worldly gain, and have developed our strength to overcome that impulse, our strength has been trumped by suffering and now by Death. If this were a pessimistic tale it would end here. In all the known early orders of the trumps Death is always number thirteen. As thirteen is a number associated with bad luck and death, this suggests that Death was given this number for symbolic reasons. It also shows that this is not a story that ends with Death. Death is always in the second act of the story, not in the last—it is not even the final trump in the second act. It is always a story about the mystic goal, the transcendence of Death, the hero's search for immortality.

TEMPERANCE

As we said, the final trump in this second act is not Death but the virtue Temperance. Often when faced with death and suffering one may become wrathful or angry with the apparent unfairness of life. In Renaissance allegories Temperance was commonly the virtue that was depicted conquering Wrath, and she is in the same position in the trumps.

The figure of Temperance in the Tarot of Marseilles and all earlier decks is consistently that of a woman pouring water from one vessel to another (see figure 7 on page 36). The only significant change in the figure in the Tarot of Marseilles is that she has wings like an angel, suggesting a higher spiritual nature, and in the earliest decks she is unwinged like the other virtues. This image is not familiar to us today, but it was a common image in the Middle Ages and the Renaissance.

Figure 35. Death and the Hermit from *The Dance of Death* by Hans Holbein, 1538[7]

It is often suggested that Temperance was depicted mixing water with wine, to avoid getting drunk. This was one interpretation of the image. In the Renaissance, however, temperance of attitude and emotion was considered to be dependant on the proper balance of the four humors, which were believed to be the vital liquids in the body: blood, phlegm, black bile, and yellow bile. This connection between the humors and temperament is still part of our language. For example, when we say that someone is melancholy, we are saying that they have too much black bile, which in Latin is called *melancholia*. Likewise, when these four liquids are in proper balance we are said to have a good temperament, which is derived from the Latin *temperamentum*, "correct mixture."

This balanced state of composure and tranquility is the virtue that will now allow us to progress to the third act and into the soul of reason.

THE DEVIL

The Devil is the first card in the last act. This is the act ruled by the soul of reason and, therefore, we may be surprised to find this embodiment of chaos and illogic introducing this act. The final card in this section is what Plato would call the One, the Good, and the Beautiful. The Devil is the exact opposite. He is the Selfish, the Bad, and the Ugly. The woman on the final trump may also represent Prudence, Wisdom, or Reason, and the Devil is imprudent, unwise, and unreasonable. He is what must be cleansed and purified to reach our goal.

The Devil does not appear in any of the early hand-painted decks, but he is included in the oldest woodcut decks and in all of the printed decks thereafter. The Devil in the Tarot is the horned demon who is the Christian personification of evil and who is common in medieval and Renaissance art. In contrast to the virtues, he is associated with the seven vices. As the embodiment of disorder, he is composed of an illogical combination of details. In the earliest decks, he appears human but has horns on his head and the feet of a bird. At times, he has a hairy body, batwings, and a face where his genitals should be. His weapon of choice is a three-pronged pitchfork.

In the Tarot of Marseilles, the Devil has male genitals but female breasts, the wings of a bat, the taloned feet of a bird of prey, and the antlers of a stag. His weapon is a torch, a symbol of unbridled passion (see figure 9 on page 37). He is standing on a pedestal. On each side, an antlered minion is chained by the neck to the pedestal. In most editions of the Marseilles Tarot, one of the minions appears to be female and the other male. In scenes depicting the vices in Renaissance art, we sometimes find devils making prisoners of men and women and the image of bound captives is common in scenes of hell. The choice of two captives that we find in the Marseilles deck, however, seems to suggest a deeper symbolic theme. The female minion may be thought of as a sensual figure, representing the first act and the soul of appetite, and the male minion as a harder, more threatening figure, representing the second act and the soul of will. From the perspective of the soul of reason, both lower aspects of the soul can now be seen to be in the control of the irrational.

The last act ended with the virtue Temperance triumphant. But now she is trumped by the Devil. The fact that the Devil appears now shows that we are approaching our goal. The Devil is the guardian of higher realm. In the hero's quest, there is always a definitive final challenge before the goal can be reached. When Christ went into the desert to find his calling, the Devil came to tempt him. In the stories of saints, there are similar scenes with the Devil acting as the final challenge. Buddha, as well, had to confront Mara, the Buddhist Devil, before he could reach enlightenment. It is easy to lose hope at this impasse on the mystic journey. It is often called the dark night of the soul.

The famous German Renaissance artist Albrecht Dürer (1471–1528), who is celebrated for his woodcuts and engravings as well as his paintings, created an engraving on this same theme, entitled *Knight, Death, and Devil* (see figure 36). Dürer was an avid proponent of the use of symbolism in art, and every detail in his works was intended to convey a poetic message through symbolic interpretation. *Knight, Death, and Devil* is an image of chivalry and the heroic quest that parallels this section of the Tarot's story. The knight on his horse with his determined stance fills the center of the picture. A skull representing death lies on a stump in front of him and Death himself, a corpse on a pale horse (the horse's head and front legs can be seen on the left of the picture in front of the knight's horse) confronts him with an hourglass, a symbol of time and mortality. The knight looks straight ahead, ignoring the warning. A dog runs alongside. As we mentioned in the discussion of the Lovers, the dog represents faithfulness and duty and this is certainly why Dürer has included the dog as the knight's companion. In the Dürer engraving, the dog links the hero in the picture with Hercules. Like Hercules, the knight has chosen the difficult path and follows his duty. He is the embodiment of fortitude and strength.

There is one other small creature at the knight's feet, however, a salamander. In medieval bestiaries, the salamander was said to live in fire and to be able to extinguish it with his breath. In alchemy the salamander is a symbol of fire but, in Christian art, because of his cooling breath, he is a symbol of faith triumphing over the passions. Here the salamander of faith is departing to the rear. The Devil, with a goat's head and a single horn, seems to have noticed this clue and is approaching from the rear. The knight is headed for the dark night of the soul.

We can see that in creating his allegory Dürer made use of characters and

Figure 36. Dürer's engraving *Knight, Death, and Devil*, printed in 1513[8]

other symbols that relate to ones we have found in Tarot decks. The knight is a hero like the charioteer, the dog suggests the virtue strength, and Death and the Devil are clearly represented in the Tarot. Dürer does not give us a clue about the outcome of the knight's struggle, but the next trump indicates that in the Tarot the hero will prevail.

THE TOWER

Next we come to the Tower, which represents the fire that purifies—the process of destruction that is necessary before we can rebuild. In many of the early decks all seven of the images in the last act are related to medieval and Renaissance illustrations for Revelation, the biblical account of the second coming of Christ and the final confrontation between good and evil. The number seven, itself, is a prominent symbol in Revelation. In the text, The armies of Satan are defeated by the angels led by St. Michael the archangel. The earth is cleansed through earthquakes and hails of fire, the stars fall from the sky, and the wicked perish. In the illustrations, their proud towers are shown crumbling and burning to make way for the new Millennium. The dead are called up from their graves by trumpeting angels and all are judged for their final reward or punishment. To illustrate this point, St. Michael is given the scales of Justice in Christian iconography. This is an image found in art but not in the biblical account. It also helps to explain why Justice was placed between the World and Judgement in one early order of the trumps.

In the climax of Revelation, the good will live on in the purified world in the New Jerusalem, a city that outshines the sun and the moon because it is lit by the aura of Christ. Time will stand still and death will be abolished. These images are central to Christian mysticism. Because of its images of purification, the defeat of time and death, and a light of truth greater than the sun, its symbols were also used by alchemists and in secular narratives like the story in the Tarot. The Renaissance was a time when secular authors and artists were concerned with moral and mystical allegory and freely mixed Christian and pre-Christian symbols.

The Tower is not included in the trumps in any of the fifteenth-century hand-painted Milanese decks but a hand-painted example does exist in the fifteenth-century Gringonneur deck. In the Gringonneur deck the Tower is a large crumbling stone structure with flames emerging from its side. The early Italian printed decks contain a flaming Tower, with the flames clearly coming from a flaming disk in the sky. In the Italian decks, this card was usually called Fire or else the House of the Devil or other variations. In the Bolognese and the Belgian Tarot, it was sometimes called Lightning or Thunderbolt, and a fiery lightning bolt would be shown striking a person or tree instead of the tower.

In the French Jacques Vieville deck, one of the earliest French decks, this card depicts a shepherd hiding his flock under a tree while lightning hits the tree. After this, the French decks in the Marseilles tradition are mostly consistent. There is a Tower, called the House of God, and a flamelike lightning bolt knockower. The crenellated top is depicted in a way that suggests a falling from the top and another appears to be jumping out bottom or to have landed on the ground behind the Tower on page 37).

In the mystical quest, the Tower represents the burning away of the egotistical urges that stop one from joining with the One. It is the breakthrough to the higher realm. In the myth of the death of Hercules, he willingly burned his body on a pyre. As his body burned away Mercury came and brought his soul to Olympus, where he became a god. To reach a vision of the One, the great Neoplatonic philosopher Plotinus believed that he had to strip away or destroy all thoughts of physical reality. He accomplished this by thinking of physical reality as being composed of dualistic pairs and asking himself what was beyond any pair that he could think of. In his meditation, he would ask: "What is there that is not masculine or feminine, that is not pain or pleasure, joy or fear?" The more ideas and preconceptions he could cut away, the higher his spirit rose. In the Tarot also, we will now make an ascent to the heavens past all duality.

THE STAR

The Star is the first of three cards that represent celestial bodies of greater and greater brilliance and light: the Star, the Moon, and the Sun. This section of the trumps represents the ascent to the heavens that is part of the symbolism of the mystical quest. The increasing brilliance of each celestial body indicates that we are approaching the source of light and clarity that is the goal of the mystic—this is why the experience of this source is called enlightenment.

In the Visconti-Sforza deck, there is a woman on the Star card who is wearing a long blue dress speckled with gold stars and holding a large eight-pointed star above her head. The woman in blue is likely to be Urania, the muse of astronomy. There is a similar figure in blue painted by the famous Renaissance artist Raphael (1483–1520) on the ceiling of the library of Pope Julius II, where she is presented as the link between philosophy and theology, the secular and the religious. All of the examples from early Italian woodcut decks have different images for this card. The most common example from the end of the fifteenth century depicts a seminude youth holding a six-pointed star above his head. In the Rosenwald Tarot, which is from the same time, the illustration on the Star only contains an eight-pointed star with clouds above and below. In the Rothschild Tarot, another printed deck from the end of the fifteenth century, three figures are depicted below an eight-pointed star. These three men are likely to represent the three Magi who followed a star to Bethlehem in the story of Christ's birth. The same theme of three Magi is illustrated on the Star in the Florentine Minchiate. As we can see, when choosing their symbols, the Tarot artists did not allow themselves to be constrained by one biblical narrative.

In the seventeenth-century French Jacques Vieville Tarot, we find an astronomer with calipers pointed at the sky on the Star. But in the Jean Noblet Tarot and all of the Marseilles decks after, we find what is perhaps the most symbolically evolved allegory for the Star in any Tarot (see figure 8 on page 36). The Star in the Marseilles tradition depicts a female nude pouring water from two pitchers, one on the land and one on the sea. Above her are seven stars situated around a larger eighth one. Here we find a Neoplatonic nude as a symbol of the soul. Above her head is the Neoplatonic ladder of the planets, which are represented by the seven stars overhead. The eighth star represents the eighth sphere on which the fixed stars revolve and is considered the gateway to Heaven. Behind her a large bird, another symbol of the soul, sits in a tree, another symbol of the celestial ladder of ascent. The image of the woman holding pitchers that pour on the land and the water is related to an image from Revelation in which an angel is seen standing on the land and the sea. In the seventeenth century, alchemists also seized on this symbol to represent the combination of opposites that is a necessary feature of their mystical Great Work: dry and wet, hot and cold, masculine and feminine, and red and white.

Figure 37 is the author's rendering of a woodcut from the 1659 Parisian alchemical text *L'Azoth des Philosophes* by Basil Valentin. This text was created at the same time and in the same country as the Tarot of Marseilles. This image is called the Siren of the Philosophers. It depicts a mermaid, a common alchemical symbol for the Anima Mundi, the Soul of the World, expressing a stream of blood and a stream of milk from her breasts. Blood and milk represent the alchemical red and white but also suffering and nurturing or death and life. As in Plotinus' meditation described in the last section discussing the Tower, the alchemist finds the Anima Mundi by going beyond all duality. The siren's breasts are related to the pitchers on the Star. Figure 38 is another rendering from the same text. Here we can see the seven stars labeled with astrological symbols as the seven planets in the Neoplatonic ladder, from left to right: Venus, Mars, the Sun, Mercury, the Moon, Jupiter, and Saturn. Below the ladder there are several symbols for the transcendence of opposites: the quadrangle and triangle are combined in the winged circle, the evil and poisonous dragon who has been transformed into the medicine stands on the circle, and the king and queen combined as one hermaphrodite stand on the dragon. The hermaphrodite is holding

Figure 37. A rendering of the Siren of the Philosophers from *L'Azoth des Philosophes*, Paris, 1659

a square and a compass, symbols for the squaring of the circle, yet another symbol of the transcending of duality in which the circle represents the celestial or spiritual world and the square represents the fourfold physical world. On either side of the hermaphrodite the Sun and the Moon are more distinctly drawn than the other planets. The Sun is paired with the male head and the Moon with the female, demonstrating that they are masculine and feminine in nature. This brings us to the next two trumps, the Moon and the Sun.

THE MOON AND THE SUN

As we saw in the alchemical illustration of the hermaphrodite with the planets in the last section, the Moon and the Sun are symbolically a pair—they are the principal feminine and masculine couple. We will, therefore, discuss them together as we did with the two pairs of temporal rulers that we encountered in the first act: the Papesse and the Pope, and the Empress and the Emperor.

Because the Marseilles Star symbolically included the Moon and the Sun as two of the seven planets illustrated in the heavens above the nude, we may find it

redundant that they are each illustrated again on their own trump. But
it is common in Renaissance alchemical and astrological illustrations for
the Sun and the Moon to perform
double duty in this way. Besides being part of the celestial ladder leading to Heaven, the Moon and the
Sun are multileveled symbols of duality and we must progress beyond
duality to achieve oneness. Besides
representing the feminine and masculine, they represent the opposites:
wet and dry, passive and active, dark
and light, and night and day. As the
rulers of night and day, the Moon
and the Sun are the ultimate timekeepers and it is the goal of the mystic to conquer time.

Figure 38. A rendering of the Envenomed Dragon,
the material of the stone, from *L'Azoth des
Philosophes*, Paris, 1659

As with the Star, the Moon and the Sun are depicted in various ways in the earliest decks. In the earliest example in the Visconti-Sforza Tarot, a woman in a red
dress, who is similar in appearance to the woman on the Star, holds a crescent moon
aloft on the Moon card, and, as the Sun is masculine, a male figure is depicted holding the Sun on the Sun card. The male is a nude youth with small wings, often
called a cherub but more accurately termed a putto in Renaissance art.

In the hand-painted Gringonneur Tarot, the images on both trumps refer to
the Moon's and the Sun's roles as keepers of time and, therefore, as guardians of
Fate. The Gringonneur Moon depicts two astronomers, one holding calipers
toward the Moon and the other using his calipers to plot its movement in his
book. This illustration demonstrates how astronomers use the movement of the
Moon to plot the progression of time in their calendars. On the Gringonneur
Sun, a woman holding a distaff is depicted standing under the Sun. A distaff is a
rod used to hold wool or other fiber that will be spun into thread. As this was a
tool used by the three Fates, who spun threads representing the lives of mortals, it
is a symbol of Fate in medieval and Renaissance art. The message of these cards is
that to go beyond the Sun and Moon is to go beyond Time and Fate.

In Italian woodcut decks from the end of the fifteenth century the Moon,

Figure 39. A rendering of the Sun card
with a woman representing Fate from
an uncut sheet of Italian Tarot cards,
circa 1500, in the Bibliothèque de
l'École Nationale Supérieure des
Beaux-Arts, Paris

personified with a face, is held aloft by a semi-nude youth, and the Sun, also personified with a face, radiates over a landscape. The Moon and the Sun in the Rosenwald Tarot of the same period also have faces but no other details except clouds that frame the celestial orbs from above and below.

In the fragmented Rothschild Tarot that was also printed in the late fifteenth century, the Moon seems to be based on the Gringonneur model. On the Rothschild Moon there are two astronomers, one holding a caliper toward the moon in the sky and one holding a square toward the earth. As we saw in the discussion of the alchemical illustration in the section about the Star (see figure 38), the caliper, used to make circles, is the symbol of the heavens and the spiritual and the square, used to draw right angles when creating squares, represents the physical world. Together they are a symbol of the squaring of the circle, the spiritualization of the world. While these astronomers are keeping track of the moon, to measure time, they also seem to have a higher spiritual goal. In the Bibliotheque de l'Ecole Nationale Superieure des Beaux-Arts in Paris, there resides an uncut sheet of six late fifteenth-century printed trumps that are in the same style as the Rothschild Tarot and, therefore, possibly from the same deck. The Sun on this sheet of trumps depicts a woman with a distaff and a spindle sitting under a human-faced Sun—again taking the Gringonneur Tarot as a model (see figure 39). As we said above, the woman is a symbol of the Fates, particularly Clotho, who pulls a thread to measure a human life.

In the Jacques Vieville Tarot, one of the earliest French decks, the woman with the distaff has been moved to the Moon card and a nude youth riding a white horse and brandishing a red banner at the end of a long pole is depicted under the Sun on the Sun trump. The red banner is a symbol of victory in Christian iconography. It is often depicted being held by Christ in icons of his Resurrection. In this Tarot it also seems to be a symbol of victory over death. As we will see in the next chapter, this image of the boy on a horse with the banner was the model for the Sun in the twentieth-century Waite-Smith Tarot.

In the Tarot of Marseilles decks the Moon contains an elaborate allegory featuring a crayfish climbing out of a pool on the bottom of the card to follow a path that leads past two dogs and two towers toward the moon in the sky above (see figure 8 on page 36). On an uncut sheet of sixteenth-century Italian printed cards in the Yale Library, we can see one of the oldest examples of this Marseilles design, which suggests an Italian origin for the image. The only change is that in the French versions the two dogs were added. The crayfish relates to the constellation Cancer, the native house of the moon, and the dogs are Diana's companions in mythology. The Marseilles Moon does not depict the moon goddess, Diana, directly but by including her hounds it suggests her presence without showing her. In Renaissance allegory all of the qualities symbolized by the Moon can also be symbolized by the goddess Diana.

On the Sun in the Tarot of Marseilles, a human-faced sun radiates above two youths wearing loincloths (see figure 8 on page 36). In the eighteenth-century versions, because of their youth and their loincloths, their sex cannot be determined. On the earliest seventeenth-century versions of this image, however, and in an Italian card of the same image from Sforza Castle dated circa 1700, they are clearly older male and female figures—with breasts depicted on the female. The youths may represent a male and female joined together in innocence in a new golden age. Some have suggested that the later figures are the brothers Castor and Pollux, of the Gemini constellation, or the founders of Rome, Romulus and Remus. Although Castor and Pollux had the same mother, Leda, Castor's father was mortal—thus Castor was mortal—and Pollux's father was Zeus—thus Pollux was immortal. In the myth of the founders of Rome, we find the same polarity. Romulus is immortal and Remus is mortal. Whether the pair is masculine or feminine or mortal and immortal they represent the joining of opposites. They are personifications of the Sun and Moon being joined. This is what the alchemists call the greater conjunction. It is this unity beyond duality that will allow us to proceed to the next trump, Judgement.

JUDGEMENT

The Judgement trump from the earliest Italian Tarots to the Tarot of Marseilles consistently depicts the scene described in Revelation in which the dead are called up from their graves by trumpeting angels to be judged for their final reward or punishment. Alchemists and other mystics commonly made use of this image to symbolize victory over death and this trump heralds the mystical reward that is depicted in the final trump.

In all of the hand-painted and printed Italian decks, we find two angels with trumpets hovering over open graves with two to seven men and women waking from their death. This card in the Visconti-Sforza deck and one card that was a fifteenth-century copy from that deck, are the only ones to add God the Father to the scene. In the earliest Italian woodcut decks one angel flies over a cemetery as the dead begin to wake up. The Tarot of Marseilles contains the same image with the number of rising figures fixed at three: two men and a woman (see figure 10 on page 37). Except for the Minchiate, which depicts Fame for this trump, the image is always the Last Judgment based on Revelation. As we discussed in the last chapter, the Renaissance poet Petrarch made use of the Final Judgment from Revelation to create his final trump, which represented eternal life and the victory over death and time in his poem *"I Trionfi."* This scene has consistently been used in this way in poetry, alchemy, and visual allegory to represent victory over death, and the angelic trumpeter on this trump can be thought of as heralding the mystical victory depicted on the World.

THE WORLD

We now have arrived at the final reward symbolized in the Tarot of Marseilles by the image of the soul standing on the throne of God. This is a complex image that synthesizes numerous mystical themes into one image of completeness and sacredness. It is perhaps the most commonly misunderstood image in the Tarot, but by examining its history and comparing it to other works of art with related themes, we will begin to appreciate its message.

As we discussed in the last chapter, some of the oldest World cards bear a representation of the New Jerusalem, the eternal city of light and the final reward described at the end of Revelation (see figure 25 on page 122). However, this is not always the case. As we mentioned in Chapter One, there are three fifteenth-century Italian cards now in collections in England and Germany in which the World is depicted as the Arthurian Grail, the mystical cup that could heal the land and that represented the final reward in the Arthurian legend of the Grail (see figure 3 on page 21).

In the Cary-Yale Visconti Tarot, one of the oldest Milanese decks, the World card combines images of the New Jerusalem with mystical chivalry. On the card, we find the city depicted through an arch as a beautiful landscape on the edge of the sea with several buildings, a river with a boat, and in the central field a knight on horseback holding a victory banner. Above the arch, there is a beautiful richly dressed woman rising out of a cloud which in turn rises out of a crown (see figure 40). In the Bible, the New Jerusalem is described as a bride and here that aspect was seized on to create a symbolic female who is at once the bride and the Anima Mundi—the Soul of the World. The woman holds a crown and a trumpet. These symbols combined with the image of the knight suggest that she is also the Lady of Sovereignty, a romantic symbol of the soul of the land that a knight must marry to become the king.

Figure 40. A rendering of the Soul of the World from the Cary-Yale Visconti World card, Milan, circa 1450

In the fifteenth-century Gringonneur deck, the figure on the World card is also the Anima Mundi. A woman with a long dress holds the regal orb and mace while standing on a circle containing a landscape. The circle is nestled in clouds, suggesting that this is the cosmos suspended in space. In Holbein's final illustration of transcendence for his *Dance of Death,* which we discussed under the Death trump, there is a more sophisticated but related image of the concentric spheres of the ancient cosmos. In Holbein's image Christ is on top instead of the feminine Anima Mundi, but the message is related—a spiritual presence, whether Christ or the Anima Mundi, rules the world and all its inhabitants and the perception of this vision provides proof of the immortality of the soul.

In European alchemy and mysticism we likewise find that the Anima Mundi may be symbolized as a beautiful woman, as Christ, or as Hermes. In the Tarot we also find all three depicted as the final triumph. In one of the early woodcut decks now in the Bibliothèque de l'École Nationale Supérieure des Beaux-Arts, Paris, there is a World card with a figure that is possibly Hermes holding an orb and a winged mace standing on top of a circle divided into the four elements (see figure 41). The Christ figure is found in the Jacques Vieville Tarot (see figure 4 on page 24). This image is based on the standard Christian icon called Christ in Majesty, representing Christ on his celestial throne surrounded by the symbols of the four Evangelists: the lion, the bull, the eagle, and the man. It is based on de-

Figure 41. A rendering of a fifteenth-century World card depicting Hermes, from an uncut sheet of Italian Tarot cards, circa 1500, in the collection of the Bibliothèque de l'École Nationale Supérieure des Beaux-Arts, Paris

scriptions of God's throne found in both Ezekiel and Revelation discussed in Chapter One. Unlike the standard icon, however, the Jacques Vieville Christ is totally nude with long blond hair and no beard. He is more closely connected to the famous painting by the Renaissance artist Michelangelo (1475–1564) painted for the altar wall of the Sistine Chapel. In Michelangelo's Neoplatonic vision Christ and Apollo are combined into one divine being that is also nude, blond, and beardless.

Figure 42 is a drawing by the author of a traditional Christ in Majesty icon. It is from a thirteenth-century French champlevé enamel on gilded copper, created to be nailed to the cover of a Bible. Surrounding Christ, one to each corner, are the four living creatures of the Evangelists. Through their connection to the four fixed signs of the zodiac, in medieval and Renaissance thought, these symbols came to represent the four directions and the four elements and represent the limits of the physical world animated by the presence of Christ. Notice that to either side of Christ's head are the alpha and the omega symbols—the first and last letters of the Greek alphabet, symbolizing the beginning and the end. In this icon, the omega is first, suggesting that the end comes before the beginning—Christ's death before his Resurrection and everlasting life. Compare this icon to figure 43, which is the author's rendering of a sixteenth-century alchemical illustration of Christ as the Anima Mundi. The alchemical image shows how the four Evangelists were related to the four elements and that Christ could symbolize the Anima Mundi. Alchemists believed that the Anima Mundi was a fifth element that permeated and animated the more physical four. It was called the Fifth Essence, Quinta Essentia, in Latin, the source of the word *quintessence.* Christ, as a symbol of the Anima Mundi or the Fifth Essence, is depicted in this woodcut in the center of the four physical elements: earth, water, fire, and air.

The twentieth-century historian of religions Mircea Eliade has observed that in all religions and cultures there is a place believed to be sacred above all else and that this place is considered to be the center of the world. This is the place where there is a connection with higher and lower worlds and the place where the divine can manifest. In art, the symbolic fourfold structure of the physical world is used to define the sacred center and frame the image of the divine presence. Buddhists place Buddha in the center of their four-sided diagrams called mandalas and Christians place Christ in the center of the cross or a mystical diagram called a quincunx. A quincunx is a diagram of the sacred in which there are four figures representing the fourfold world placed one to each corner and a fifth sacred figure placed in the center. The Christ in Majesty icon is a quincunx, a Western mandala. Although Christian artists were influenced by the description of Christ's throne in the Bible, the icon is also informed by a sacred tradition that is pre-Christian. In the Orphic myth Phanes was the beautiful creature of radiant light, who was the first being to emerge from

Figure 42. A drawing of a thirteenth-century French enameled Christ in Majesty icon

the world egg (see figure 44). To express Oneness and Goodness, Phanes was said to be double sexed and golden winged. He had four heads representing the seasons, that of a bull, a lion, a ram, and a serpent. He created the earth, sky, sun, moon, and stars and brought love and beauty into the world. We can see that his ancient icon is also a quincunx, in which Phanes is placed in the center of the zodiac, the wheel of time and the center of the physical world, symbolized by the four winds placed in the corners. Although depicted as male, his torch, representing the sun, and the crescent behind his shoulders, representing the moon, symbolize his masculine and feminine duality.

After the Jacques Vieville deck, all of the World cards in the Marseilles tradition depict a female nude dancing on Christ's throne in the center of the creatures representing the four Evangelists. The most common image of the Anima Mundi in alchemical and mystical art was also a beautiful nude. Figure 45 is the author's drawing of a painting of the Anima Mundi from an eighteenth-century French alchemical text. Again, she is the center of a quincunx with the four ele-

Figure 43. A rendering of a sixteenth-century alchemical woodcut
depicting Christ as the Anima Mundi

ments in the corners. Like Phanes, she is depicted as transcending the fourfold world. Like a mermaid, the upper part of her body allows her to exist on land and the lower part in the water but she also has wings to allow her to transcend air. In her right hand she holds a chalice with a serpent. This image is borrowed from the symbol for St. John. In his legend, St. John was given poisoned wine to drink but when he blessed it the poison departed in the form of a serpent and he was able to drink it unharmed. The alchemists used his cup as a symbol of the alchemical transformation, which was believed to change harmful substances into a healing elixir. By holding this vessel the Anima Mundi demonstrates the power of her "secret fire," and completes her mastery of the four elements. To symbolize that she is the harmony of opposites, she has one eye open and one eye closed. One of her wings is black and the other is red in the original painting. These represent the first and last stages of the alchemical process. Like Christ she is between the beginning and the end, outside of the process, and outside of time.

In the Tarot of Marseilles, the illustration of the World is clearly related to the images we have been examining (see figure 46). The Marseilles World is also a quincunx and a symbol of transcendence. The nude dances on Christ's throne, identified by the symbols of the four Evangelists in the corners. She takes the po-

Figure 44. A drawing of a Classical relief of the Orphic Phanes, Modena, Italy

sition in the sacred center, which identifies her as the Anima Mundi and the Quinta Essentia. She is holding the regal orb and mace, symbols of the feminine and masculine, indicating that she has mastered or transcended duality. The wreath that surrounds her is a symbol of time, which she has also transcended. In some Renaissance examples, a similar wreath is divided into four sections with

Figure 45. A drawing of the alchemical Anima Mundi from Solidonius,
eighteenth century, Paris

different foliage, chosen to represent each season, depicted in each section. Although the foliage is depicted as consistent on the Tarot of Marseilles wreath, four divisions of the wreath are made clear in the earliest seventeenth-century examples.

The nude is simultaneously the individual soul, which is also symbolized as a female nude, joined to the World Soul, and the World Soul is depicted as both Christ, or Sophia his female counterpart, and the pre-Christian Venus. As Sophia, the female aspect of Christ or God, the World represents divine wisdom, which is the highest virtue, Prudence. All of these elements point to the same conclusion, the World represents the state of enlightenment, the mystical goal. Next we will examine the World's domain, the four minor suits that can be related to the symbols of the four directions and four elements that were depicted in the corners of the final trump.

THE MINOR ARCANA

The Tarot's four minor suits—cups, swords, coins, and staffs—which the occultists called the Minor Arcana were a preexisting deck to which the trumps were added to form the Tarot (see the images of the four aces of the minor suits in figure 10 on page 37). Yet symbolically they can be related to the fourfold mundane world that is symbolized by the symbols of the four Evangelists depicted in the corners of the World trump.

Figure 46. A rendering of the Grimaud Tarot of Marseilles World, 1748

Like these symbols, the four minor suits can be related to the four elements and other aspects of the fourfold division of the world.

As we have seen, the minor suits in the Tarot are based on the Islamic Mamluk decks. As these were made for Mamluk nobles in the thirteenth and fourteenth centuries, it is likely that, to their creators, the suits represented the four aspects of the life of a noble or we might call it the good life. Coins represent wealth, swords the martial arts, polo sticks sport, and cups sensuality. There have been similar four-suit decks created for nobles in Europe. One example is a hand-painted fifteenth-century deck now in the Metropolitan Museum in New York. It was created for a Flemish noble and the suits represent aspects of the royal hunt—hound collars, hound tethers, game nooses, and hunting horns.

Although the first European deck—the one incorporated into the Tarot—was influenced by the Islamic cards, the Europeans were unlikely to view the suit symbols in the same way. They transformed the deck to reflect their views and equated the four card suits to the four classes of medieval and Renaissance society. We find an example of this in the oral history of the development of the French suit symbols: hearts, spades, diamonds, and clubs. According to legend, the symbols were created by the French knight Etienne Vignoles in the fifteenth century for the game of piquet. The hearts represented the clergy, the spades were the lance points of the knights, the diamonds were actually arrowheads representing the vassals, and the clubs were clover representing peasants.

The theme of correspondences was again addressed by the French historian Pere C.-F. Menestrier who wrote in 1704 that the four French suits relate to the four classes of medieval society: hearts to the clergy; spades to nobles; clubs to merchants; and diamonds (which in France is considered a floor tile) to peasants.[9] In this same period, in French divination systems designed for a four-suit deck, each suit was designated a related theme that would color its meaning: hearts were equated to joy; spades to sorrow; clubs to money; and diamonds to country (meaning rural pursuits in contrast to money, which was traditionally associated with urban life).

Modern Tarot historian Ronald Decker points out that when one understands that it was common in the seventeenth and eighteenth century in France to equate the French suit symbols to the Italian ones—hearts to cups; spades to swords; clubs to coins; and diamonds to staffs—it is obvious that the French associations are based on older Italian ones in which the associations between the suit symbol, the class, and theme make more sense: cups to joy and clergy; swords to sorrow and nobles; coins to money and merchants; and staffs to country and peasants.[10] Knowing that it was common in medieval and Renaissance thinking to create lists of correspondences between the four classes of society, the four elements, four temperaments, and other fourfold systems, it is easy to imagine a complete set of correspondences for the minor suits that reflects the historic possibilities and would be similar to the way that Levi looked at the four minor suits.

Chart number 4 is created by the author to list correspondences between the four minor suits and various fourfold systems. The correspondences on this list are based on traditional associations for the four elements and on logical assumptions that can be drawn from these associations and other historical information. Starting with the four suit symbols and equating them with the four Evangelists and their symbols as depicted on the World card, we can use traditional associations to equate the Evangelists to the four fixed signs of the zodiac and to the four elements assigned to these signs in astrology (Levi had switched the elemental attributes for Aquarius and Taurus).

It may not be obvious at first why a particular suit relates to a particular Evangelist, but, as we proceed down the list, we find that the four suits become assigned to the elements in the same way as Levi recommended. As we will see, this is also the basis of the elemental associations for the four suits in the Waite-Smith Tarot.

SUIT	CUPS	SWORDS	COINS/ PENTACLES	STAFFS/ WANDS
EVANGELIST	JOHN	MATTHEW	LUKE	MARK
SYMBOLIC CREATURE	EAGLE	MAN	BULL	LION
ZODIAC SIGN	SCORPIO	AQUARIUS	TAURUS	LEO
ELEMENT	WATER	AIR	EARTH	FIRE
ELEMENTAL CREATURE	UNDINE	SYLPH	GNOME	SALAMANDER
SOCIAL CLASS	PRIEST	NOBLE	MERCHANT	PEASANT
DIVINATORY THEME	JOY	SORROW	MONEY	COUNTRY
VIRTUE	PRUDENCE	JUSTICE	STRENGTH	TEMPERANCE
PSYCHOLOGICAL FUNCTION	INTUITIVE	THINKING	SENSATION	FEELING

Chart 4. The Author's List of Correspondences for the Minor Arcana and the Fourfold World

The Waite-Smith minor suits also make use of four elemental creatures—undines, sylphs, gnomes, and salamanders—which are listed below the corresponding element. The famous alchemist Paracelsus (1493–1541) first identified the living spirits of the four elements in the sixteenth century. Because of his influence the elementals became an accepted part of occult lore.

As we continue down the list, we can also see that the four classes of medieval and Renaissance society can be assigned to the four elements in a traditional manner, and that the correspondences between the classes and the suits are then the same as the traditional Italian associations as listed by Decker. The chart then lists the corresponding divinatory theme associated with each class. In a Platonic-like system, each class in the late Middle Ages was also associated with a virtue. The virtue chosen is the one that is needed to move up to the next class. The peasants need to develop temperance to be entrusted with money and join the merchants; the merchants needed to develop strength to join the nobles (this is how the young St. Francis first aspired to improve his role in life); the nobles needed to develop justice to become the guardians of morality, the clergy; and the clergy needed to develop prudence to become saints.

Similarly, in medieval and Renaissance medicine the four elements were associated with four liquid systems in the body, which were called the four humors: phlegm, which is related to water; blood to air; black bile to earth; and yellow bile to fire. Each of these humors, in turn, was believed to be the cause of a psychological temperament: phlegm caused sluggishness; blood cheerfulness; black bile sadness; and yellow bile vindictiveness. Two of these temperaments, cheerfulness and sadness, seem to be related to two of the divinatory themes associated with the suits, but the two systems do not relate to the four elements in the same way, which is the reason why they are not included on chart number 4. The modern pioneer of Depth Psychology Carl Jung (1875–1961) investigated the four temperaments but found that they did not relate well to his psychological observations. He felt that the four humors and the four temperaments were an outdated and inaccurate system. In his investigations of the human psyche, however, he did uncover a fourfold division of psychological types that he labeled the four functions of consciousness. As Jung felt that the psychology contained in the theory of the humors is outdated, it will be more useful to the modern student to work with their modern counterpart, the four functions as presented in Jungian psychology, and the Jungian functions are listed on the bottom row of chart number 4.

The four Jungian functions represent abilities or talents that each person possesses in varying degrees: at birth, we are each dealt strengths in one or more function and are weak in the others. Everyone tends to use their strong suit to solve problems and is at a disadvantage when their weak suit is what the situation demands. Each function can be expressed in an introverted or extraverted way. Introverts look within for direction and extraverts look to others for direction. Throughout life, if an individual matures, he or she will develop more functions and become more versatile in their capabilities. This maturing is what Jung calls the process of individuation, a progression toward psychic wholeness that moves one away from the limited egotistical view of one's self toward the realization of the psychic connectedness that Jung labeled the Self. In dreams this process is naturally symbolized as a journey to the center. If an individual can develop all four functions and bring the entire psychic landscape into consciousness, then the fifth element, the true or higher Self, is attained. Each corresponding virtue on the list is the positive quality that is needed to bring each function into balance and progress toward this psychological and mystical goal.

The following is a list of each function and a description of the personality type in which it is dominant.[11] Although Jung speaks of the sacred model of the four elements in his book on the four functions he makes no correlation between the two. The correlations below are the author's.

Intuition: Intuition is a talent for determining how a situation developed and where it is headed in the future. It is investigation directed toward the unconscious, which is often symbolized by water. The introvert would tend toward roles like poet, mystic, or psychic. The extravert would be more comfortable investigating society's unconscious and may become an adventurer, or entrepreneur. Prudence represents the wisdom found in the unconscious; that is why Plato believed wisdom is actually remembered. Plato would recommend philosophy and meditation to develop intuition.

Thinking: All people think, but the thinking function is intellectual or analytical, in contrast to thinking that is random or focused on feelings. It asks *why* or *what* is reality. This is a decision-making function. Thinking is forceful, yet intangible, like air. The introvert may tend toward the role of a philosopher or research scientist, and the extravert toward economist, judge, or statesman. Justice represents the search for truth that is necessary to excel at thinking. Plato would recommend the study of mathematics to develop thinking.

Sensation: Sensation is concerned with perception. It allows one to ascertain whether an object exists and to determine how to manipulate it. This is an investigation of the physical world, symbolized by earth. The introvert may tend to be an artist, connoisseur, or technician, and the extravert an engineer, accountant, builder, or investigator. The discipline of strength is needed to excel at sensation. Plato would recommend physical exercise to develop sensation.

Feeling: This term is often misunderstood. To Jung, feeling is the function that makes value judgments, that decides if something is good or bad. To him, feelings are not emotions. Jung calls emotions *affects,* a term derived from the Latin *affectus,* meaning "disposition." He explains that *affects* can be observed in one's expression and posture, whereas feelings cannot. One does not need to laugh or cry to determine if one likes or dislikes something. If feelings become intense enough they may give rise to emotions, but emotions may arise from other functions as well. Jung considered emotions a shallower level of psychological activity and the functions work on a deeper level. As we said, feeling is a decision-making function that determines if something is good or bad and motivates one to action, symbolized by fire. An introvert may display a talent as a healer, a nurturer, a musician, or a monk; an extravert may become a singer or social organizer, or a politician. Temperance is needed to keep feeling from overwhelming

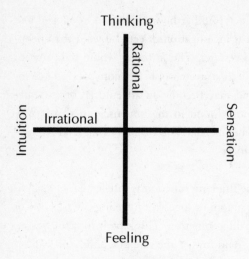

Figure 47. The Jungian four functions
of consciousness

the personality. Music is the study that Plato would recommend for developing this function.

Notice that intuition and sensation are used to investigate reality but not to make decisions. Because of this, Jung called them irrational, a label that may be equated to "passive." In this list the irrational functions are equated to the feminine, passive elements, water and earth. The other two functions, thinking and feeling, are decision-making functions. Jung called them rational, which may be equated to "active." In the list the rational functions are associated with the masculine, active elements, fire and air. The irrational and the rational functions are polarities of each other, as we can see in figure 47.

Jung found that the rational functions, thinking and feeling, are polar opposites of each other, and that the irrational functions, sensation and intuition, are also opposites. This meant that the person in whom the thinking function is dominant—as in our chart, which depicts thinking at the top—will have the most difficulty developing the feeling function, which would be his or her inferior function, depicted at the bottom. Similarly, if sensation was dominant, intuition would be inferior, and we can see that no matter which of the four functions was in the dominant position the polar opposite will be in the inferior position. Jung found that most people have an easier time developing the functions that reside on the opposite pole from their dominant trait than they do developing the one that is on the opposite end of the same pole. Therefore, a person dominant in thinking, for example, will be likely to develop both irrational functions before developing feeling. The same relationship applies for the other three functions.

The associations presented in this section can become useful tools for using the cards to describe personalities during divination. Also, when we associate the four minor suits with the fourfold world in this way we can see that the entire Tarot deck is a quincunx with the four minor suits in the four corners and the Major Arcana in the center. It is like a sacred mandala and its entire structure is illustrated by the Marseilles World card.

We are now going to turn away from the Renaissance and toward a later era in which fascination with the Tarot became reignited, partly due to the late nineteenth-century efforts of the innovative English-American occult society, the Hermetic Order of the Golden Dawn. We will also look at the work of two members of the Golden Dawn, Arthur Edward Waite and Pamela Colman Smith, who collaborated to create the innovative twentieth-century Waite-Smith Tarot. Their deck has done more to shape current perceptions of the Tarot than any in recent history and when most people think of the Tarot today, it is Smith's haunting images and Waite's commentary that come to mind.

THE WAITE–
SMITH TAROT

The Tarot embodies symbolical presentations of universal ideas,
behind which lie all the implicits of the human mind, and it is in this
sense that they contain secret doctrine, which is the realization by
the few of truths imbedded in the consciousness of all.

—A. E. WAITE, *THE PICTORIAL KEY TO THE TAROT*

Despite the proliferation of Tarot decks in the twentieth century, one Tarot, published at the end of the first decade, has remained the most popular throughout the century and become the model to which other Tarots are compared. This is the Tarot that was envisioned by the famous occultist Arthur Edward Waite, created with Waite's direction by the visionary artist Pamela Colman Smith, and first published in 1909 by William Rider and Son of London. For most of the twentieth century, it has been titled the Rider Waite Tarot, but Tarot historians now commonly refer to it as the Waite-Smith Tarot, to honor its designer, Pamela Colman Smith. In 1910, Rider also published Waite's book written to accompany the deck, *The Key to the Tarot,* and the following year they published an expanded edition, which included black-and-white versions of Smith's illustrations and was titled *The Pictorial Key to the Tarot.* From 1909 to the present, the Waite-Smith Tarot has reached millions of people, and due to this success, Waite and Smith have become the most influential occultists in modern history.

Because the Waite-Smith Tarot was the inspiration of Arthur Edward Waite we will discuss his life first. Waite (1857–1942) was born in Brooklyn, New York, but after his first year, his father died and his mother brought him back to her homeland, England. There he was brought up Catholic and remained so the rest of his life. As an adult, Waite became a translator, a reviewer, a poet, and a writer on mysticism and the occult. In 1886, he published the first book on the occult Tarot in English, *The Mysteries of Magic,* which was his translation of selections from Levi's first two books. Later, he translated the entire two-volume work under the title *Transcendental Magic.* He also translated Papus's *Tarot of the Bohemians* and numerous works on alchemy, Rosicrucianism, and other subjects.

In 1891, Waite joined the occult society founded in 1888 by William Westcott and Samuel MacGregor Mathers, the Hermetic Order of the Golden Dawn, which we discussed in Chapter Two. The Golden Dawn was a magical occult organization that offered a path to personal development through scholarship and study, ritual practice, and the development of psychic abilities. As each member progressed in knowledge and ability, he or she could pass an oral examination and rise in rank within the society.

Rank in the Golden Dawn was measured with ten grades which corresponded to the ten sephiroth on the Kabalistic Tree of Life (see figure 14 on page 63). Each rank had its own secret ritual of initiation that marked one's acceptance into that grade. The ten grades were further divided into three levels. Although Golden Dawn is commonly used as the name of the society it more precisely referred only to the first or outer level, which comprised the first four grades. The next three higher grades comprised a second level called Ordo Rosae Rube et Aureae Crucis, and the three highest grades belonged to the third level, called the Secret Chiefs. The Secret Chiefs were said to be humans who had attained a superhuman level of existence with immense magical powers and only MacGregor Mathers claimed to have any contact with them. It is doubtful that Westcott and MacGregor Mathers ever envisioned anyone actually reaching the highest level. Because of his intelligence and occult scholarship, by 1892 Waite had achieved the highest rank in the first or outer level, but then he resigned out of dissatisfaction. In 1896 he rejoined the order, and by 1899 he reached the first grade of the second level.[1]

During its first year the Golden Dawn was divided into three affiliated institutions called temples. The original London branch, to which Waite belonged, was called the Isis-Urania Temple. There was also the Horus Temple in Bradford, and the Osiris Temple in Weston-super-Mare. As the society grew, the Amen-Ra Temple in Edinburgh and the Ahathoor Temple in Paris were added. By 1897, MacGregor Mathers had taken sole leadership of the Golden Dawn and situated himself in the Paris temple. Riffs between MacGregor Mathers and other prominent members had developed and dissatisfaction with the leadership of the Golden Dawn was growing among the members of the London temple. In 1900, the Isis-Urania Temple voted to expel MacGregor Mathers and placed the prominent poet and member of the Golden Dawn William Butler Yeats in command. Because MacGregor Mathers was still in control of the Paris temple and the other existing temples remained loyal to him, this vote effectively split the Golden Dawn into two splinter groups. By 1903 further riffs occurred and Waite with the help of two other members took control of a faction of the Isis-Urania Temple, and again split away from the other groups.

Waite was an occultist, but his interest in the occult was mystical. He believed that the true goal of occult ritual was the spiritual transformation of its participants and that the true purpose of symbolism was to elevate one's consciousness. Waite looked at magic—ritual used to transform the environment instead of the individual—as degraded occultism, a trap that lured one from the true purpose of occult ritual, spiritual rebirth. His disapproval of magic was one factor that motivated him to leave the initial Golden Dawn and create a splinter group. Under Waite's direction, magical practice was frowned on in the Isis-Urania Temple and the occult rituals that were practiced could be viewed as components of a new mystical religion—an occult version of Catholicism. If Waite had thought of the Tarot as only a tool for fortune-telling, he would not have had any interest in it either. As he wrote in *The Pictorial Key to the Tarot:* "I hate the *profanum vulgus* of divinatory devices."[2] It was because he recognized that the Tarot contained a series of symbolic images that expressed the archetypal mystical journey that he valued and studied the Tarot.

Waite was too much of a scholar to be fooled by the erroneous claims made by Court de Gébelin, Levi, and Papus. Yet he realized that their crooked paths—their unfounded claims of the Tarot's origin, for example—sometimes led to truth, primarily that the Tarot does contain a mystical philosophy. On several occasions he wrote that the correlations made by occultists between the trumps and the Hebrew alphabet are all false. He did entertain the idea that there might be an accurate correspondence but he realized that all of the ones that had been offered did harm to the mystical story by making associations with each trump that led one away from a true understanding of the Tarot. Waite sums up his position in his Introduction to *The Pictorial Key to the Tarot:*

> The true Tarot is symbolism; it speaks no other language and offers no
> other signs. Given the inward meaning of its emblems, they do become
> a kind of alphabet which is capable of indefinite combinations and

makes true sense in all. On the highest plane it offers a key to the Mysteries, in a manner which is not arbitrary and has not been read in. But the wrong symbolical stories have been told concerning it, and the wrong history has been given in every published work which so far has dealt with the subject.[3]

It is because of his perception that the Tarot was a valuable mystical text and that it had been misrepresented by occultists before him that he longed to give birth to a new Tarot that rectified its symbolism and would stand as a valued work of art as well. During the later part of first decade of the twentieth century, Waite began looking for a gifted artist who could due justice to this project, but, before we go on, it is time to introduce the artist who was destined to accept this challenge.

Pamela Colman Smith (1878–1951) was born in Middlesex, England, to American parents who were followers of the mystical teachings of the Swedish philosopher and psychic Emanuel Swedenborg (1688–1772). Because of her father's duties while working for the West India Improvement Company, Smith's early life was spent in London, New York, and Kingston, Jamaica. She studied art at Pratt Institute in Brooklyn, and as an adult, she settled in England and made her living as a set and costume designer for the theater. She was also known as a storyteller, an illustrator, and a fine artist.

In the early 1900s, she regularly showed her paintings and other work in New York at the gallery owned by the famous American photographer Alfred Stieglitz (1864–1946). She enjoyed critical acclaim, particularly for her visionary drawings of mythical and otherworldly subjects. Smith was part of the Symbolist art movement that was prevalent in Europe at that time. Symbolism was a movement in poetry and visual art that originated in France and Belgium in 1885 and quickly spread through the German-speaking countries and then the rest of Europe at the end of the nineteenth century. Symbolist artists were noted for the sensual beauty of their work and for the portrayal of subjects based on dreams, mythology, and the imagination. As both an occultist and an artist Smith was at home in this style. When she was not illustrating a particular legend or story, she would allow herself to fall into a light trance while listening to classical music and draw what she saw. For example, while listening to a composition by Beethoven she painted a majestic queen in flowing robes standing on the sea carrying a small ball-like moon in her hands.

Among Smith's friends were many artists and writers including Bram Stoker, Florence Farr, and William Butler Yeats. It was Yeats who introduced her to the

Golden Dawn. In the early 1900s, she joined the Isis-Urania Temple of the Golden Dawn, the same splinter group to which Waite belonged. It was here that she met Waite. When Waite split his faction of the Isis-Urania Temple away from the other Golden Dawn groups, she went with him into the new order.[4]

Pamela Colman Smith impressed her friends and acquaintances with her open-hearted friendliness and her childlike innocence. Yet they recognized a depth behind the innocence, especially in that she had a gift as a psychic as well as an artist. Many believed that she had the ability to directly perceive the spirit world while she worked at her art. John Butler Yeats, the father of her friend William Butler Yeats, described her in a letter to his son: "She will go far because she believes in all her ideas. . . . She has the simplicity and naïveté of an old dry as dust savant (but) with a child's heart."[5]

Waite took notice of Smith's artistic talent and psychic ability while she was a member of his group and believed that he had found in her the artist he was looking for to design his rectified Tarot. Waite, however, seemed to misread her spontaneity and naïveté as a lack of depth. In his memoirs, he expressed both his confidence in her artistic abilities and doubts about her intellectual ability:

> Now, in those days there was a most imaginative and abnormally psychic artist, named Pamela Colman Smith, who had drifted into the Golden Dawn and loved its ceremonies—as transformed by myself—without pretending or indeed attempting to understand their sub-surface consequence. It seemed to some of us in the circle that there was a draughtswoman among us who, under proper guidance, could produce a Tarot with an appeal to the world of art and a suggestion of significance behind the Symbols which would put on them another construction than had ever been dreamed by those who, through many generations, had produced and used them for mere divinatory purposes.[6]

Although Waite admired Smith as an artist, he seems to have been guilty of the common prejudice that ideas expressed in words are more intelligent than ideas expressed in pictures. As Tarot historian Stuart Kaplan wrote in his biography of Smith:

> Pamela's conscious awareness of the elements of religious symbolism and ritual is indicated by her paintings, her wide reading as evidenced by her letters, her familiarity with music and theater, her long involvement in the Order of the Golden Dawn and, later in her dedicated activ-

ity in the Roman Catholic Church. What Waite and others may not have realized was that Pamela's apparently simple approach to the meta-physical was not due to a lack of depth of intellect. Her writings indi-cate that, for her, ritual and symbolism derived their power to illuminate from the senses, emotion, and the imagination, not from the mind.[7]

In 1909 Waite hired Smith to create a new artistic Tarot. As he stated, he was hoping that with Smith's talent she would make a deck that was both an appeal-ing work of art and one that clarified the mystical story in the Tarot. Like a Re-naissance artwork, it would have body and soul, beauty and meaning. Waite was relying on Smith for the body and hoped to supply the soul himself. Perhaps Waite was hoping that Smith was as shallow as he first perceived her to be, for then she could be easily directed. But a talent as dynamic as Smith's could not easily be contained. And in his memoirs, Waite acknowledges the challenge.

> I saw to it therefore that Pamela Colman Smith should not be picking up casually any floating images from my own or another mind. She had to be spoon-fed carefully over the Priestess card, over that which is called the Fool and over the Hanged Man.[8]

Waite picks out these examples as ones where he was more involved in the out-come but we cannot assume that he was as involved in every design.

Smith was in New York attending a show of her work at Stieglitz's gallery in March of 1909. By necessity, she would have been working in January and Febru-ary on the pieces that she would need for her show. On November 19, 1909, Smith wrote a letter to Stieglitz in which she mentions finishing her Tarot.

> I've just finished a big job for very little cash! A set of designs for a pack of Tarot cards 80 designs—I shall send some over—of the original drawings as some people may like them!—I will send you a pack— (printed in color by lithography)—(probably very badly!) As soon as they are ready—by Dec. 1—I think—[9]

The deck did come out in December. It is unlikely that Smith's artwork could be transferred to plates and printed in less than two weeks, and at the time that Smith is writing she seems to already have the original art back from the printer. We therefore can assume that she worked on the designs sometime between

April, when she returned from New York, and October, the latest she could have delivered the art to the printer—within a six-month period. It is common for an artist to take a year or more to create a Tarot deck and six months or less is a short time to produce eighty designs (there are seventy-eight cards in the deck and no one is sure what the other two designs were but perhaps they were a title card and an advertisement card) even for a spontaneous artist like Smith.

Many people assume that Waite oversaw every aspect of the design of the Waite-Smith Tarot and attribute even the smallest details on each card to his direction. This type of interaction between an artist and a director, however, would have been tedious and time-consuming, and given the short amount of time in which the deck was created it would actually have been almost impossible for Waite to have had this much input in all seventy-eight cards. It would have been highly impractical for Waite to be standing in Smith's studio looking over her shoulder every day during the months that she was working and he would have to choose which images merited his attention. Waite continually expressed in his writing that he was most concerned with the symbolism of the Major Arcana, which he saw as expressing the mystical quest, and we can also infer from his writing that he would have been less concerned with the Minor Arcana, which he associated with divination.

It is most probable that for the Major Arcana Waite described the design that he desired for each card, complete with the symbolism it should contain and the significance of each symbol, and then he would have stepped out of the picture and let Smith work in her usual spontaneous and intuitive manner. It was Smith's intuitive psychic ability that convinced Waite that Smith was the right person for the task in the first place. Although the original art for the deck no longer exists, we can see from the printed copies that Smith drew the designs in black ink and colored them with watercolors in her usual manner. Art produced in this manner cannot be edited. If Waite desired changes once a design was complete, Smith would have had to recreate the entire piece, and considering the short time in which the work was completed that cannot have happened often.

The symbolic connections that Waite decided to include in the Waite-Smith deck include the astrological and elemental associations of the Golden Dawn's system of correspondences (see chart 3 on page 81). He even switched the positions of Justice and Strength from the way they appear in the Marseilles order, so that Justice would correspond with Libra and Strength with Leo as listed on the Golden Dawn's table of correspondences. But in *The Pictorial Key to the Tarot*, Waite goes against the Golden Dawn's recommendation by placing the Fool, which he had numbered zero, in the penultimate position, before the World, as

Levi did. If he was embracing the Golden Dawn's alphabetical associations as well as the secondary correspondences, this placement would not make sense, and although Levi placed the Fool in the penultimate position so that it would correspond to the Hebrew letter shin, Waite did not follow the rest of Levi's correspondences.

Waite continually expressed his dissatisfaction with any system that correlated the trumps to the Hebrew alphabet and in *The Pictorial Key to the Tarot* he clearly states: "I have also not adopted the prevailing attribution of the cards to the Hebrew alphabet . . . because nearly every attribution is wrong."[10] Waite continually stated that the Tarot's power was based on visual symbolism, on the power of the images to connect with universal archetypes in the psyche. He realized that the alphabetical association flattens the symbols and leads away from their power. Realizing that the Tarot's power was visual, Waite chose a gifted visionary artist to design his deck.

It seems that Waite gave Smith more freedom to express her visionary talent in the creation of the fifty-six Minor Arcana, which comprised the bulk of the work. Unlike earlier Tarots, which commonly display only a repetition of the suit symbol and possibly some decorative details on the pip cards, the Waite-Smith pips are illustrated with complete scenes in which figures interact with the correct number of suit symbols on each card. These scenes are allegorical and express the intended divinatory meaning of each card. As this innovation is one of the outstanding characteristics of the deck, it is likely that Waite requested it. We can also gather that he explained the general elemental and symbolic structure of the four suits, and provided a list, from Etteilla and other sources, of traditional meanings that are associated with each card. These lists are included with each minor card in *The Pictorial Key to the Tarot.* Many of the meanings are contradictory and Smith's illustrations convey only some of the listed meanings. As we will see, Waite seems to have formed his opinion on which meaning is being conveyed after Smith created the illustrations. It is therefore likely that Smith chose from Waite's list the meaning that she wanted to convey for each card.

Further evidence for Smith's independence in the creation of the Minor Arcana can be gleaned from the fact that many of the characters and symbols that she incorporated in the pips are modeled on her own paintings that she completed sometimes years before receiving the commission. Many observers have also mentioned that besides the Tarot of Marseilles many of Smith's illustrations for the Minor Arcana are clearly modeled on the fifteenth-century Sola Busca Tarot, the only Renaissance deck to have figures and complete scenes on the pips. A complete set of photos of the Sola Busca engravings had arrived at the British

Museum two years before Smith's commission and was certainly available for Smith to study. It is known from Waite's memoirs that he was a frequent visitor to the museum and he may have recommended the Sola Busca deck to Smith. In *The Pictorial Key to the Tarot* Waite acknowledges that there is an historic precedent for the fully illustrated pips.

The pips in the Sola Busca deck contain scenes in which figures interact with the correct number of suit symbols for each card in the same way as Smith's pips. Although we have no evidence that the images on the Sola Busca pips were intended to illustrate their divinatory meaning, this is the only Tarot that made use of this novel approach before the Waite-Smith deck. Besides taking the same approach as the Sola Busca, the Waite-Smith cards are also the same proportion as the Sola Busca cards, and many individual cards are obviously modeled on individual Sola Busca cards. The most obvious example is Smith's three of swords which contains an image of a heart pierced by three swords that is almost identical to the image on the Sola Busca three of swords. Besides the pips many of Smith's royal cards are also modeled on Sola Busca royal cards, and even her Fool seems to be modeled on the Sola Busca five of cups, which contains a similar figure with a small dog at his feet. There are many more examples but we can describe them as we discuss individual cards.

Tarot scholars often speculate that Smith was also influenced by her famous and knowledgeable friends, particularly Florence Farr and William Butler Yeats. Farr was a close friend of Smith's as well as a prominent member of the Golden Dawn, and is known to have been involved in Tarot divination. There is evidence that she made use of the Celtic cross spread for divination, the spread that was later recommended by Waite in *The Pictorial Key to the Tarot*.[11] It seems that Waite did not practice divination personally and the inclusion of this spread in Waite's book may indicate Farr's influence. Yeats was another close friend of Smith's, and also deeply interested in the Tarot. It is known that he created his own versions of the cards in his unpublished Golden Dawn notebook, and Smith is likely to have had the privilege of inspecting his book.[12]

It seems that when Waite saw the finished art for the cards, he wrote his impressions and added these before the lists of meanings in his book. The fact that these descriptions were only written after the art was complete is evident in the nature of the text. It reads like a description of a first-time observer, one who at times misunderstands what he is looking at. This is especially obvious in his description for the Knight of Wands. Waite says that the knight is "passing mounds or pyramids." This gives the impression that he is not sure what Smith depicted. His statement lacks the certainty that it would have if he were the author of the symbol. For the Ace of Cups, Waite says that there are four streams pouring from the cup and the picture shows five. For the Six of Swords, Waite says that "the course is smooth" but the water is smooth on the viewer's left and choppy on the viewer's right. It is different on each side of the boat, which suggests another meaning. There are numerous other examples but we can explore these under the descriptions of each card below.

We will now discuss the symbolism and divinatory meaning of each of the Waite-Smith cards.

THE MAJOR ARCANA

Figure 48

THE FOOL

As in the Sola Busca Tarot, and in the Golden Dawn's system, Waite assigned the Fool the arabic numeral zero although all of the other cards in the Major Arcana are assigned roman numerals. In traditional decks other than the Sola Busca the Fool is not numbered and in the traditional game that is played with the deck he is considered a wild card that is not part of the series of trumps but can be played instead of a trump. Because the Fool is unnumbered, Levi felt free to assign him the penultimate position in the Major Arcana just before the World, where the Fool would correlate with the penultimate Hebrew letter, shin. In *The Pictorial Key to the Tarot*, Waite, like Levi, places the Fool in the penultimate position when he describes each Major Arcana, but in another list in the book he places the Fool in the first position. In his introduction to the Major Arcana in *The Pictorial Key to the Tarot*, Waite acknowledges that he is not satisfied with either solution.

In *The Mystical Tarot*, modern Tarot scholar Rosemary Ellen Guiley recounts a story of uncertain origin in which Smith was said to have protested Waite's placement of the Fool. Smith was said to prefer that the Fool be placed in the initial position in the Major Arcana, and as a sign of protest to Waite's placement, she refused to sign this illustration.[13] A close examination of the illustration will reveal that Smith's characteristic monogram does, however, appear intertwined in the cross-hatched shading representing the side of the cliff in the lower right corner of the image, although on all other cards Smith was careful to leave a clear space for her signature, and this is the only card in which she hid her signature in this way. This detail may still represent her protest. Some observers claim that the Hebrew letter shin—the letter that corresponds to the penultimate position—is depicted in the circle on the far right of the Fool's tunic just above the hem. The three strokes in the circle, however, do not clearly form the Hebrew letter, and if the story of Smith's protest is true, it would be unlikely that she would include this detail.

In the Golden Dawn's correspondences, the Fool, the Hanged Man, and Judgement are linked to the elements air, water, and fire, respectively, while all of the other Major Arcana are linked to planets or the zodiac. The fact that these three have elemental associations while the other Major Arcana are associated with celestial symbols differentiates these three cards from the others and also suggests that they form a separate group within the Major Arcana. Tarot historians Decker and Dummett have gathered from Waite's initial companion book, *The Key to the Tarot,* that Waite saw these three as a unique group in the same way and that for him they represented the three stages of the mystical quest.[14] The Fool is a new soul when he is at the beginning of the suit but in the penultimate position he is the soul redeemed. Waite called him "a prince from another world on his travels through this one."[15] Smith's picture shows him high on a mountaintop immersed in his element. As a novice, he is about to fall from the cliff that he is walking toward but not looking at. As a master, he has climbed to the summit, a symbol of the sacred center, and regained his innocence. His trials are over and he can bask in the golden sunlight of the dawn.

Smith's depiction of the Fool seems to be influenced by the figure on the Sola Busca Five of Cups, who is looking up to the sky with a similar expression while supporting a bundle of reeds on his shoulder, and who also has a small dog tugging at his leg. In her image she has transformed the bundle of reeds into a pole with a traveling bag that is similar to the one held by the Marseilles Fool, and reinterpreted the dog as a companion. In the modern printing of Smith's card, the bag on the end of the pole bears the image of a hawk's head, a connection to the Egyptian sun god Horus, but in the original it is indistinct. In his left hand, the Fool holds a white rose, a Golden Dawn symbol of silence and rebirth.[16] His tunic is covered with fruit or flowers and the dog in the picture has become his joyful companion. The feather in his cap is a symbol of air and it points to the sun, a symbol of enlightenment. The Fool looks away from the sun. Is it because he is foolish and ignores wisdom or is it because he has absorbed its lessons and does not need to look directly into the light? To decide which Fool is meant in a reading, look at the cards that flank him and particularly the one he may face.

THE MAGICIAN.

Figure 49

THE MAGICIAN

The wide-brimmed hat of the Marseilles Juggler has disappeared and only the edge of the brim remains. It forms a mystical lemniscate—a figure eight on its side—floating above the head of the Magician. The lemniscate is a symbol of infinity. It illustrates that the Magician is connected to the timeless. This is reinforced by the fact that his belt is an ouroboros, a circular symbol of time formed by a snake biting its tail.

Waite points out in his commentary that Gnostics and Martinists associated the number eight with Christ and he links the lemniscate to Christ consciousness. Perhaps he is referring to the fact that early Christians determined through gematria—an ancient practice in which symbolic associations were determined by equating letters with numbers and finding the sums of the letters in words—that the letters in the name Jesus added up to 888, a number that they equated to the logos, or the spiritual sun, a symbol of enlightenment. Alternatively, he may have been referring to the medieval association of the number eight with Christ, derived from the fact that Easter, the feast of the Resurrection, is the eighth and final day of the celebration of Christ's Passion, Holy Week, and the beginning of the first eight days of the Easter season, called the Octave of Easter.

The Magician stands in a garden of roses and lilies. Tarot historian Robert O'Neill points out that this symbol is derived from the Song of Songs, 2:1, "I am the Rose of Sharon, the lily of the valleys."[17] The red and white flowers, however, are also the alchemical opposites: red being equated to masculine and the fixed polarity and white to the feminine and volatile polarity. The objects on the Magician's table are the four magical tools, which have become the suit symbols for the minor suits in this deck and are linked to the four elements: pentacles to earth, cups to water, swords to air and wands to fire. The Magician's relationship with these symbols aligns him with the fifth element, the spirit. Three symbols also appear to be carved on the edge of the table. The first appears to be a seascape and possibly represents water. The second seems to be a representation of the element fire, and the third is the dove, a Christian symbol for the Holy Spirit—the divine force that is beyond the physical elements, and, therefore, also the fifth element. At the top of the table leg, there seem to be three letters which possibly spell *vin*. This is Latin for "wilt thou?"—the question that the Magician poses.

This card represents will, initiations, and beginnings. The Golden Dawn correspondence for this card is Mercury, and like Mercury, or Hermes, the Magician holds his wand toward heaven and points his left hand toward earth in the Hermetic axiom "as above, so below." He says that the way of Heaven should be manifested on Earth. The Hermetic texts tell us that it is our purpose, given to us by God, to complete His creation by making the world beautiful. The Magician points the way.

Figure 50

THE HIGH PRIESTESS

The High Priestess dressed in blue sits on the cubic stone, the alchemical raw material, on the edge of the sea of the unconscious. The view is almost completely obscured by the veil hung between the two columns. The columns, from left to right, are Levi's Boaz and Jakin, the two symbolic pillars that in the account in *I Kings* 7:15–22 are said to have stood to the north and the south of the door of Solomon's Temple. The meaning of their names in Hebrew is uncertain but it is believed that Boaz means "in his strength" and Jakin (also spelled Joachim) means "he establishes." The pillars are important symbols in both Rosicrucian and Masonic ritual, and like the Chinese yin and yang, they represent dark and light, and feminine and masculine.

The pomegranates and date palms on the veil are symbols of fertility that were also found carved into Solomon's Temple. But compare the placement of the pomegranates with the sephiroth on the Tree of Life in figure 14 on page 63. It is obvious that this is the Kabalistic tree with the lower sephiroth hidden by the Priestess's body. The palms suggest the paths and the pomegranates the sephiroth. In the Golden Dawn lessons that were distributed to its members, there is an illustration of a man whose body is covering the lower three sephiroth of the Tree in the same way.[18] It illustrates a magical exercise in which a human forms the middle pillar of the Tree of Life.

In the Golden Dawn's system, this card is associated with the moon and we find a large crescent at the Priestess's feet. Yet she also has a solar cross on her breast.[19] This suggests that she is the woman clothed in the sun and standing on the moon, an image of the Madonna found in Revelation 12:1. By giving her the headdress of Isis, which is also composed of a sun and a moon, Waite and Smith have made an archetypal connection between Mary and Isis. In her lap she holds the scroll of the law, labeled TORA, in the style of Levi, who created symbolic anagrams from the letters TARO as we saw in Chapter Two.

This card represents inner, esoteric religious experience, or mystery. A true mystery is something that the more we learn about it the more we know that we cannot know it. We understand mystery when we accept that we cannot know it. The development of a fetus in the womb is such a mystery, and that is why a woman best symbolizes it. In its simplest form it is intuition.

THE EMPRESS.

Figure 51

THE EMPRESS

The Golden Dawn relates the Empress to Venus and we find the glyph of Venus on the Empress's heart-shaped shield. But this is the earthly Venus of Botticelli's *Primavera,* not the celestial Venus. She sits in sensuality on plush cushions in a field of grain next to a waterfall, symbols of abundance and sexuality. Her white dress is covered with what are most likely stylized pomegranates that are sliced open to reveal their red seeds. This is a symbol of fertility and Waite says that the Empress is "the fruitful mother of thousands."[20] She holds a scepter and wears a crown with twelve stars. This is the crown of the woman clothed in the sun, which was replaced by the crown of Isis on the last trump. It shows her connection to the High Priestess. She is the mother aspect of the virgin depicted on the last trump. The Empress represents the feminine principle, the principle that is attractive and attracts what she desires. She is fertility and sensuality.

Figure 52

THE EMPEROR

In the Golden Dawn correspondences, the Emperor is linked to Aries, the sign of the Ram, and we find four rams' heads carved on his stone chair and one on his shoulder. The Emperor is armored under his robe. Iron and the color red that dominates the landscape and the Emperor's clothes are symbols of Mars, the ruler of Aries. The martial Emperor sits on a cold throne in an arid, rocky landscape. He is the complement to the Empress. Whereas she is sensual, he is ascetic; she is comfortable and he is disciplined. Alchemically he is the red king and she is the white queen. In his hands are the symbols of his office, the feminine orb and the masculine mace. But his mace is an ankh, the Egyptian emblem of life. His is designed to illustrate that the ankh is composed of the first and last letters of TARO. This is a card of power that comes from self-control. It may also represent someone in authority.

Figure 53

THE HIEROPHANT

The word *hierophant* is Greek for "high priest," and refers to the priest who guided the initiation into the Eleusinian Mysteries. Although Waite chose the occult name, the figure on the card is clearly the Pope. He wears the triple crown, and the crossed keys of St. Peter, both of yellow gold, are at his feet. Three nails project from the top of his crown, a symbol of Christ's Passion and that, like the Magician, he is one with Christ consciousness. Two tonsured priests kneel at his feet, one wearing a chasuble decorated with roses and the other with lilies. Alchemically, the Hierophant is marrying the red and the white. He wears a pallium, a white band around his shoulders and down his front, with three crosses in a vertical row down the center. At the base is a diamond, a symbol of the fourfold physical world. This is like the central column of the Tree of Life, a theme repeated by the Hierophant's placement between two equal pillars. To the Pillar of Severity, on our left, he offers the sign of blessing and to the Pillar of Mercy, on our right, the triple cross of martyrdom. The Hierophant is like the central pillar connected to God and bringing the spirit down to earth. The Hierophant represents the exoteric aspects of religion versus the esoteric represented by the Papesse. He represents moral judgment, the determination of what is right and what is wrong. When used in divination, notice if he is blessing another card in the spread.

Figure 54

THE LOVERS

The Tarot of Marseilles Lovers card depicts a man standing between two women, each of whom represents a choice. Above, a Cupid hovers ready to strike with his bow. On the older Italian Lovers cards only a man and one woman stand under Cupid. This older image is of marriage or betrothal and takes the form of a standard Renaissance betrothal portrait. The Waite-Smith Lovers follows the form of the older Italian model but they have transformed it into a mystical vision of the marriage of Adam and Eve.

The duality of the Waite-Smith image was suggested by the Golden Dawn correspondence with Gemini, which in its older symbolism was a masculine and feminine pair. Here, Eve stands in front of the Tree of Knowledge with its apples and snake, a symbol of sexuality and forbidden knowledge. Adam stands in front of the Tree of Life, a symbol of divine love with twelve flames like the ring of the zodiac. As with the High Priestess's pillars, the feminine one is on our left and the masculine on our right, and there is a representation of the third pillar between them, the mountain of the sacred center. Above, an angel with flaming hair and wings opens the way to the true sun of enlightenment. This angel is sometimes identified as Raphael, but O'Neill points out that in the Golden Dawn's rituals, the great angel of solar fire is called Michael. As in Plato's Symposium, here love is depicted as one continuum, a divine force that impels us to pursue the Good from the physical to the spiritual. This card represents sexuality and other forms of love.

Figure 55

THE CHARIOT

W aite says that the charioteer is carrying a drawn sword and that "on the shoulders of the victorious hero are supposed to be the Urim and Thummim."[21] Urim and Thummim are the stones used as divinatory tools by the ancient Israeli priests. Smith's picture is true to Levi's model and contains neither detail. As in Levi's drawing (see figure 16 on page 76), the charioteer is carrying a wand or a scepter, and, on his shoulders, Smith has depicted the same hammered metal faces that serve as part of his highly decorative Classical armor, although, depicted in profile as they are, they may be interpreted as waxing and waning crescent moons.

Smith has switched the positions of the dark and light sphinxes from the way Levi presented them but, like Levi, she includes a Tantric sexual emblem on the shield surmounted by the solar disk of Horus and gives the charioteer a scepter and a star-covered canopy. The three stars on his crown in Levi's illustration have been reduced to one eight-pointed star. His Chariot is clearly the cubic stone and he is the spirit emerging from the stone. The leather pteruges that form his skirt are covered with alchemical glyphs, as is his belt. The square, the symbol of fourfold matter, appears on his chest. He is the conquering hero who has transformed sexual energy into a vehicle that can carry him toward his spiritual goal, the spiritual Sun, which is the meaning of the crest on the front of his Chariot. He is still, however, concerned with the physical world. To proceed he has to pull together the opposing forces represented by the two sphinxes. The Chariot represents confidence, preparedness, travel, and victory.

Figure 56

STRENGTH

The Marseilles woman on the Strength trump has a hat similar to the Magician's. She is, therefore, given the same lemniscate in this deck. In the Golden Dawn's table of correspondences this card is linked with the astrological sign Leo (see chart 3 on page 81), which is why Strength, with her lion, was placed here in what is the traditional position of Justice. Switching the positions of Strength and Justice disrupts the Platonic meaning and suggests that Waite was unaware of it. The image itself, however, is in harmony with the Platonic concept of Strength.

Alchemically the woman is white, the higher feminine aspect of the soul, and the lion is red, the lower physical aspect. She gently but firmly closes the lion's mouth. The higher aspect controls the physical strength but this is accomplished through love, not force. This is shown by the lion licking the woman's hand and by the chain of roses that connects them. This card represents self-mastery through love. The distant mountain is the goal, the sacred center. These symbols are prominent in Rosicrucian imagery. A woman in white holding a symbol of love while sitting on a lion with a mountain in the distance can be found in an alchemical illustration for *The Golden Tripod*, which is one of the alchemical texts that Waite translated and included in his *Hermetic Museum*, a collection of alchemical texts.

Figure 57

THE HERMIT

The Waite-Smith Hermit is based on the Marseilles image, except that his robe is dark and his hood is up, which strengthens the mood of isolation and contemplation. Also, he is on a mountaintop. He has mastered the virtue of the last trump and climbed to the top of the distant summit. This image is also influenced by a picture in the *Hermetic Museum.* On the title page there is a print of an alchemist in a long robe with a stick and a lantern following the Anima Mundi, symbolized as a beautiful woman. She is holding a glowing six-pointed star, a symbol of the masculine upward-pointing triangle and the feminine downward-pointing triangle joined as one power. Here the star is in the Hermit's lantern. The Hermit represents seclusion for the purpose of meditation and attainment, but he can also simply mean the state of being alone or of going outside of the group. He is a pioneer who lights the way for others.

WHEEL of FORTUNE.

Figure 58

WHEEL OF FORTUNE

This image is strongly influenced by Levi. The letters on the rim of the Wheel may read ROTA, Latin for wheel, when read from the bottom, and TARO, when read from the top. Between the Latin letters are the four Hebrew letters that spell the name of God, the Tetragrammaton. Levi calls it the wheel of Ezekiel, which explains the inclusion of the four living creatures in the corners. This detail turns the image into a quincunx related to the World.

The alchemical symbols on the crossbars of the inner circle are, proceeding clockwise from the top, mercury, sulphur, solution, and salt. These can be translated as soul and spirit in combination with the body. The Marseilles monkeys have been transformed into Hellenized Egyptian deities. The human figure with the head of a jackal is Hermanubis, a combination of Hermes and Anubis. He is the guide of the soul and represents the good. The snake is Typhon, the Greek name for Set, who is the evil brother of Osiris. The sphinx on top represents wisdom and equilibrium. The Waite-Smith Wheel represents the forces of change in the world. It is like the philosopher Hegel's dialectical process composed of a thesis, an antithesis, and a synthesis. The world of time and impermanence is seen here as permeated by the spirit and as the spirit at work. This card represents change, the awareness of change, and good fortune. The good god is rising, and the evil god descending.

Figure 59

JUSTICE

Justice is placed here to correspond to Libra just as Strength was given her former position to correspond to Leo. Justice is another figure sitting on a stone between two pillars. Like the High Priestess, she has a veil between her pillars but Waite warns that it does not open on the same vista. Instead of the sea of the unconscious we see the yellow glow of the dawn behind her. A material square appears on her fortresslike crown but a symbol for the squaring of the circle is on her breast. In her left hand, near the left pillar, she holds the scales, representing impartial judgment. In her right hand she holds the upright sword, a symbol of responsibility and mercy. Justice is a fortress of virtue. She represents truth, right judgment, and dealings with the law.

Figure 60

THE HANGED MAN

As we mentioned under the discussion of the Fool, the Hanged Man is related to water, the second elemental correlation, and he is, therefore, symbolically connected to the Fool and Judgement, the other elemental Major Arcana. Waite sees the Hanged Man as a key figure in the soul's journey. He represents initiation. The giblet of the traditional card has been transformed into a tau cross, a symbol that unites the man's suffering with the martyrdom of Christ. This is reiterated by the halo. In the Golden Dawn, the initiates would suffer a simulated ritual execution as a rite of passage into the higher grades and be asked to identify with Christ. The position of the Hanged Man's arms and legs even forms a glyph representing the Golden Dawn, an upward-pointing triangle, like the man's arms, with a red cross extending from the top, like the man's crossed legs with red leggings. An image of the sun rising out of the sea was placed in the triangle. The man's halo is like the sun (see figure 61).

Figure 61.
The symbol of
the Golden Dawn

The upside-down position of the Hanged Man represents a reversal in attitude and perception, but it can also be a loss of position. He is going through an ordeal but willingly, to further his goal.

Figure 62

DEATH

Death is fittingly linked to Scorpio, the astrological sign associated with death and rebirth. The corpse in black armor riding a pale horse is related to the image in Revelation. A king, a bishop, a woman, and a child all fall prey to him. None are immune. Yet Death is holding a flag emblazoned with the white rose, the Golden Dawn symbol of rebirth. In the distance, a ship, a symbol of the afterlife, sails toward a sun rising between two towers, the new dawn. Here the towers are the equivalent of the twin pillars. This is the logical conclusion to the ritual of the Hanged Man. Death is not the end but a new beginning. He represents the passing of the old, the natural end of a situation, and the dawn of new opportunity. All things end but the cycles of the world teach us that all endings are followed by renewal.

Figure 63

TEMPERANCE

Among the older printings of this card, there is a rainbow arching across the sky behind the angel. O'Neill points out that the flowers in the picture are named after the Greek goddess Iris, who is the goddess of the rainbow. Iris is the messenger of the gods, the female equivalent of Hermes. Her rainbow connects heaven and earth: "as above, so below." She was Classically depicted with wings and was also the goddess who poured the rain from her vessel. In Hebrew, the word for "rainbow" is *tav-shin-qoph* and the same word was used by the ancient Hebrews for the sign Sagittarius, the archer, which was depicted as only a bow and arrow in ancient Persian and Semitic star charts. This symbolic connection helps to link the angel on the card with the Golden Dawn's correspondence for this card, Sagittarius.

The angelic figure, whom Waite acknowledges is neither masculine nor feminine, has red and violet wings and the symbol of the sun on his head, which would indicate that besides being the goddess Iris he is also the archangel Michael. In Revelation 10:1–2, there is a great angel, thought to be Michael, who stands on the sea and the land with a rainbow on his head and a face that radiates like the sun. The sea and land are also the alchemical wet and dry, symbols of the outer and the inner world. The triangle in the square on Michael's chest is a symbol of spirit contained in matter. It is related to the symbolism of the tetractys discussed in Chapter Three (see figure 18 on page 93). Also notice that while the sun is on the angel's head, a glowing crown appears in the sky where the sun should be. The landscape wears the crown and the head wears the sun. Temperance mixes the inner world of the psyche with the external physical world. This connection between the internal and external is what Jung calls synchronicity. This card represents timing, connectedness, balance, beauty, and higher consciousness.

Figure 64

THE DEVIL

This card is connected to Capricorn, the goat, and this goat-headed image borrows from both Levi's Baphomet and the traditional Marseilles card. Waite says that there is a sign of Mercury at the pit of the stomach, but it is not there. It seems that he wanted it to be more like Levi's drawing of Baphomet, the Sabbatic Goat (see figure 17 on page 76), which has Mercury's staff, the caduceus, rising from his groin. Perhaps Smith left it out because they were using the Golden Dawn's correspondence with Capricorn for this card, and not Levi's correspondence with Mercury. The Devil has bat's wings, bird's feet, and brandishes a torch as in the Marseilles card (see figure 9 on page 37). The inverted pentagram between the horns, suggesting the shape of the horned head, is borrowed from another of Levi's drawings.

The Devil makes a perverted sign of benediction to mock the Hierophant (*Star Trek* fans will recognize it as the Vulcan sign of greeting). He is perched precariously on a narrow pillar to which a man and a woman are chained. The man and the woman are Adam and Eve from the Lovers card but their angel of love and light has become a fallen angel of selfishness and darkness. Here their nudity represents unbridled passion instead of innocence, and, as further evidence that they are ruled by their animal nature, the couple has grown tails and horns. Their tails are tied to the symbolism of their respective trees in Eden—the woman's tail bears fruit like the Tree of Knowledge and the man's tail bears a flame like the Tree of Life. This is Adam and Eve in their fallen condition, chained to what is base. This card represents imprisonment, addiction, selfishness, and generally the bad and the ugly.

THE TOWER

The Waite-Smith Tower is essentially similar to the Marseilles model except the top of the Tower is more clearly a crown being toppled and the Tower itself is built on a mountaintop. Two figures are falling to either side. One in a crown and a long blue dress is female and the other in a red cape and blue tunic is male. They are like Adam and Eve being freed from the trap of egotism that was presented in the last trump. The background is black, linking it to the Devil

Figure 65

card, which has the same dark setting. Alchemically the Devil represents the nigredo, the black stage, of the Great Work, in which the gross material is presented that needs to be purified and now fire, wind, and rain are cleaning it away. Small bits of fire that are depicted in the form of the Hebrew letter yod—the seminal form all of the other Hebrew letters are formed from—fertilize the earth. This card represents transformation, the shattering of illusion, and sudden change. This kind of transformation is abrupt and may be discomforting or unsettling. It may mark the loss of a position, or the shattering of illusions.

THE STAR.

Figure 66

THE STAR

The Star is the quiet after the storm presented in the last trump. The purified, therefore nude, soul gently washes away the remaining dark matter and the ladder to the stars is visible in the sky. O'Neill points out that Waite wrote in *The Secret Tradition in Alchemy* that the final reward comes in the stillness that follows a tempest. Again, this is essentially the same as the Marseilles model except that the anima figure is not only pouring onto the land and the sea, she is standing on both, like Temperance. She is completing Iris' mission and nurturing the world. The connection between the inner and the outer world is more complete. The water offers a better footing now. The Golden Dawn equates her to Aquarius, the water bearer. This is an opportunity to ascend to a higher state. It represents a breakthrough, an opportunity suddenly becoming available, calm after a storm. It is like forgiveness after an argument or clarity after the disillusionment of the last trump.

THE MOON.

Figure 67

THE MOON

Except for small details, the Moon image follows closely the Marseilles model. The primary difference is that the two dogs have been transformed into a dog and a wolf. An illustration appears in Waite's *Hermetic Museum* taken from *The Book of Lambspring* that depicts a dog and a wolf as the two warring opposites that are resolved to form the alchemical medicine. The Moon is rising between two towers. These are the same two towers, each with a single window, that we saw in the distance on the Death card. Then they were on the other side of the water. We have now crossed over but our experiences have reduced us to a primitive state, like the crustacean climbing from the water. We are entering on the path that leads to the place of the dawn but the Moon is there now. It is a time to rest and to prepare. The moon has thirty-two rays—the Kabalistic number of the ten sephiroth combined with the twenty-two paths of the Tree of Life. The Moon fertilizes the earth with dew. Alchemists sometimes gathered dew as the prime material for the Philosopher's Stone. Like the flames on the Tower, the dewdrops take the form of the core Hebrew letter, yod. The Moon indicates that it is not yet time to act but the seeds of action are being planted.

Figure 68

THE SUN

Although, at times, the Golden Dawn's correspondences for the Major Arcana seem symbolically strained, the Golden Dawn's correspondence for this card is the sun—an obvious choice. The Waite-Smith card retains the walled garden of the traditional Marseilles card but instead of the two nude youths, there is only one riding a horse and carrying a red victory banner. This figure is based on the Sun card in the older Jacques Vieville Tarot. The human-faced Sun casts twenty-two rays (one of which, at the top, is half obscured to make room for the roman numeral). This may correspond to the twenty-two cards of the Major Arcana, which may also be thought of as rays emanating from one glowing truth. The four sunflowers are the earthly reflection of the image of the Sun and they may be seen as the four minor suits and as the fourfold world—of the four elements, the four directions, and the four seasons. The embryonic crustacean of the Moon card has now been reborn as a child and is departing this Tarot garden to share his joy with the world. The red feather connects the child with the Sun and with the Fool, who has the same feather. This is the dawn of the inner light. This is a card of victory, achievement, and joy.

Figure 69

JUDGEMENT

This is the third elemental card and it is associated with fire. Waite believed that it represented the successful accomplishment of the mystic goal. In the Golden Dawn, the mystic goal was the identification of the self with what they called the Good Genius. We might call it the Higher Self. Here this inner consciousness is symbolized by the trumpeting angel calling a man, a woman, and a child from the tomb of ego consciousness. The angel of Judgement is usually identified as Gabriel. The white banner with the red or orange cross that is attached to the trumpet is a standard Christian symbol derived from the victory banner of Constantine, the first Christian emperor. When held by Christ or Gabriel it represents victory over death. With his red wings and flaming hair, the Golden Dawn would also identify this angel with the archangel Michael.

The three figures in the foreground, which are reflected again in the background, can be thought of as personifications of the three pillars of the Kabalistic Tree of Life, but here the masculine/active and feminine/passive pillars have been reversed. In earlier Major Arcana which depicted clearly defined masculine/light and feminine/dark polarities—the High Priestess, the Lovers, the Chariot, and the Devil—the feminine or dark symbol is on our left and the masculine or light symbol is on our right. Here instead the man is on our left and the woman is on our right. The Golden Dawn lessons tell us that although the diagram of the Tree of Life should have the feminine pillar on the left and the masculine on the right, when you identify with the Tree as yourself the sides are reversed, because you are looking out of it from the inside instead of looking at it from the outside.[22] This is what is being depicted here and it is repeated in the background to show that this experience is available to all who reach this level of understanding. On the center pillar, the child, who has been reborn under the Sun, is now ready to ascend to God consciousness. We are invited to identify with the child. This card represents higher consciousness, freedom, renewal, and judgment based on the past.

Figure 70

THE WORLD

This is Smith's interpretation of the Tarot of Marseilles quincunx, which we discussed in detail in Chapter Four (see figure 46 on page 169). The symbols of the four Evangelists in the corners indicate that we are viewing God's throne, situated in the center of the fourfold world. The wreath represents the sensual world. In the sacred center, the purified soul is at one with the World Soul. She dances on God's throne. Instead of the scepter and orb of the standard Marseilles image, the soul has two equal wands, derived from an older French card. These wands are like the twin pillars of duality, now equalized and reduced. They have become tools for the creative expression of the soul. This card represents the Anima Mundi at work and the goal achieved. Whenever it comes up, it represents what is truly desired. It is the One, the Good, and the Beautiful.

THE MINOR ARCANA

Figure 71

ACE OF WANDS

In the Tarot of Marseilles, the Ace of Staffs and the Ace of Swords both depict a hand coming out a cloud holding the suit symbol. Smith uses this device for all of her aces. Here, the traditional staff has become the magician's wand. All aces are a beginning or a renewal. Wands are linked to fire, and fire represents the feeling function. Sometimes people think of feelings as emotions, but Jung viewed emotions as something more shallow than a psychological function like feeling. Feeling is a fiery, decisive function that determines what is good and what is bad. Feelings may turn into emotions if they are intense enough, but it is not necessary to become emotional to decide if we like or don't like something. In addition, emotions may also emerge from other functions. Feeling motivates one to action and many of the pips in this suit depict people involved in new ventures or competitive activity. Smith has symbolized the fire in the wands by depicting the wand as a living branch with green leaves, attesting to the life force within. This is the beginning of an enterprise or a love affair. It is related to energy, feeling, passion, and work.

Figure 72

TWO OF WANDS

A wealthy merchant or noble stands on the rampart of his castle looking over the parapet and out to the sea. His banner is made of the red rose and the white lily joined in a cross. These alchemical opposites were depicted in an alternating check pattern on the back of each card in one of the oldest printings of this deck. One wand is strapped to the parapet. It represents a project that is complete and now supports the man. From this secure position he now grasps a new wand and project. In his right hand he holds a globe. He looks out with optimism and anticipation. He literally has the world in his hand.

Figure 73

THREE OF WANDS

A knight in a cape with a heraldic pattern stands on a cliff with three wands planted in the ground. With an armor-clad arm he grasps the one farthest away. On the sea below, there are three sailing ships, one for each wand. The knight may be setting in motion the plan that was envisioned in the last card or he may be witnessing the ships returning with news of their success.

Figure 74

FOUR OF WANDS

The project that has been initiated in the last pip is now established. With four wands, the number of physical manifestation, a new structure can be erected. The castle is now in the distance. The bridge on the right signifies that we have crossed over the water and the structure is being erected in the new territory. A symbolic roof of rose garlands has been attached and the erection is celebrated with festivities. This is the first of many of Smith's illustrations for the Minor Arcana in which the foreground is a flat surface, like a stage, and a straight horizontal line separates it from the scene in the background, as it would if the scene were a stage backdrop and this were a performance. As Smith was a theater designer, it is not surprising that she would make use of this convention. This card represents commitment and celebration. As the structure is made with the symbol of feeling and compassion, it can represent a marriage.

Figure 75

FIVE OF WANDS

Five men with wands use them as weapons in a battle. With the addition of a fifth element the stability and joy of the last card are dissolved in competition and strife. Five is the number of the Quinta Essentia, the Anima Mundi, or the spirit that animates matter. Although it is the Good, the Anima Mundi desires growth and dislikes complacency. Sometimes it works against our comfort to further the greater good.

Figure 76

SIX OF WANDS

A man on a white horse wears the victor's wreath and hoists another laurel wreath as a banner at the top of his wand. Other men stand at the side of his path and salute him with their wands. It appears that one man has emerged victorious from the struggle. Now he is enjoying the pleasure of success and the admiration of his peers. This is the growth that the Anima Mundi desired for us.

Figure 77

SEVEN OF WANDS

One man stands on top of the hill using his wand to defend his position from six attackers. Only the attackers' wands are visible. The victory of the last card has now placed the victor in the position of having to defend himself from those who desire what he has gained. This is a warning not to rest on our laurels, although, as the attackers are not visible, this threat may only be in our imagination.

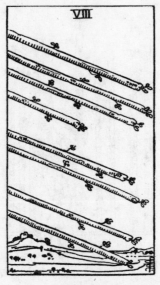

Figure 78

EIGHT OF WANDS

Eight wands hang in the air like arrows or spears in flight. An attack has been launched or what was settled is now in the air. The wands cannot stay in the air. They are already beginning to descend. This is a card of transition and new possibilities. This situation cannot last long.

Figure 79

NINE OF WANDS

A man with a bandaged head looks suspiciously over his shoulder and clutches his wand. Eight other wands form a defensive barrier behind him. This man has been successful in holding his position against attack. He has learned to strengthen his position and keeps himself prepared for action. He is a strong opponent. He has learned from his experiences but they have also left him scarred both physically and emotionally. He may be alert and able to defend himself but he may also be overly defensive and unable to relax and enjoy life. Smith again makes use of a stagelike foreground with the background separated like a painted backdrop, suggesting that this is a play performed for our benefit.

Figure 80

TEN OF WANDS

Aman struggles to carry a bundle of wands. He appears to be straining his back. He has taken on more than he can handle. The man may be a workaholic or circumstances may be demanding a heroic effort. This is one of the cards that Smith based on the Sola Busca Tarot. Seven Sola Busca cards are similar, particularly the Five, Six, and Seven of Staffs and the Ten of Swords. Because this card also makes use of a stagelike setting, like the Nine of Wands, and the man's tunic is similar to the one worn by the man on that card, it may be that the man on the Ten of Wands is removing the barrier or fortification that was depicted in the previous pip.

Figure 81

PAGE OF WANDS

In keeping with Levi's idea that the royal cards represent a family with the first representing the youngest child, this card was named the Page in English. A page is a young noble who was put in the service of a lady. When he reached his teens he was apprenticed to a knight and his title changed to squire. The figures on the cards are actually too old to be pages. They are squires or possibly knaves, a title often used on cards, who are servants, though not of noble birth. On later cards the title *Jack* was also used for Knave. In *The Pictorial Key to the Tarot*, Waite acknowledges the fact that the Page should correctly be labeled a Squire, or as he writes, an "esquire, presumably in the service of a knight."[23]

In the Golden Dawn's teachings on the Tarot, the Pages are called Princesses and they are said to represent "reception and transmission." Smith's Page is a richly clothed man walking into a desert landscape clutching his living wand as if transferring his wand to a new uncultivated area. This image is influenced by the Sola Busca Knave of Staffs or Batons. The Page is dressed in red and yellow to represent fire and his tunic has a beautiful design made of salamanders curving to bite their tails like an ouroboros. The salamander is the elemental spirit of fire. This card represents enterprise. Waite feels that the Page is making a proclamation though his hand is not extended and his mouth is closed.

Figure 82

KNIGHT OF WANDS

In the Golden Dawn's teachings on the Tarot, the Knights are called Princes and they are said to represent "power in action." All of Smith's Knights are depicted engaged in action. The Knight of Wands with his red horse and plume and holding his wand in his bare hand rides into the desert looking for new territory. His action is similar to the Page's but more forceful because of his steed. The Knight has the same salamander on his surcoat as the Page had on his tunic. Waite was not sure if the landscape contained mounds or pyramids. Although Smith's depiction is intentionally ambiguous, perhaps if he had known that Smith based it on the Sola Busca Knight of Batons, he would have seen that this detail is based on the three mounds seen behind the Knight on that card. The Knight is on a quest for new territory for his creative endeavor, or he may be searching for a mate.

Figure 83

QUEEN OF WANDS

In the Golden Dawn's teachings on the Tarot, the Queens are said to represent "brooding power," but Smith's Queen of Wands is the least brooding of the four. Waite points out that the wands in this suit are always in leaf because this is "a suit of life and animation."[24] These qualities are expressions of the feeling function, and the Queen is depicted as the mistress of feeling. She has made the desert her home. The leaves from the wand have spread to her crown. Like the earth mother and goddess Cybele, the Queen sits on a throne with lions on either side. The banner behind her also depicts lions. Lions are related to Leo, a fire sign, and the house of the sun, the ultimate ruler of fire. Although the Queen is a powerful ruler connected to the sun, she expresses her solar connection in a friendly and domestic way. Her scepter is a sunflower and her feline companion is the domestic representative of the lion.

Figure 84

KING OF WANDS

In the Golden Dawn's teachings on the Tarot, the Kings are said to represent "potential power," but the Golden Dawn also switched the rank of the Knight and the King, putting the Knight in the highest position. Smith's Kings are the masters of their elements, and with their thrones and crowns they are clearly in the most powerful position. The King of Wand's companion is the living fire elemental, the salamander. He is comfortable and at home, like the Queen, and looking out with anticipation, like the Knight and Page. His emblem is both the lion and the salamander. He is dressed in red and green—fire and leaves. He has a gold pendant in the form of a lion's head. All of the Kings relate to one of the symbols of the four Evangelists found in the corners of the World card. The King of Wands is related to the lion of St. Mark, which is also associated with Leo, a fixed sign of the zodiac connected to the element fire. Like Leo, the King of Wands is brave, generous, enthusiastic, and dominant—he knows what he likes and what he does not. He represents the best of all aspects of the feeling function.

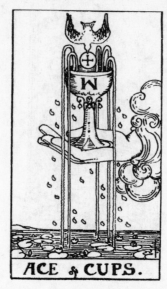

Figure 85

ACE OF CUPS

The Ace of Cups in the Tarot of Marseilles displays an elaborate hexagonal chalice with turrets like a castle. It seems that it represents the Holy Grail. The Waite-Smith Ace of Cups is definitely an allegorical image of the Grail. A hand holds the cup over its element, water, where there are lilies growing, symbolizing the alchemical feminine. Water corresponds to the intuitive function, a feminine, passive function that investigates the unconscious. The initial *M* on the cup identifies it with Mary. It is upside down to show that it is receiving the Host delivered by the dove. The dove is the standard Christian symbol for the Holy Spirit and the Host with the cross is the body of Christ. Here the Grail is being depicted as the body of Mary, which was the vessel for the body and blood of Christ. The five streams represent the five wounds, which he bled to bring eternal life to the world. Waite wrote that there were four. It appears that he wanted to connect the symbol to the fountain in the center of Eden from which four rivers flowed toward the four cardinal directions.

This card represents the initiation of a search within the soul for one's true purpose or desires. When we find our true desire, we will discover that we are not its author. It is like a seed planted in us by the divine, a seed that needs to be nurtured and allowed to grow.

Figure 86

TWO OF CUPS

From the earliest examples, the Two of Cups in the Marseilles tradition depicts a flowering stem in the center between the two cups. Near the top, two tendrils branch to either side and terminate in dolphin heads, which turn inward and lick the flower. This is a Tree of Life design. The Waite-Smith card reinterprets this symbol as the snake-entwined caduceus of Hermes terminating in a winged lion head. The winged lion is like an anthropomorphized Egyptian solar disk. Together with the caduceus it has ties to the lion-headed god of the Mithraic mysteries, a winged human figure with the head of a lion and a snake spiraling around its body. It represents divine power.

As in many of Smith's illustrations for the Minor Arcana, the people in the picture stand on a flat surface like a stage and a straight horizontal line separates them from the scene in the background, as it would if the scene were a stage backdrop. A distant house with a red roof can be seen painted on the backdrop. A similar house will also appear on the Ten of Cups. The two cups on this card are held by a man and a woman, as if they are toasting one another in a performance. Waite says that they are pledging. The man reaches out with his right hand to touch the woman. This is a card of sexual attraction.

Figure 87

THREE OF CUPS

Three maidens dressed in the alchemical opposites, red and white, dance in the center of a garden, which is cornucopialike in its abundance of fruits and vegetables. They hold up their goblets to offer a toast. This is a card of prosperity, celebration, and friendship. Perhaps the greatest wealth that these women possess is their mutual support.

Figure 88

FOUR OF CUPS

A man sits under a tree as in meditation but his arms are folded defensively. His mood is open for interpretation. He is contemplating three cups but another unexpectedly is delivered out of a cloud. This card represents a message, such as a telephone call. It is further news about a situation that has already developed. The man's mood may suggest that the news is unwelcomed.

Figure 89

FIVE OF CUPS

Aman stands like a pillar in a black cloak. His head is low and dejected as he contemplates three spilled cups. Behind him are two more upright, but he ignores them. In the distance, a bridge leads over the water and to a castle, but the man is unable to take this path because he is frozen in sorrow. Again we may interpret this scene as one being presented in a play. This card represents loss of perspective, sorrow, and inaction. It cautions that we are focusing too strongly on loss or what is negative and not seeing what we have.

Figure 90

SIⰅ OϜ CUPS

In the garden behind a manor, there are six cups, each with one star-shaped flower planted in it, as in a flowerpot. A boy gives a girl one of the cups with a flower. A guard walks away on the path to the left. This card represents innocence, generosity, love, trust, and sharing. It is the achievement of the pure mind of the beginner, unfettered by preconception. The departing guard means that for better of worse we have let our guard down.

Figure 91

SEVEN OF CUPS

A man stands with his back to us. He is in the dark but a vision of seven cups glows in front of him. Each cup tempts him with a different fate—love, property, wealth, or revenge. One cup holds the wreath of victory but the skull of death appears below. In the center there is one cup with a figure emerging. Its arms are spread in welcome and there is a red glow coming from the figure but it is veiled. All of the choices except for the veiled figure are tainted by egotism and selfishness. The unseen figure is the Higher Self, the guardian angel. This is the best choice, the one that invites us to live up to our destiny and to make choices outside of egotism.

Figure 92

EIGHT OF CUPS

It is night and there is a full moon—drawn in a medieval style—looking out over a landscape by the water. The night is a time of rest. A man walks away. He has a walking stick, which suggests that he is on a long journey. In the foreground, eight cups are neatly stacked. These represent past accomplishments and emotional complexes stored in the psyche. There is a space where a ninth cup can be placed, and this space allows us a view of the man. The man has put his past in order and, "letting bygones be bygones," he continues on his way. Perhaps the experiences of this journey will supply the ninth cup.

Figure 93

NINE OF CUPS

A man sits on a stool in front of a banquet table with nine cups in a row. Waite says that he is a goodly person, who "has feasted to his heart's content."[25] But Smith has drawn him fat and smug. This card can represent satisfaction but it can also represent greed or excessive pride.

Figure 94

TEN OF CUPS

In a rainbow above, ten cups arch across the sky. Below there is a country cottage by a stream. It appears to be similar to the cottage that was depicted in the background on the Two of Cups only now it is closer. Again, the background is divided from the foreground by a straight line, suggesting that it is a stage set. A man and woman embrace as each holds one hand out toward the rainbow. Their two children dance to their right. The scene appears to be the happy ending to a play. Perhaps the man and woman are the same two who toasted each other on the Two of Cups card. This card represents family life, joy, contentment, and faithfulness.

Figure 95

PAGE OF CUPS

The Page stands at the edge of the sea of the unconscious, which again appears to be painted on a stage backdrop—this is the only royal card with this type of composition. His tunic is blue like the water but it has tulips on it that show he is still connected to the land. He seems to have captured some of the water in his cup. As he examines it, a messenger from the depths emerges. Out of all of Smith's Pages, the Page of Cups most exemplifies the Golden Dawn's theme for the Pages, "reception and transmission." This card can represent a message. It can also represent a message from the unconscious such as a dream or one arrived at through divination. The Page is exploring his mind as an actor does when delivering a soliloquy.

Figure 96

KNIGHT OF CUPS

Unlike the Page with his tulips, the Knight has fish on his surcoat. Like Hermes, the messenger of the gods, he has wings on his helmet and on his feet. The Sola Busca Knight of Cups also has wings, and a similarly posed horse. The Knight has crossed over. He is no longer one who just receives messages from the unconscious. His purpose is aligned with the unconscious and he brings the message to others. He is on an errand to deliver his cup. This card represents a message or a messenger but it can also represent one who practices divination.

Figure 97

QUEEN OF CUPS

The Queen of Cups in the Sola Busca Tarot sits in a similar pose in a dolphin throne, intently staring into a chalice. Here, the Queen's throne is placed on the edge of the sea facing the water. There is a fish lying on the ground in the lower right corner. There are waves on her cape and it has a shell for a clasp. She is no longer identifying with the messenger from the deep but with the water itself. Of all of the Queens, she most exemplifies the act of brooding, but not in the gloomy sense. Her brooding is more like that of a hen when she sits on her eggs patiently waiting for them to hatch.

The Queen's throne has a scallop shell carved at the top supported by two fishtailed children. These are undines, the elemental spirits of water. Paracelsus (1493–1541), the great alchemist and physician, was the first person to identify the living spirits of the four elements, and afterward they became an accepted part of occult lore. When Smith was in Ireland, she had seen elementals and fairies for herself and enjoyed incorporating them into her work. Another undine talks to a fish on the side of the throne.

The Queen's elaborate Gothic chalice has angels flanking it and a lid with a cross on top. These elements identify it as a symbol of the sacred center. The Queen knows that the center is in herself. She does not open the cup. The Queen knows that it will open on its own, like an egg, when the time is right. Meanwhile, she is psychically in tune with its contents. This is a symbol of mystery and intuition.

Figure 98

KING OF CUPS

The King of Cups is the master of his element. He is dressed in blue. He has a fish for a pendant and a live one for a companion. An Egyptian lotus column is carved on his throne and he has another for a scepter. The lotus is a water flower from the desert. It connects him to Scorpio, the water sign with a desert animal for its image and through this fixed sign of the zodiac he is connected to the eagle of St. John on the corner of the World card. He has waves on his crown. His throne is no longer on the edge of the water; it is in it. He is literally "out to sea." The King is so at home with the unconscious that he allows it to support him. To the rest of us this seems as impossible as walking on water. We need a ship to visit him. The King is a spiritual master but he may be out of touch with mundane affairs. Like Scorpio, he is emotional and intense.

Figure 99

ACE OF SWORDS

Except for the landscape, the details of this card are entirely derived from the Marseilles Ace of Swords. This is the suit of air and the thinking function. The sword represents a new thought or an idea. It is positive and singularly focused and it wins the crown of victory. The crown is decorated with a vine bearing berries and an evergreen, symbols of prosperity and lasting achievement. Hebrew yods descend from the crown; they are the seeds of new words and ideas.

Figure 100

TWO OF SWORDS

A woman sits on the edge of the sea with her back to it. Like several others of Smith's pips, she appears to be sitting on a stage in front of a backdrop as if she were a character in a play. The waxing moon is out. It is a time of rest but action will come in the future. She is holding two swords as if deciding between two alternatives. Her position is awkward and she will not be able to hold them long. She is like Justice without her scales and faced with two courses of action. Without the information from her scales the woman will have to base her decision on intuition instead of logic. She is not comfortable with this method.

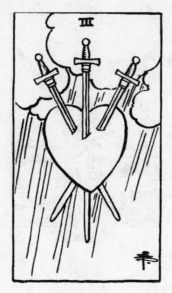

Figure 101

THREE OF SWORDS

The image of three swords piercing a heart is derived from the Sola Busca Three of Swords. Smith added the clouds and rain. This image depicts negative thoughts and cutting words bringing pain to the heart. The storm in the background reminds us that pain is like rain. We may prefer the sunshine of joy but both rain and sun are necessary for our growth.

Figure 102

FOUR OF SWORDS

In a practice called incubation, ancient mystics would lie lifeless imitating the state of death, sometimes for days, in order to enter a deep trance.[26] Although this card depicts a knight's tomb, it is a card of meditation, the process by which thought enters the physical world. Four is the number of physical manifestation and this is the suit of thought. Three swords with the points down in the negative position are hung on the wall, signifying that negativity is put aside. On the window, a man kneels praying to the Madonna or another saint. The knight carved on the sarcophagus lid is also praying. The lid is open, not sealed. This is a place where temporally we can be "dead to the world." A place of rest, prayer, and meditation.

Figure 103

FIVE OF SWORDS

Under wind-torn clouds and on the edge of the sea two men turn their backs to us and look dejected. A third picks up the swords that have been left lying on the ground. He smiles in the direction of the other men. Their loss is his gain. This may be the aftermath of a battle. Whether or not the third man is the victor or an opportunist is open to interpretation. This is a card of gain, but at another's expense.

Figure 104

SIX OF SWORDS

A ferryman guides his boat across a waterway. He and his passengers have their backs toward us. The passengers appear to be a mother and a child, perhaps his family. Waite says that "the course is smooth,"[27] but it is only smooth in the distance on the left and choppy in the foreground on the right. They are leaving troubled waters for a better life. The posture of the figures and the boat-load of negative swords suggests that they are weighed down by sorrow. Although they are moving to a better place, their thoughts are too much in the past and on their troubles.

Figure 105

SEVEN OF SWORDS

This image seems to be influenced by the Sola Busca Seven of Swords. In the background, there is an armed camp with bright colored tents. Again the background appears to be a stage backdrop. The men of the camp are pictured far in the back circled around a campfire. In the foreground, a man tiptoes away carrying the majority of their weapons. He has a look of satisfaction on his face. He is a thief but the interpretation of his action depends on the nature of his motivation and the motivation of the army. Like numerous characters in plays, he may be a trickster hero. This may be a card of dishonesty or of heroism.

Figure 106

EIGHT OF SWORDS

A woman is blindfolded and bound standing in the marshy wasteland outside of a city. Eight swords are stuck in the ground around her like the bars of a cage. The swords are like negative thoughts that have cut the woman off from others and bound her in her fear, anger, or depression. This card can also mean incarceration and isolation. Waite suggests that the situation is temporary.

Figure 107

NINE OF SWORDS

A woman sits up in bed with her hands over her face as if she has been crying. Nine swords hang in the air above her pointing to the future as a somber warning. The quilt on the bed has a checked pattern. In the yellow squares, there are red flowers with a fourfold structure. These are poppies, the symbol of dreams and remembrance. Poppies have also been associated with fallen soldiers since the nineteenth century but this aspect of the symbol did not become popular until after World War I. In the alternating blue squares, there are astrological glyphs, which suggest divination. In a carving on the side of the bed, one man thrusts at another as if to stab him with a sword. This card represents nightmares, fear, and foreboding.

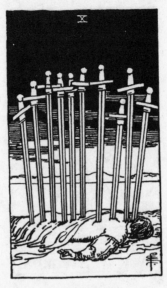

Figure 108

TEN OF SWORDS

A man lies facedown in his blood with ten swords piercing his body. This card represents pain, severe criticism, or being "stabbed in the back." The worst has happened. Now it is time to heal. Accepting pain is often an important part of the healing process. With his right hand the slain man is making the sign of benediction, a gesture that allows him to identify with Christ and Christ-like forgiveness (see the right hand of Christ in figure 42 on page 165 and figure 43 on page 166). Forgiveness is also an important part of healing.

Figure 109

PAGE OF SWORDS

Although Waite says that the Page is walking swiftly, we can see by his stance that he is not. The birds, the storm clouds, the trees, even the earth, seem to be moving, but in the center of all of this action, the Page stands his ground. He has taken the high place. He lifts his sword into an upright and positive position and is prepared for action. The scene is filled with air and turbulence but for the Page the movement is internal and mental.

Figure 110

KNIGHT OF SWORDS

This card also has windblown clouds and trees and birds, the messengers from the air, flying above. There are birds on the Knight's surcoat and on the horse's reins and breastplate. Along with the birds on the horse's breastplate there are butterflies. These represent sylphs, the elemental spirits of air. The Knight charges ahead with his feathered crest trailing. He is like a personification of the wind, and he expresses better than any of Smith's Knights the Golden Dawn's theme for the Knights, the "power of action." Waite compares him to Galahad. The Knight has identified what is evil and intends to destroy it. He is a hero but this type of judgmental behavior must be reserved for true threats and not become a habit.

Figure 111

QUEEN OF SWORDS

S mith's Queens are generally influenced by the Queens in the Sola Busca Tarot. This Queen is wearing a cape covered in clouds and clasped with a golden bird. There are butterfly sylphs on her crown and the side of her throne. Below the arm there is a winged head, which is the original way a cherub was depicted in Christian art. The clouds have settled and the tassel on the Queen's wrist attests to the fact that the wind has died down. One bird flies overhead. The Queen is settled on the high ground looking out to our right with her sword held in the upright positive position. Her left hand is held out as if she has just finished making a proclamation. Her mouth is closed with a stiff lower lip. This card can represent self-confidence or the desire for revenge. It can also signify an official statement.

Figure 112

KING OF SWORDS

The King is the master of his element. The landscape has become calmer and two birds in the sky glide on a gentle breeze. The back of the King's throne is decorated with sylphs in their butterfly form and in the more evolved form of fairies. The King's crown has a cherub across it like a band. These evolved forms of air spirits are symbolic of the King's highly evolved intellect. The winged human images connect him with Aquarius, the air sign, and with the man, the symbol of St. Matthew, on the World card. He holds his sword upright and is positive about his decision. This card represents Aquarian qualities, such as analytical intelligence, decisiveness, and independent authority.

Figure 113

ACE OF PENTACLES

L evi referred to the traditional suit of coins as "pantacles," meaning "talis-mans." Waite and Smith transformed the talismans into actual magical pen-tacles with a five-pointed star in a circle on each one, but the themes expressed in this suit are still connected to the original suit symbol, the coin. This is the suit of earth and the sensation function. Sensation is a technical function that deter-mines how physical systems work and how they can be improved. This suit can pertain to matters of money and wealth but also to the body and health and other physical matters. The Ace represents a new path that opens up promising success in the future, as is suggested by the fertile landscape.

Figure 114

TWO OF PENTACLES

In the Tarot of Marseilles, the Two of Coins has a lemniscatelike banner with the maker's name written on it wrapped around the two coins. Here it becomes an actual lemniscate and the coins, or pentacles, are held in the hands of a juggler jumping from one foot to another in a kind of dance. Again he is on a stage like a performer. In the background two ships sail on a turbulent sea, echoing the up-and-down position of the two coins and the juggler's feet. This card represents gaiety in the face of hardship and the ability to get by with little resources by juggling our funds.

Figure 115

THREE OF PENTACLES

The three pentacles in this image are part of the tracery in a Gothic arch. This suggests money connected to an establishment. The rose with the cross in the center found in the lower triangle suggests the Rosicrucians. Two men, one dressed as a monk and the other in a secular cape, present plans to a third man, who appears to be an artist carving an image or a design in the stone wall. This represents creative work done for a salary or a commission and for an established organization.

Figure 116

FOUR OF PENTACLES

Four is the number of physical manifestation and this is the suit of earth. This card is too heavily grounded in materiality. A noble sits on a stone with pentacles under his feet, a pentacle clasped to his chest and another on top of his crown. The symbolic nature of this display may be explained by the fact that the noble appears to be a performer on a stage. He stands on money, holds on to his money, and has money on his mind. His attitude has made him an outcast from the city. He is a miser or, as the Renaissance *Book of Trades*—a sixteenth-century illustrated text listing common occupations—would call him, a "money fool." His is the opposite sentiment from the Six of Cups.

Figure 117

FIVE OF PENTACLES

Five pentacles form a tree design in a stained-glass window. The light coming through the window suggests the glow of warmth within the establishment. On the outside, a crippled beggar with a bell around his neck is trudging through the snow accompanied by a poor woman clutching a tattered shawl around her neck. This card represents poverty, and exclusion. It is the natural consequence of the actions taken by the noble on the Four of Pentacles. As the stained-glass window suggests a church, this card may also signify physical poverty combined with spiritual wealth.

Figure 118

SIX OF PENTACLES

A richly dressed merchant weighs out coins with a scale and distributes the money to those in need dressed in patched cloaks. This is an enlightened solution to the problem and imbalance depicted on the last two cards. The fact that he is also on a stage like the miser on the Four of Pentacles suggests that the Four and the Six of Pentacles represent alternatives being presented in a play. Unlike the miser, the wealthy man chooses to create balance by giving money where it is needed. This card can represent giving and receiving. The interpretation depends on who is identified as the merchant and who is identified as the recipient.

Figure 119

SEVEN OF PENTACLES

A man rests on his hoe and admires the fruits on his vine, which are depicted as seven pentacles. Waite mistakenly calls the man's hoe a staff, and, therefore, interprets him as looking at the pentacles with desire. The addition of the hoe suggests that the man is actually a farmer who has worked to cultivate the pentacles, and he is now ready to enjoy the fruits of his labor. This card represents profit, reward, and a welcomed rest.

Figure 120

EIGHT OF PENTACLES

Smith's image for this card is based on the Sola Busca Six of Coins, which represents a metalworker raising the shieldlike disks that are the suit symbols for that deck. Here the craft worker is sitting at a bench and using a small hammer to chase the stars on the metal pentacles. When he is done, he hangs them from a board to display them for sale. Waite calls him "an artist in stone at his work."[28] But the pentacles are too thin for stone, his bench is too light, and the pentacles are hung by a cord or a wire that would be difficult to attach to stone and too weak to hold its weight. Waite wanted him to be the apprentice to the artist on the Three of Pentacles. The man, however, is doing production work in contrast to the highly creative work of the artist on the Three of Pentacles. This card represents production and routine. He is literally making money.

Figure 121

NINE OF PENTACLES

A woman of wealth and leisure stands in her garden with her gaming hawk. The garden is abundant with grapes and pentacles, symbols of sensuality and wealth. This card represents prosperity, comfort, and the time and ability to enjoy it. The hawk suggests that she has resources for further gains.

Figure 122

TEN OF PENTACLES

A white-haired and bearded patriarch sits at the entrance to the courtyard of his manor house petting his dogs. Behind him are three figures, who are possibly his male and female heirs and his grandchild. Like the patriarch the child reaches out to pet a dog. Their interest in the dogs unites them. The young man—the heir—holds a spear as if standing guard. The patriarch has the grapes of sensuality and abundance on his robe and heraldic emblems representing balance and security on his arch. This card represents family, generations, wealth, and security.

Figure 123

PAGE OF PENTACLES

The Page stands in a fertile field with part of the ground plowed for planting. But he does not look at the earth solely as a source of wealth. He holds a pentacle lightly in his fingertips out in front of his gaze. He looks at it lovingly as if he were admiring its beauty. This card represents aesthetic appreciation, study, and reflection. This Page is one that Pythagoras would describe as a lover of wisdom.

Figure 124

KNIGHT OF PENTACLES

The Knight sits astride a black horse in the midst of fertile plowed fields. He has oak leaves, sacred to the Druids and to the Classical god Jupiter, for the crest on his helmet and on his horse's head. The Knight holds out a pentacle as if looking for a place to plant it. This card represents investment and the search for a new job or means of livelihood.

Figure 125

QUEEN OF PENTACLES

The Queen sits on her throne in a flowering field under a rose arbor on a hill-side by a stream. There is a red rabbit, the messenger from the earth, in the right foreground. The upholstery that covers the Queen's seat and back is deco-rated with pears and there are leaves and a flower on her crown. There is a goat's head on the arm of her chair and cherubic figures with horns, and goat's legs are carved on the upper back and side of the throne. These are gnomes, the elemen-tals of earth. The Queen holds her pentacle gently in her lap and tilts her head to admire it. She has wealth and she appreciates it. The Queen looks at herself as the caretaker of her possessions instead of their owner.

KING of PENTACLES.

Figure 126

KING OF PENTACLES

The King sits in a walled garden next to his castle. There are flowers and grapes growing in the garden and he has flowers on his crown and grapes on his robe. He has four bull's heads on the back and arms of his throne and he rests his armored foot on another more primitively carved one. The bull is the sign of Taurus, an earth sign, and it connects him with the bull representing St. Luke on the World card. Like Taurus, the King is wealthy and pleasure loving. He is conservative but dependable. From under his sensual robe he displays an armored leg, which attests to his preparedness to defend his property.

ROT 269

HIEROGLYPHS FROM THE SOUL

The true Tarot is symbolism; it speaks no other language and offers
no other signs. Given the inward meaning of its emblems, they
do become a kind of alphabet which is capable of indefinite
combinations and makes true sense in all.

—A. E. WAITE, *THE PICTORIAL KEY TO THE TAROT*

The word *divination* literally means "to get in touch with the divine." It is derived from the Latin *divinus,* which meant "soothsayer," which, in turn, was derived from *deus,* meaning "God." We often think of the ancient soothsayers or oracles as making predictions. We have, however, written records from Delphi and other oracles, and they show that the majority of statements of the oracles were not predictions but advice on how to make improvements and keep the favor of the divine.

In the ancient world, it was generally believed that the gods desired to communicate with people, and divination was how that communication happened. Techniques for divination included dream interpretation, the interpretation of the flight of birds and other omens, the examination of the entrails of sacrificial animals (particularly the liver), the declarations of oracles (the spokesperson for a specific god, located at the appropriate shrine, also called an oracle), astrology, and throwing dice or drawing lots. All important decisions at a personal or state level involved divination. As there was no central authority to decide religious issues, often the questions that were asked were concerned with the will of the gods, and the use of dice and lots allowed divination to be available to everyone on an immediate and personal level.

In the Renaissance, cards began to replace dice as the common tool for divination. There were books that explained how to use playing cards for divination and the Merini Cocai sonnets, published in 1527, describe the Tarot's trumps being used to depict the fate of individuals.[1] Thanks to the eighteenth- and nineteenth-century occultists, in modern culture the Tarot has become the common tool for divination. As in the past, this tool is best used for determining the will of the gods or God, although we may prefer to label the origin of this inner wisdom the Higher Self, or the voice of the unconscious.

It is likely that the main reason that the Tarot has replaced dice as a popular divinatory tool is that the Tarot offers a set of visual symbols instead of the bare numbers offered by dice. The eminent psychologist Carl Jung observed that there is a difference between a true symbol and what he labeled a sign. True symbols flow naturally from the unconscious. We find them in our dreams and in the myths of our culture. Jung refers to signs as consciously crafted images that have one standard meaning, such as the logo of a corporation. Symbols are also used by artists in their creations, but in the strictest sense, they are not created by the artist, they emerge from the unconscious. This is why artists often have trouble describing their work or explaining the meaning of their images in words, and this is also why artists from cultures separated by time and geography often use the same symbols. Words tend to be signs; they are created to have specific meaning. The natural language of the unconscious is more direct. As we can see in our dreams, the unconscious prefers to use sensual imagery or sounds and smells. When it uses words, they do not always mean what they appear to on the surface, they may point to other things beyond themselves.

As we learned in our discussion on the history of the Tarot, the cards in the Major Arcana were originally symbolic images created by Renaissance artists. In the Renaissance this type of symbolic image would have been referred to as a hieroglyph. *Hieroglyph* stems from the Greek word, *hieorglyphikos,* which means a "sacred carving or picture." The Greeks used this term to describe the picture writing of the ancient Egyptians, the well-known hieroglyphics. Although the prevailing opinion of modern historians is that most Egyptian hieroglyphs were designed to have limited meaning or to be signs, in the ancient world only the Egyptian priests could read them. Like the common Egyptians, the ancient Greeks could not read the Egyptian hieroglyphs, but observing that they were used for spiritual purposes, they believed that hieroglyphs were a set of true symbols, containing unlimited depth of meaning. The Greeks believed that Egyptian hieroglyphics were a sacred writing, which used pictures to communicate directly with the gods and the soul, or as the Greeks would say, the psyche.

In approximately the fifth century C.E., a Hellenistic author named Horapollo recorded the Greek understanding of Egyptian hieroglyphs in a text entitled the *Hieroglyphica*. A copy of the *Hieroglyphica* was brought to Florence in 1422, where it caused a sensation among Renaissance artists.[2] Inspired by the *Hieroglyphica*, Renaissance artists began to create new hieroglyphs, or true symbols, and this creative endeavor helped to popularize allegorical and symbolic imagery in Renaissance art. One result of this trend was the creation of the Tarot. From its origin, the Tarot has been designed as a set of symbols or tools that the unconscious can use to communicate with the conscious mind. When Pamela Colman Smith redesigned the Minor Arcana in 1909, she effectively created hieroglyphs for the entire Tarot deck.

When making decisions about relationships or career, everyone has wished for a wise friend to turn to, a friend who has perspective on the situation and insight into what others are feeling. Each of us does have such a friend. Inside ourselves, we have a higher, wiser Self who can guide us toward our goals. The key to communicating with this wise friend is our intuition. The Tarot is a tool that we can use to develop our intuition. As we have demonstrated in the previous chapters, this group of hieroglyphs that comprises the Tarot's Major Arcana also illustrates the archetypal story of the hero's journey toward enlightenment, and the entire structure or the Tarot with its five suits is a sacred mandala. The Tarot, therefore, provides a spiritual tool with a complete set of archetypal images that can be used by our Higher Self to guide us toward more enlightened choices and spiritual wisdom. Instead of predicting the future, the cards work best when they are used to help to create a more fulfilling future. Used in this way, Tarot readings are healing and instructive.

Now we will focus on some techniques and card spreads that will help us to use the Tarot to communicate with our Higher Self.

THE THREE-CARD MESSAGE

To allow the Higher Self to make use of the Tarot as a set of hieroglyphs, we must get our ego out of the way and let the unconscious use the cards to create concepts or stories in which each card acts as a word, a phrase, or a sentence. The simplest and most powerful reading that we can do is perhaps the three-card reading. Once we have learned this technique, it can be used to build many different types of spreads, to address different issues.

As a symbol, three represents creativity. Three is considered a sacred number in most ancient cultures. The ancient Pythagoreans defined three points as necessary to make the first geometric form and begin creation. They believed that creation itself was governed by a trinity of three principal gods, and, as we have seen in Chapter Three, Plato believed that the soul was composed of three parts. The ancient Celts also considered three a sacred number. They associated it with a triple goddess of the sun and used it as a base to create their intricate designs. In Christianity, three is related to the mystery of the Trinity. When constructing a sentence, we find that every complete sentence needs a subject and a predicate. To go beyond the most rudimentary form, it will also need a third part, an object. Every story or situation has a beginning, middle, and an end. The Tarot trumps themselves are a three-part story. A layout of three cards follows an archetypal pattern that allows communication to happen, and in this chapter, we will learn how to construct and interpret that layout.

To start, make sure that none of the cards in the deck are upside down in relation to the others. This will make it easier to place the cards right side up in your reading. Right-side-up cards allow the pictures to communicate more clearly and are less likely to impose unnecessary negativity onto a reading. Some people believe that it is necessary to use upside-down cards to increase the vocabulary of the cards by allowing for more possibilities, but in fact this only doubles the possibilities. When we use three cards as one statement instead of a single card, however, we find that we have 456,456 possible combinations. If we use three cards for each position in a more complex reading, we have 456,456 for the first place, 405,150 for the second, and 357,840 for the third place. With one card for each, with upside-down possibilities, we only have 156 for the first, 154 for the second, and 152 for the third. It is not necessary to confuse the reading with upside-down images.

Next, the querent must decide the purpose of the reading. Of course, it is both possible and advisable to read for oneself, in which case, you are the querent as well as the reader. The purpose can be a clarification of a past or present situation, to attain wisdom or advice, to investigate the possible outcome of a course of action, to gain perspective, or to gain insight into another person's view. Let the querent cut the cards once with his or her left hand (symbolizing the unconscious) while stating the purpose of the reading. The statement should be simple and specific. One of the most common problems that beginners encounter when reading the Tarot is that they find the answer confusing or muddled. Usually a clear statement of purpose at the beginning of the reading can avoid this problem. Do not be afraid to declare the statement in an audible voice. If you want advice, say, "I desire advice on (state the specific issue)." If you want to know where a situation is headed then ask, "What is the likely outcome of the present course of action?"

Take the cards and shuffle them by holding the deck in the left hand, cutting the deck with the right, and letting the cut cards fall in among the remaining cards held loosely in the left hand. If this is difficult then simply cut a block from the bottom of the deck and place some of it on the top of the remaining cards and some on the bottom. Some people with smaller hands find it easier to hold the deck vertically when shuffling instead of horizontally. Continue this action in a meditative rhythm until you feel the intuition to stop. One can also let the querent shuffle, but watch until the process comes to a natural state of completion and instruct him or her to stop. When we are shuffling in this way, we are not consciously in control of the ordering of the deck. The unconscious will take over and place the cards in the right order. It is important to develop an intuitive sense of when the process is complete. With practice, you will find that this is easier than it sounds. Let yourself trust your feelings. I find that when the deck is ready, my hands become reluctant to shuffle. I could force them to continue but they don't seem to want to. At this point, I stop.

Let the querent cut, again with the left hand, by removing a block of cards from the top of the deck and setting it aside. Lay the next three cards out in a line from left to right. Now look at the cards as one picture; look at the flow of energy in the picture, and interpret it as you would a dream or a story in a picture book. At this point, one should forget everything one has learned about the meaning of the cards. Simply look at the layout. Often this causes a momentary panic when one realizes that one does not know what the cards mean. I often feel this myself. This is good; it is a sign that the ego is letting go. Take a deep breath, relax, and continue to simply look at the cards. You will find that with patience, the cards will start to make sense in their own way. Allow yourself to sit quietly until they do. You will begin to notice in what direction the characters are facing.

There are six basic patterns that can come up, although each has subdivisions, and at times, two patterns can merge. The center card is most important to the action—it is like the verb in a sentence. The characters on each card can be facing left, right, center, up, or down. At times, the body is in one direction but a head or gesture points to the other side, or the figure may be pointing to either side. Now allow yourself to think about the meaning of each card, but remain open to new insights contained in the picture. By combining the direction of the action with the meaning of each card, it is usually possible to state the action as one sentence or expand it into a more detailed story.

THE SIX PATTERNS

1. **Linear:** The cards could show a story, which begins on the left and ends on the right, or the action could start on the right and proceed to the left. The figures will tend to be facing in the same direction, left or right. Sometimes the end card may be facing forward or the opposite way—meeting the action.

2. **Choice:** The central figure may have his or her back toward the back of the figure on one of the flanking cards. When two figures are back-to-back in this way it indicates that the central figure is moving away from one side and all that that symbolizes, and toward the other—choosing one direction and rejecting the other.

3. **The central origin:** Perhaps the central figure is looking directly at you or up to a higher plane. This may indicate that the action starts in the center and moves out to both sides or to one side and not the other. Look at the direction of the flanking cards. If they are moving away from the center, this is the central origin pattern.

4. **The central destination:** When the central figure is looking at you, up, or down, and the end figures are facing the center, the action may start on both sides and converge in the middle. Thus the middle has become the destination for the action.

5. **The central problem:** At times there may be no flow of energy. The central card may be blocking the action or dispersing the energy. For example, if placed in the center, the Eight of Swords may represent a block and the Tower may represent dispersion.

6. **The central teacher:** The central figure may be instructional and commenting on or pointing to two possibilities illustrated by the cards that flank it. The center card may be illustrating that two choices are available or recommending one choice over the other.

As mentioned above, sometimes the layout may be interpreted as fitting more than one pattern. Use your intuition to determine which is being suggested. If a card confuses you, you may expand it for clarification. This involves shuffling and obtaining another three cards, which are an expanded message related to the card in question. It is best to place these three above the card that they refer to. To find out the causes of a situation we may also place three cards below any card we need to know more about.

EXAMPLES

To help clarify how the six patterns manifest in readings and how they would be interpreted, this section contains examples of each pattern. In the following examples, we will make use of the Waite-Smith Tarot deck. Most modern decks follow the example of the Waite-Smith deck when it comes to including scenes on the pip cards. However, not all agree with Waite's and Smith's interpretation. When reading using different decks by different designers, the same cards may have different meanings in each deck. One should become familiar with the unique qualities of the deck and always interpret the cards based on the pictures that are presented by the designer.

When using an older-style Tarot deck, with only repetitions of the suit symbol on the pip cards of the minor suits, when pip cards come up, one should observe which of the numbers presented is higher or lower than the others. The direction of the action can be determined by the numerical sequence of the cards combined with clues provided by the figures on the trumps and the royal cards. The antique pips also contain decorative designs such as vines, flowers, shields, or banners that are helpful in interpreting them. Often one of the suit symbols is singled out in the design in a way that adds meaning or direction. In the Tarot of Marseilles, for example, two swords cross on the Ten of Swords and one central sword cuts into the design on the Nine. On the Ten of Cups, the top cup is lying on its side pouring to the viewer's left.

One—Linear

In figure 127, we see a clear example of the linear pattern with the action proceeding from the left to the right. The central character, the Page of Swords, is the most active card and can be thought of as the verb in this sentence. Swords are related to air and therefore thoughts and words. Because all of the cards are swords, the commentary seems to be about a line of thought and its consequences. It can also, however, pertain to the actions that stem from this line of thought, and the emotions that are engendered.

The first card on the left, the Nine of Swords, depicts a woman sitting up in bed with her face in her hands expressing grief and fear. The nine swords hang

Figure 127. The linear pattern

heavily in the air over her like unpleasant thoughts that can't be banished. As she is on the left and the action proceeds to the right, she represents fear about upcoming events. The second card, the Page of Swords, depicts a youth who lifts his sword upright in a positive direction. He seems to be preparing himself mentally for positive action in his stormy environment. Perhaps he represents someone who is presenting an argument on a debated issue. His body faces right and continues the action, but his head faces left toward the figure representing fear. Although he attempts to right a bad situation, inwardly he is consumed with fear and doubt. Bravely, he summons up a confident veneer to hide his doubts. On the right is the likely outcome of this behavior, the Ace of Swords.

Aces represent a birth or the beginning of a new direction. In this case, the sword is upright and positive and is crowned at its tip. This sword is like a magnification of the one in the hands of the Page. It is an image of his debate or line of reason existing beyond its author and winning the crown of triumph. To read the entire layout, it says that in spite of fear and doubts the querent should present his or her ideas. The ideas will triumph and lead others into a new and positive direction.

This could be a welcomed answer to a question such as, "What is the likely outcome of my present course of action?" Or it may be in answer to a request for advice from the higher self, in which case it would be suggesting a course of action. In either case, the result is favorable. Let us suppose that the last card was not favorable. It might be the Three of Swords shown in figure 128. In this case, the cards would be suggesting that this course of action will bring criticism on the

Figure 128. The linear pattern with the Three of Swords as the outcome

querent, and as a result, further pain and fear. If this is what the higher self chooses to warn us about, the querent should next ask the higher self, "How can my goal best be achieved?" or "What is the best that I can accomplish in this situation?" Then shuffle and lay out the cards once more.

Two—Choice

In the next example, figure 129, we see that the central character, the Two of Wands, is back-to-back with the Page of Wands. They are moving away from each other. Instead of choosing to take up arms and argue his case like the Page, the man on the parapet chooses to head to the left and toward the World. Wands are related to the element fire, which corresponds to feelings, motivation and work. The man has two staffs or wands. One is behind him and attached to the fortress that he is standing on. This represents what has been accomplished. He holds the other wand in his left hand and a globe in his right as he looks out through the embrasure, an opening in the wall designed to allow the firing of weapons. The man looks past the kingdom and toward the sea with its promise of future adventure. This is an aggressive image. The man does not rest on his accomplishments but continues to forge ahead feeling the thrill of adventure. The central character could be interpreted as heading for disaster or triumph, depending on what cards are flanking it. Here the card that the Two of Wands is headed for is the World.

As explained in earlier chapters, the World represents the achievement of the spiritual goal, the experience of the mystical presence at the heart of the physical

Figure 129. The choice pattern

world. It is the most important card in the deck. It may be called the Soul of the World or simply the Good. On the most mundane level, it represents the achievement of any goal. With this layout, the Higher Self would be advising that we should not rest on our laurels or attempt to defend our position to others. The key to success is to focus totally on the future. If we look to the world, the world will respond. If this were to appear in a reading for a businessperson worried about competition, it would be advising him or her not to cut prices and compete but to search for new markets, particularly foreign markets.

Three—The Central Origin

In figure 130, we find the strong figure of Temperance facing us in the center of the layout. To either side of Temperance are figures facing away from the center. This is the central origin pattern. Temperance is represented in the Renaissance custom as an angel pouring water from one vessel into another. To the ancients, Temperance meant the regulation or balance of desire and was considered one of the four principal virtues. In the Renaissance mind, the balancing of desire was closely connected to the physical balance of the four humors. The humors were part of Renaissance medicine, consisting of four bodily liquids (phlegm, blood, black and yellow bile) that were related to the four elements. When these liquids were in proper balance one was said to be in "good humor" or able to "hold one's temper." Temperance is making balance by proportioning liquid between her two vessels.

In this layout the cards are saying that once the virtue of Temperance is

Figure 130. The central origin pattern

achieved, two courses of action will emerge, each of equal importance. Both courses are represented by pentacles. This suit was originally called coins. It represents the element earth and psychologically the sensation function, which deals with physical reality. Because it was originally called coins and deals with the material world, the cards in this suit often speak about matters of money. On the right, we find the Eight of Pentacles with a depiction of a metalsmith, who, through his discipline and skill, is literally creating wealth.

On the left we find the Six of Pentacles on which a wealthy merchant uses a scale to weigh out money and distribute it to the poor. The message suggested by this image is close to that of the fifteenth hexagram of the Chinese oracle, the I Ching. The hexagram is titled Modesty, and the commentary for it contains the following words:

> High mountains are worn down by the waters, and the valleys are filled up. It is the law of fate to undermine what is full and to prosper the modest. . . . The superior man does the same thing when he establishes order in the world; he equalizes the extremes that are the source of social discontent and thereby creates just and equable conditions.[3]

These three cards together are saying that the virtue Temperance is the source of the discipline necessary for creating wealth and of the generosity of spirit necessary for distributing and maintaining it.

Figure 131. The central destination pattern

Four—The Central Destination

Figure 131 depicts the pattern called the central destination in which the action starts at both ends and converges in the middle. On the left we find the Empress, a figure of sensuality and authority, seated on a throne in the midst of earthly abundance. On the right we find the Fool, a gaily attired young man with a dog at his feet, strolling along with his head high and seemingly unaware of the precipice immediately ahead of him. He seems to be an idealist following his dreams and unaware of practical concerns. They are both facing toward the Two of Cups in the center. The suit of cups symbolizes water. Psychologically it refers to the intuitive function, where we are in touch with feelings and ideas emerging from the unconscious. On the central card we find a male and a female figure, both of whom bear some resemblance to their counterparts to either side. The couple on the Two of Cups looks into each other's eyes as they hold up their goblets and pledge devotion to each other. From their union the caduceus emerges surmounted by the winged head of a lion, a solar symbol.

The caduceus is the staff of the god Hermes. In mythology, Hermes was given the staff by Zeus as a sign that he was the herald of the gods. The caduceus was said to have magical powers to heal and bring peace. One day while Hermes was on an errand, he came across two serpents fighting. Perhaps to test the powers of his staff, he thrust it between the intertwined snakes. They immediately ceased their combat and affixed themselves to the staff, alternating, each to an op-

Figure 132. The central problem pattern

posite side, as they spiraled up the staff in perfect balance. With the serpents on either side, the caduceus became a symbol of the Axis Mundi, the mystical center of the world and the elixir of life.

Together these three cards speak about love between a well-situated woman and a carefree, idealistic man. With the caduceus in the center, these two seem well matched. From their union peace and harmony should emerge. They seem to satisfy an unconscious need in each other. If these cards were in answer to a request for advice about a possible mate, then this would be a welcome go-ahead from the higher self. The same cards, however, may at another time be speaking metaphorically or they may be saying that if one wants to live a carefree life following one's inspiration, it is good to be married to wealth. Conversely, it may be saying that if one is wealthy one should use this advantage to follow one's ideals.

Five—The Central Problem

In figure 132, we find the same two outer cards as in figure 131, but here the central card is the Five of Cups with its black-cloaked, brooding figure blocking the Fool from reaching his love interest. This is the central problem pattern in which the flow of energy is stopped.

On the Five of Cups, there is a depiction of a man in a black cape hanging his head sorrowfully as he contemplates three spilled cups. Two cups remain upright at his back. In the background, there is a bridge leading over a river toward a castle. Visually the black cape turns the man into a monolithic slab of inactivity.

He contemplates what he has lost but seems unaware of what he still has. The bridge suggests a journey, the castle a destination, but the man is frozen in his somber contemplation, unable to continue.

By combining this card with the Empress and the Fool we now have a different story from the one in our last example. Here as before, the Fool seems to be progressing toward the attractive and wealthy Empress. This time, however, before he can attain the object of his desire, it is necessary for him to make some sacrifices. Perhaps he is required to act more responsibly, to consult the Empress about his plans instead of spontaneously going wherever his whims carry him. Whatever the sacrifice, the Fool finds it is too much to bear. He loses sight of what he will be gaining and is unable to progress. If our querent is the Fool, this would be a good time to ask the Higher Self what the best course of action would be. Again, depending on the question asked, the cards may be speaking metaphorically. They may be saying that the quality of spontaneity that we value so highly is also our flaw in that it stops us from making a commitment and creating prosperity.

Six—The Central Teacher

At first glance figure 133 seems to be an example of the central origin pattern. However, on closer examination, we find that the charioteer in the center has two sphinxes on either side of himself, one white and active and the other black and passive. These can be thought of as a comment on the two cards to either side of the Chariot, and with that insight, we see that the pattern is the central teacher instead of the central origin.

The Chariot depicts a prince or perhaps someone who has completed a mystical initiation. He is well armored and prepared for a challenge. His Chariot appears to be an immovable block of stone, which suggests that he is prepared for an inner journey versus an outer one. To either side are two knights riding away from him on their individual quests. The layout suggests that the knights are an extension of the charioteer's steeds into the material world. On the right the Knight of Cups proceeds slowly, holding his cup before him as if he were on quest for sustenance or spiritual fulfillment. On the left the Knight of Swords charges ahead in a quest for battle. His is an extraverted quest to slay monsters and conquer the evil he finds in the world.

Notice that the active sphinx is on the right with the passive introverted knight and that the passive sphinx is on the left with the active extraverted knight. This layout is telling us that to gain spiritual strength and courage we need to spend less energy finding evil in the world—criticizing others—and use more of our resources to find guidance and sustenance from within.

Figure 133. The central teacher pattern

FURTHER EXERCISES

Now that we have reviewed the six patterns, lay out the same cards that are illustrated in this chapter and see what happens when you change one of them. Next, create the six patterns for yourself with alternative cards. Another useful exercise is to predetermine a statement that you wish to make and find three cards that express that meaning. If you continue to play with your deck in this fashion, in a few days you will become accustomed to the visual language of the deck, and will be ready to use the deck as a tool for communicating with the Higher Self.

If you are a beginner at reading the Tarot you may find it useful to ask the Higher Self for guidance in reading the cards. For your first reading simply ask, "What do I need to know about reading the Tarot?" When you start handling life questions, read for yourself or someone close to you and about situations that you know about. In this way, you can see how the cards handle familiar information.

Next we will learn how to use the three-card message to build more complex readings and handle the kind of life situations that call for inner guidance.

THE RELATIONSHIP SPREAD

The Relationship Spread is a useful reading for analyzing a situation and giving advice. It deals with a specific question and brings it into focus. It can be applied to relationships between two persons, or between a person and a job, home, fambridge

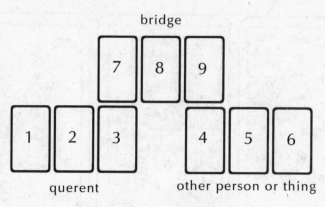

querent   other person or thing

Figure 134. The relationship spread

ily, culture, city, or other environment. It can be a health reading showing the relationship between the querent's mind and body. It not only gets to the heart of a
situation but it can be used creatively to solve problems. As most people go to a
card reader to obtain advice on their love life or career and this reading deals easily with either subject, this is the reading that I use most often.

Start by letting the querent shuffle and cut as before. On the left, lay out the
first line of three cards. These represent the querent. Put the remaining cards back
in a stack and let the querent cut again. Now skip a space, and on the right lay out
the second line of three cards, which represent the other party in the relationship—a person, a job, or something else. If you feel that the three cards representing the other party belong to the left of the querent instead of the right, then
follow your intuition, or you may lay out the first three and ask the querent on
which side the other three should go. On top, after letting the querent cut again,
place a third line of three cards bridging the gap between the two sides. The first
will be over the last card of the group on the left, the second will be over the gap,
and the third will be over the first card on the right, as illustrated in figure 134.
This will represent the relationship itself, and reveals the dynamics at work. This
reading can also be done for two people at the same time, if their relationship is
the subject. In that situation, ask each querent to shuffle and cut for the three
cards that represent him or her. The card reader may shuffle and cut to obtain the
three cards for the bridge.

Look at all three lines to see a whole picture and observe the energy patterns.
Then use the story approach to read each line of the three as one picture. It is
helpful to notice how each side's cards change as they approach each other—from
the outside into the center. Once you have analyzed the relationship, you can replace the bridge with three additional cards to show where the relationship is

Figure 135. A relationship spread analyzing a romantic relationship

likely to be heading in the future or you may ask the Higher Self for three cards that represent the best that can be achieved in this relationship. You can also expand on or underline any ambiguous cards or cards that need more details for their story to unfold. With all readings always end with three additional cards of advice from the Higher Self. Again, it is best to practice this reading on yourself and your own relationships before doing it for others.

Figure 135 is an example of the relationship spread. In this example, the cards on the left represent a male querent. The relationship is with a woman, in whom the querent has a romantic interest. He had met her at work and is contemplating asking her out on a date. She is represented on the right. When we first look at the spread, we can see that although not all of the cards are consistent in their direction, there is a general directional pattern suggesting that there is a coming together of the two subjects. If the directional patterns for the two parties were aiming in opposite directions, it would show a weak relationship. If all of the cards were headed left or right it would show that one party is dominant in this relationship. Here there is a good chance that each party will be interested in the other and that there will be a giving and taking on both sides of the relationship.

Starting on the far left, the Three of Cups suggests that the querent first became interested in the woman at a festive occasion. Perhaps it was an office party or perhaps when he interacts with her at work he likes to joke and creates a more festive mood in the office. It seems that the woman is drawn into his mood, which is why he feels that she may be interested in him. The next card, the Six of Cups, depicts childlike innocence. In the ancient world, six was associated with Aphrodite, the goddess of love, and, as if expressing the goddess's influence, the boy on the card lovingly offers flowers to the girl. It seems that the querent has developed a boyish infatuation for the woman and is moving in her direction. The third card, the Three of Wands, represents fire and passion. The man is reaching out in the direction of the woman and contemplating setting his ships sailing, in other words, asking her on a date. He is not, however, actually looking in the direction of the woman's cards, and the ships are sailing in the opposite direction. This suggests that at this point the date is a fantasy in his mind and that he, as yet, does not know the real woman.

On the woman's side, on the far right, the Page of Swords suggests that the woman is usually focused on her job and intellectual challenges when she is at work. The page's head is turning, however, in the direction of the querent, which indicates that he has captured her attention. The Page of Cups indicates that she welcomes the querent's festive interaction, and the Eight Wands landing in her direction say that she is expecting him to ask her out.

On the bridge, we see the Knight of Pentacles coming in from the querent's side. He is contemplating offering a pentacle. This represents something physical and tangible. In this case, it is a definite date with a time and a destination. The Ace of Pentacles is the date being offered. Aces are the start of something and this is a good card to have in this location. It suggests that this action will blossom into something bigger. The Knight of Wands on the woman's side suggests that she is looking for the offer and is likely to accept. The bridge is projecting slightly into the future and it shows where the activity is heading. However, this is not a prediction of the future. The querent may decide not to ask the woman out. This reading only shows the likely outcome of one course of action. The bridge could also be only about the present or we could choose to replace it with a projection of what this event is likely to lead to in the more distant future. Again this would only be a projection based on a course of action. If the action is changed the outcome will change. In fact, we may ask the Higher Self for advice on actions that may improve the situation. In any case, it is wise to end with advice from the Higher Self.

Figure 136 depicts three additional cards that were drawn for advice. The Eight of Cups on the right depicts the man leaving this situation behind—the cups are undisturbed—and going on his way. The man on the Two of Wands in the center turns his back on that prospect and embraces the challenge with confidence. This is the recommended action. The Seven of Swords suggests that by asking the woman on a date the querent will steal a prize. Perhaps there are others interested in the same woman and the Higher Self is recommending that the querent act quickly.

Figure 136. Three cards of advice

Next we will learn some more complicated spreads that will give insight into the querent's psyche and that can be used therapeutically. Again it is best to do these for oneself at first and become familiar with reading the spread before attempting to analyze another person. We will not use a specific example but the cards should be read in the same way as the three-card message spreads illustrated above.

THE SEVEN SOUL CENTERS READING

Although many people think of the seven soul centers or chakras as a mystical system that the West has adopted from India, there is evidence that the seven soul centers were known to the ancient Pythagoreans and they have been part of Western culture for centuries. In the ancient world, the seven soul centers were related to the Neoplatonic ladder of the planets that we discussed in Chapter Three (see figure 19 on page 94). In modern Western culture, we have merged the ancient Western concepts about the soul centers with Asian teachings on the chakras. In our modern conception, the soul centers and chakras have been synthesized into one system. The soul centers or chakras are thought of as seven energy centers located in ascending order from the base of the spine to the top of the cranium. They may be blocked or flowing freely and their proper functioning is necessary for psychic and physical health.

This reading gives us a picture of what is happening in the querent's soul. Just seeing the energy patterns in these centers is healing. But we can go a step further and with additional cards suggest changes in behavior that will begin to

7. Crown	20	7	21	cosmic mind destiny
6. Head	18	6	19	thinking intuition
5. Throat	16	5	17	self-expression communication
4. Heart	14	4	15	relationships love
3. Solar Plexus	12	3	13	self-idenity ego
2. Genitals	10	2	11	individual mind desire
1. Sacrum	8	1	9	group mind survival

Figure 137. The seven soul centers spread

dissolve blocks. The spread always gives a picture of the soul at the moment of the reading. The picture should not be considered the permanent state of the soul centers. Even if one were to do a reading immediately after completing the first, there would be changes, possibly caused by the first reading. The possibilities for therapy that this reading offers would merit a book of its own. Here we can only introduce the subject. Further knowledge can be gained form reading various books on chakra therapy.

Start, as before, by having the querent shuffle and cut with the left hand. After a block of cards is removed draw from the top of the remaining block and lay out seven cards in a column from the bottom up, as indicated by the numbers on the cards in figure 137. As you lay down the cards, describe each soul center for the querent. This is just a description of each center and what energies are associated with it, without any attempt to analyze what is happening there. Analysis will come later when we lay down the cards that flank this central column. Here is a list of each soul center and its associations. The names are given in English based on the Latin names for these centers. The names tend to describe the part of the body where the center is found.

1. **Sacrum:** This center is located at the base of the spine, which is called the sacrum. It is interesting to note that the modern name for these bones, *sacrum,* is Latin for "sacred." This is the group or tribal mind. It is the first part of the psyche that is developed in an infant. This center deals with issues of survival and self-preservation and is important for physical health and prosperity. Here we may find patterns that tell us about the childhood of the querent. At first, we are dependent on our parents, our family, and our culture, and try to conform, and those conservative patterns, or patterns that stem from the rejection of conservative values, are found here. The more conservative and the less individuated the querent is, the more influence this area has on the other chakras.

2. **Genitals:** This center is located on the spine at the level of the genitals. This is the area of desire, not just sexual desire but all desires—comfort, wealth, respect, and so on. Plato said that there was a connection between the mind and the genitals and that vital force could be directed in either direction. The ancients believed that this is why the genitals seem to have a mind of their own. It is desire that pulls one out of the group mind and helps one to become an individual, and this is where we begin to define our individuality. It contains patterns that show how one goes about satisfying desire. Often these patterns were formed in adolescence. This area is important for our emotional well-being and for developing the ability to find pleasure.

3. **Solar plexus:** This center is located on the spine at the level of the upper abdomen. This is where we digest our food and begin to create our body and this is where we create our self-identity. Plato believed that this was the location of the soul of appetite. In modern psychological terms, it is the center of one's ego. This center is fully developed in young adulthood. The patterns here describe the querent's will, self-esteem, and power. We will find patterns that indicate if the querent is weak and shy, dominating and aggressive, or self-confident with a good self-image and a sense of humor. A healthy ego is a necessary stage of development and allows one to progress to higher states of consciousness. Blocking the development of the ego is not the same thing as overcoming egotism. Although enlightenment is described as letting go of the ego one must first have an ego in order to let go of it.

4. **Heart:** This center is located on the spine at the level of the heart. This is the area of true maturity where we go beyond thinking only about ourselves and develop compassion. Plato believed that it was the location of the soul of will.

The heart is where we interact with the world and others. It is the center of feeling, which is not emotion but something deeper—a deep decision-making function where our values are created. The heart is of central importance to the whole system. It allows the energy from the sacrum to rise to the crown, the energy from the crown to descend to the sacrum, and it allows one's energy to interact with the energy of the others. The heart is the door. We may find patterns here that depict jealously, shyness, love, grief, empathy, or courage.

5. **Throat:** This center in located in the cervical vertebrae of the neck. This is the center of self-expression and communication. Plato believed that the throat was the boundary between the higher soul and the lower souls associated with the body and desire. This center has to do with our occupation, creativity, and ability to speak. The centers above the heart tend to mirror the centers below the heart. The throat center relates to that of the solar plexus. A healthy ego supports eloquence and creative expression. A negative self-image will lead to the inability to speak or to express our emotions or may lead us into a stifling job. What we do for a living and how we express ourselves will also affect our self-image. We may find patterns here of shyness or excessive talking, an energy block, or artistic ability and free expression.

6. **Head:** In the Vedic system, this center is thought of as the third eye and located in the center of the brow, but in Western Platonic thought, it is the head and the brain. Plato placed the soul of reason here. It is the center of thinking and intuition. This is where we develop our perception and philosophy and make decisions. I have found that thinking is a product of the energy rising up from the lower centers. It parallels the desires of the genitals and seeks ways of fulfilling these desires or it can go beyond thinking about hopes and fears and allow this energy to ascend to the crown, its ultimate goal. Intuition stems from the energy that comes down from the crown. It is a message from the Higher Self and can help to clarify our thoughts. This energy wants to descend to the sacrum and manifest in physical reality. In this area we may find patterns of obsession, delusion, or denial, or clear-sightedness, intelligence, imagination, and intuition.

7. **Crown:** The crown is located at the top of the cranium. But this center is actually the place where the system opens beyond the body to the psychic energy of the cosmos and transforms this energy into the individual personality. It pairs the tribal group of the sacrum center with the universal collective of the unconscious. This is where we are in contact with the Higher Self. When this

center is fully awakened the experience is compared to internal sunlight, which is why the experience is called enlightenment. Just as the patterns that are found in the sacrum have to do with the past, the patterns found in the crown have to do with the future. This is advice from the Higher Self about the direction we should take. We may call it destiny. We do not have to listen to the advice or proceed in that direction, but life will be easier if we do.

This reading is like a picture of what is happening in the querent's soul. There is also a psychic connection between this picture and the actual energies in the querent's soul centers. At this point, pass your left palm over the cards, keeping it about two inches above the surface. Repeat this process as many times as necessary to allow yourself to become sensitized to the energy in the cards. With practice this will become easier. When you are sensitized, you will notice a flow of energy in the cards. Over certain cards you may feel a large mass of energy or a hot spot. This area may feel spongy or slow up your hand. In other places we may feel a depression or a cold spot and other areas may seem slippery or free flowing. Once you have done this you may invite the querent to do the same and share his or her impressions. I have found that every time I have done this, the querent was able to feel something and it almost always was the same as what I felt.

Ideally the energy in the centers should be free flowing and unobstructed. The energy from the base wants to liberate itself in the crown and the energy in the crown wants to manifest in the base. At the heart there should be a free flow with the hearts of others. When this is the case we have health, confidence, and creativity. This, however, is almost never totally the way we will find the energies in the reading. When we hold on to certain patterns of thought and behavior, we create blocks in our psyche and this creates thick or hot spots where the energy is being hoarded, and thin or cool spots in the areas that are being starved of energy. Our job as a healer is to help dissolve these blocks and to promote the flow of energy.

To complete the layout, have the querent shuffle the cards again and cut. Lay out cards to the left and the right of the card at the base of the column, as indicated in figure 137. Replace the block of cards that was removed from the top of the deck back to the other block of cards and ask the querent to cut again. Now lay cards to the left and the right of the second card of the column. Repeat this process until the entire layout is complete.

Each section of the column can be read as a three-card message that will give information about the energy patterns and behavior that are held in each soul center. Pay special attention to the thick or hot spots that you discovered earlier. The reading will tell you what preconceptions or false expectations are causing this blockage. They may be the result of positive expectations as well as negative. Also give special attention to the advice from the Higher Self in the crown.

After all of the chakras have been discussed and the querent has absorbed the information, it is time to work creatively with the energy blockages. Have the querent shuffle the remaining cards while asking the Higher Self how he or she may heal the area in question. When the querent cuts, place three cards directly over the three cards representing the blocked center so that the original cards are covered by the new cards and are now out of sight. Again read this new section as a three-card message. Repeat this with any problem areas. I have found that often problems in the sacrum create other problems in the chakras above. Therefore it is a good idea to work on the sacrum no matter where problems show up. As in all readings, it is also a good idea to finish with three cards of advice.

THE TWELVE-HOUSE READING

This is another reading designed for analyzing what is happening in the querent's psyche, but here an astrological model is used instead of the soul centers. In astrology, the houses are twelve divisions of a person's personality or psyche that deal with twelve different aspects of life. An astrological chart is divided into twelve sections representing these aspects and then signs of the zodiac and planets are placed within the houses to provide information on each aspect. In this reading we will use the cards to replace the signs and planets in the chart. As this spread may use seventy-two or more cards it will be useful to do it with two decks, one deck for the description of each house and another deck for the three cards of advice for each house.

Starting on the left with the first house, shuffle, cut, and lay out three cards to represent the house. Then proceed as in figure 138 to lay out three cards for each of the houses. Starting with the first house, proceed in a circle in a counterclockwise direction until the cards for the twelfth house are placed directly above the cards representing the first. When all of the houses are laid out, each can be read to gain insight into how this aspect of the querent's life is manifesting. Then the querent should shuffle while asking the Higher Self for advice on how to improve any aspect that needs development or redirection. The deck should be cut and three more cards can be placed on top of the ones for each house for which the advice is needed. One may desire to gain advice for every house but it would be best to use a second deck for the advice if this is the case. Read the advice cards as before. A study of astrology is helpful for those who would like to go deeper

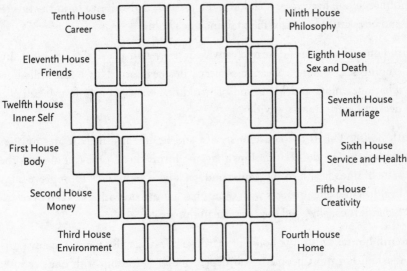

Figure 138. The twelve-house reading

into this subject. Here is a list of each house with a discussion of the aspects that each one represents.

First house: This is the house of the body and of the self. It refers to one's relationship with one's body, self-image, and mannerisms, as well as one's likes and dislikes. This house can also depict one's goals in life. It is helpful for learning how we present ourselves to the world and how the world perceives us. Self-image underlies all of the other aspects and colors the entire reading.

Second house: This is the house of money and possessions. It concerns what one owns, earning power, and one's relationship to money and finance. This house can provide useful information about what endeavors may be lucrative for the querent. If there is a problem, be sure to get advice.

Third house: This is the house of environment. It deals with family ties and early education. It can give insight into one's relationship with one's parents, sisters, and brothers. It also deals with travel, especially to work. As much of our modern environment is filled with machines, this house can also show our relationship with machines.

Fourth house: This house symbolizes home life, including matters of family, ancestry, inheritance, and tradition. Here we can find out about one's relationship to one's family in the present as well as the past. It also deals with the type of home one lived in as a child, at the present, and will live in in the future, and one's attitude toward maintaining one's home.

Fifth house: This is the house of creativity. It deals with all the aspects of love, including sex, children, creative projects, business, art. This house will show what one enjoys and what kind of world one wants to manifest. It can also deal with parties and festivities.

Sixth house: This is the house of service and health. It usually relates to one's workplace and the relationships that one forms there. One can also see the state of one's health in this house and get advice about how to improve one's health. How one interacts with others has a lot to do with one's ego development. It is usually good to get advice in this area.

Seventh house: This is the house of marriage but it can also pertain to any partnership. For most people it will depict one's relationship with one's spouse. Here we can see the querent's ability to harmonize with others and we can get advice about how to improve relationships. Advice is recommended because it is not always easy to know what one's partner values, and the cards can help.

Eighth house: This is the house of sex and death. As we learned in the earlier chapters, sex and death are deeply connected to the mystical quest. Death represents endings, and if the life energy or sexual energy is strong, one has the power to overcome endings with new beginnings. This is called regeneration. Ultimately the mystic learns to overcome mortality itself by ceasing to identify with what is temporary. This house can depict where one stands in relationship to desire and loss but it can also show one's psychic ability.

Ninth house: This is the house of philosophy. It depicts the querent's mental exploration and higher education. It may also depict foreign travel and the ability to speak another language. This house can be thought of as the higher aspect of themes that were introduced in the third house.

Tenth house: This house deals with career. It has to do with how one lives in the world outside of the home and we should compare this house to the fourth to see if there is a healthy balance between home and work in the querent's life. This house can represent ambition and show one what others respect about her or him.

Eleventh house: This is the house of friendship but it is also depicts one's hopes and fears. It may show how the querent relates to groups and professional or political organizations. The friends depicted here are ones who can help further one's ambitions or dreams.

Twelfth house: This is the house of the inner self. This is the secret self that one does not often share with others. This house can depict sorrows and limitations. We might call it the house of karma. But it is also a spiritual house that can represent our psychic gifts and rewards.

MEDITATION

*Their symbols—or at least some among them—were gates which
opened on realms of vision beyond occult dreams.*

—A. E WAITE, *SHADOWS OF LIFE AND THOUGHT*

The images in the Tarot are connected to an ancient tradition of magical art that was designed for meditation, and this is one of the best ways to make use of the Tarot. As Waite suggested, the Tarot images are capable of unlocking experiences in our psyche that are powerful and transformative. As we progress through the trumps in meditation, we are initiated into the true mystery tradition that is contained in the Tarot.

Pick a card whose symbolism you wish to enter into more deeply. Find a safe comfortable room where you will not be disturbed. Sit with your back straight and upright on a pillow on the floor or in a chair that does not cause you to slouch. Now pay attention to your breath until you find yourself breathing deeply and rhythmically from your abdomen. This may take some time at first. In this relaxed state, take the card and place it in front of you in a way that makes it easy to gaze on it. Now simply look at it without attaching any thoughts to it. Thoughts will naturally arise, but let go of each one as they do, watch them drift away, and then return to looking at the card. Begin to hold the image of the card in your mind. Visualize the border of the card as a doorframe, and the colored rectangle as a painting on a door. Visualize a handle on the door, reach out and grasp the handle, open the door and picture yourself walking through the doorway.

Look around. If you see darkness, look into it and wait—be patient. Feel free to allow yourself to interact with whatever images arise. The vision will come to a natural conclusion. When you are done, you may want to write your experience down.

To perform the entire initiation, meditate on the Fool and each trump consecutively. This is the Fool's Journey. It is best not to work on more than one in a day.

Figure 139. Final advice

A FINAL READING

Now that I have completed this book I asked the Tarot for some final advice that would help my readers when using the Tarot. The result is depicted in figure 139. The three cards, the Lovers, Death, and Temperance, with the central figure strongly carrying the energy from the left to the right, can be read as a linear pattern starting on the left. It says that the initial love and enthusiasm that one has for the Tarot will eventually come to an end—a death. To go beyond this initial infatuation and learn the Tarot, one needs regular and continuous practice. It has to become a comfortable part of one's daily life as represented by the activity of Temperance. Temperance will lead to a deeper love, and eventually to mastery.

NOTES

CHAPTER 1: Tꞑe Hꞁstꝋꝛy ꝋf tꞑe Tꝋꝛꝋt

1. Dummett, Michael, "Tarot Triumphant," *FMR/America,* no. 8, Franco Maria Ricci International, New York: 1985, page 50.
2. *Microsoft® Encarta® Encyclopedia,* see under "Paper."
3. The information on Chinese cards in this section is derived from W. H. Wilkinson, *The American Anthropologist,* vol. 8, January 1895, pages 61–78.
4. Kaplan, Stuart R., *The Encyclopedia of Tarot,* vol. 1, U. S. Games Systems, Inc., New York: 1978, page 53.
5. Ibid., page 24.
6. Kaplan, Stuart R., *The Encyclopedia of Tarot,* vol. 2, U. S. Games Systems, Inc., New York: 1986, page 1.
7. Kaplan, Stuart R., 1978, page 345.
8. Dummett, Michael, *The Visconti-Sforza Tarot Cards,* George Braziller, Inc., New York: 1986, pages 3–4.
9. Decker, Ronald and Michael Dummett, *A History of the Occult Tarot 1870–1970,* Duckworth, London: 2002, page ix.
10. This information is from Franco Pratesi, "Italian Cards—New Discoveries: The Earliest Tarot Pack Known" in *The Playing Card,* vol. 18, no. 1, August 1989, and continued in the following issue, September 1989.
11. Dummett, Michael, 1986, page 6.
12. Ibid., page 5.
13. Kaplan, Stuart R., 1986, page 3.
14. Ibid., page 11.
15. Moakley, Gertrude, *The Tarot Cards Painted by Bonifacio Bembo for the Visconti-Sforza Family an Iconographic and Historic Study,* New York Public Library, New York: 1966, page 37.
16. Dummett, Michael, 1985, page 46.
17. Dummett, 1986, page 9.
18. Kaplan, 1986, pages 8–9.
19. Opsopaus, John, *Guide to the Pythagorean Tarot,* Llewellyn Publications, St. Paul: 2001, pages 21–22.

CHAPTER 2: The Mythical History of the Tarot

1. The historic facts about Court de Gébelin's life in this chapter are derived from Chapter Three in Ronald Decker, Thierry Depaulis, and Michael Dummett, *A Wicked Pack of Cards: The Origins of the Occult Tarot*. New York: St. Martins Press: 1996.

2. Ibid., page 58.

3. Ibid., page 57.

4. Kaplan, Stuart, *Tarot Classic*, U. S. Games, Inc., Stamford, CT: 1972, page 38.

5. Decker, Depaulis, and Dummett, page 62.

6. Budge, E. A. Wallis, *Egyptian Magic*, Dover Publications, New York: 1971, page 165.

7. These illustrations from *Monde Primitif* in figures 2, 3, 4 , 6, 7, and 8 are used with the permission of William M. Voelkle.

8. Hornblower, Simon and Anthony Spawforth, editors, *The Oxford Classical Dictionary*, Third Edition, Oxford University Press, New York: 1996, page 691.

9. Scott, Walter, *Hermetica*, Shambala, Boston: 1985, page 123.

10. Ibid., page 123.

11. Yates, Frances A., *The Art of Memory*, Pimlico, London: 1999, page 151.

12. Scott, page 127.

13. This list is based on Faivre, Antoine, "Renaissance Hermeticism and the Concept of Western Esotericism," found on pages 199–120 in van den Broek, Roelof and Wouter J. Hanegraaff, editors; *Gnosis and Hermeticism: From Antiquity to Modern Times*, State University of New York Press, Albany: 1998.

14. The historic facts about Etteilla's life in this section are derived from Chapter Four in Ronald Decker, Thierry Depaulis, and Michael Dummett, *A Wicked Pack of Cards: The Origins of the Occult Tarot*.

15. Decker, Depaulis, and Dummett, page 88.

16. This information is drawn from an unpublished essay by Ronald Decker titled "The New Etteilla."

17. O'Neill, Robert V., *Tarot Symbolism*, Fairway Press, Lima, Ohio: 1986, page 234.

18. *The Oxford Classical Dictionary*, Third Edition, Oxford University Press, Oxford: 1996, page 1,391.

19. Barry, Kieren, *The Greek Qabalah*, Samuel Weiser, York Beach, Maine: 1999, page 180.

20. The historic facts about Eliphas Levi's life in this chapter are derived from Chapter Eight in Decker, Depaulis, and Dummett.

21. Levi, Eliphas, translated by Waite, A. E., *Transcendental Magic; Its Doctrine and Ritual*, Samuel Weiser, Inc., New York: 1970, page 10.

22. Ibid., page 103.

23. This illustration is found on page 56 of Levi and is used with the permission of Samuel Weiser Inc.

24. Levi, footnote 1, page 382.

25. This illustration is found on page 389 of Levi and is used with the permission of Samuel Weiser Inc.

26. This illustration is found on page 186 of Levi and is used with the permission of Samuel Weiser Inc.

27. Levi, page 394.

28. Decker, Depaulis, and Dummett, page 157.

29. Ibid., pages 205–206.

30. Decker, Ronald and Michael Dummett, *The Occult Tarot,* Duckworth, London: 2002; page 53.

31. Ibid., page 76.

32. Ibid., page 86.

33. Regardie, Israel, *The Golden Dawn,* Llewellyn Publications, St. Paul: 1995, page 542.

CHAPTER 3: The search for meaning

1. Honderich, Ted, editor, *The Oxford Companion to Philosophy,* Oxford University Press, New York: 1995, page 613.

2. Fideler, David, editor, Kenneth Sylvan Guthrie, translator, *The Pythagorean Sourcebook and Library,* Phanes Press, Grand Rapids, Michigan: 1988, page 307.

3. Dummett, Michael, "Tarot Triumphant," *FMR/America,* no. 8, Franco Maria Ricci International, New York: 1985, page 46.

4. De Botton, Alain, *The Essential Plato,* Quality Paperback Book Club, New York: 1999, page 361.

5. Hornblower, Simon, and Anthony Spawforth, editors, *The Oxford Classical Dictionary,* Third Edition, Oxford University Press, New York: 1996, pages 186–87.

6. De Botton, page 375.

7. Pegis, Anton C., editor, *Introduction to Saint Thomas Aquinas,* The Modern Library, New York: 1948, page 589.

8. Hall, James, *A History of Ideas and Images in Italian Art,* Harper & Row, New York: 1983, page 21.

9. Ibid., page 230.

10. Burckhardt, Jacob, *The Civilization of the Renaissance in Italy,* vol. 2, Harper & Row, New York: 1958, page 411.

11. The quotes from *I Trionfi* in this chapter are from: Kaplan, Stuart R., *The Encyclopedia of Tarot,* vol. 2, U. S. Games Systems, Inc., New York: 1986, pages 142–47.

12. This image is an edited version of Brueghel's *Triumph of Time* found in Klein, Arthur H., *Graphic Worlds of Peter Bruegel the Elder,* Dover Publications, New York: 1963, page 177.

13. Shakespeare, William, *Four Tragedies by William Shakespeare,* Washington Square Press, New York: 1961, page 417.

14. This illustration is reproduced from Kieren Barry, *The Greek Qabalah,* Samuel Weiser, York Beach, Maine: 1999, page 80.

CHAPTER 4: Interpreting the Major and Minor Arcana

1. Moakley, Gertrude, *The Tarot Cards Painted by Bonifacio Bembo,* The New York Public Library, New York: 1966, page 72.
2. This illustration is from Linda Fierz-David, *The Dream of Poliphilo: The Soul in Love,* Spring Publications and Princeton University Press, New York: 1987, page 192.
3. This illustration is from Stanislas Klossowski de Rola, *The Golden Game: Alchemical Engravings of the Seventeenth Century,* George Braziller, Inc. New York: 1988, page 94.
4. Pegis, Anton C., editor, *Introduction to Saint Thomas Aquinas,* The Modern Library, New York: 1948, page 563.
5. Thomson, Leslie, *Fortune: All Is but Fortune,* The Folger Shakespeare Library, Washington: 2000, page 15.
6. Ficino, Marsilio; Jayne Sears, translator, *Commentary on Plato's Symposium on Love,* Spring Publications, Woodstock, Connecticut: 1985, page 13.
7. This illustration is from Gundersheimer, Werner L., *The Dance of Death,* by Hans Holbein the Younger, Dover Publications, New York: 1971, page 29.
8. This illustration is from Ernst and Johanna Lehner, *Devils, Demons, Death, and Damnation,* Dover Publications, New York: 1971, frontispiece.
9. Menestrier, C.-F. *Bibliothèque Curieuse et Instructive de Divers Ouvrages, Anciens et Modernes, de Litterature et des Arts,* 2 vols.; Trevoux: 1704, vol II, pages 175–176.
10. This information is derived from an unpublished paper by Ronald Decker titled *From Alliette to Etteilla.*
11. The information in this list is based on C. G. Jung, *Psychological Types,* Princeton University Press, Princeton: 1990, pages 330–408.

CHAPTER 5: The Waite-Smith Tarot

1. The facts of Waite's life are derived from his memoirs: Waite, Arthur Edward, *Shadows of Life and Thought,* Kessinger Publishing; and from Decker, Ronald and Michael Dummett, *The Occult Tarot;* Duckworth, London: 2002; pages 120–123.
2. Waite, Arthur Edward, *The Pictorial Key to the Tarot,* Harper and Row, New York: 1971, page 42.
3. Ibid., pages 4–5.
4. The facts of Smith's life are derived from Kaplan, Stuart R., *The Encyclopedia of Tarot,* vol. 3, U. S. Games Systems, Inc., New York: 1990, pages 1–45.
5. Greer, Mary K., *Women of the Golden Dawn: Rebels and Priestesses,* Park Street Press, Rochester, Vermont: 1995, page 406.
6. Waite, Arthur Edward, *Shadows of Life and Thought,* page 184.
7. Kaplan, 1990, pages 29–30.
8. Waite, *Shadows,* page 185.
9. Kaplan, 1990; pages 30–33.

10. Waite; 1971, pages 160–161.
11. Greer, page 405.
12. Kaplan, 1990, page 30.
13. Guiley, Rosemary Ellen, *The Mystical Tarot*; Signet, New York: 1991, page 38.
14. Decker, Dummett, pages 140–141.
15. Waite, 1971, page 152.
16. Decker, Dummett, page 140.
17. Historian Robert O'Neill's insights on the Waite-Smith Tarot that appear in this chapter are drawn from his article "Sources of the Waite/Smith Tarot Symbols," which appears on the Tarot Passages Web site: *www.tarotpassages.com.*
18. Regardie, Israel, *The Golden Dawn,* Llewellyn Publications, St. Paul: 1995, page 89.
19. Waite, 1971, page 76.
20. Ibid., page 80.
21. Ibid., page 96.
22. Regardie, page 81.
23. Waite, 1971, page 32.
24. Ibid., page 172.
25. Ibid., page 208.
26. Kingsley, Peter; *Reality,* The Golden Sufi Center, Inverness, California: 2003, page 45.
27. Ibid., page 242.
28. Ibid., page 266.

CHAPTER 6: Hieroglyphs from the soul

1. Kaplan, Stuart R., *The Encyclopedia of the Tarot,* vol. 2, U. S. Games, Inc., New York: 1986, pages 8–9.
2. Klossowski de Rola, Stanislas, *The Golden Game: Alchemical Engravings of the Seventeenth Century,* George Braziller, Inc., New York: 1988, page 9.
3. Baynes, Cary F., editor, and Richard Wilhelm, translator, *The I Ching: or Book of Changes;* Princeton University Press, Princeton: 1950, page 64.

BIBLIOGRAPHY

The following volumes were quoted or consulted in the preparation of this book:

Barry, Kieren. *The Greek Qabalah.* York Beach, Maine: Samuel Wiser, 1999.

Baynes, Cary F., editor, and Richard Wilhelm, translator. *The I Ching: or Book of Changes.* Princeton: Princeton University Press, 1950.

Berti, G., and A. Vitali. *Tarocchi Arte e Magia.* Bologna: Edizioni le Tarot, 1994.

Bonner, Anthony. *Doctor Illuminatus: A Ramon Llull Reader.* Princeton: Princeton University Press, 1985.

Budge, E. A. Wallis, *Egyptian Magic.* New York: Dover Publications, 1971.

Burckhardt, Jacob. *The Civilization of the Renaissance in Italy.* Vol. 2. New York: Harper & Row, 1958.

Burke, Peter. *The Italian Renaissance: Culture and Society in Italy.* Princeton: Princeton University Press, 1986.

Clark, Kenneth. *The Nude: A Study in Ideal Form.* Princeton: Princeton University Press, 1984.

De Botton, Alain. *The Essential Plato.* New York: Quality Paperback Book Club, 1999.

Decker, Ronald, and Michael Dummett. *A History of the Occult Tarot 1870–1970.* London: Duckworth, 2002.

Decker, Ronald, Thierry Depaulis, and Michael Dummett. *A Wicked Pack of Cards: The Origins of the Occult Tarot.* New York: St. Martin's Press, 1996.

Dummett, Michael. "Tarot Triumphant." In *FMR/America*, 8. New York: Franco Maria Ricci International, 1985.

Dummett, Michael. *The Visconti-Sforza Tarot Cards*. New York: George Braziller, 1986.

Eliade, Mircea. *Images and Symbols: Studies in Religious Symbolism*. Princeton: Princeton University Press, 1991.

———. *Myth and Reality*. New York: Harper & Row, 1975.

———. *The Sacred and the Profane: The Nature of Religion*, New York: Harper & Row, 1961.

Englebert, Omer. *St. Francis of Assisi: A Biography*. Ann Arbor, Mich.: Servant Books, 1965.

Ficino, Marsilio. *Commentary on Plato's Symposium on Love*. Woodstock, Vt.: Spring Publications, 1985.

Fideler, David, ed., and Kenneth Sylvan Guthrie, trans. *The Pythagorean Sourcebook and Library*. Grand Rapids, Mich.: Phanes Press, 1988.

Fideler, David. *Jesus Christ Sun of God: Ancient Cosmology and Early Christian Symbolism*. Wheaton, Ill.: Quest Books, 1993.

Fierz-David, Linda. *The Dream of Poliphilo: The Soul in Love*. New York: Spring Publications, and Princeton University Press, 1987.

Godwin, Josclyn. *The Mystery of the Seven Vowels: In Theory and Practice*. Grand Rapids, Mich.: Phanes Press, 1991.

Gombrich E. H., *Art and Illusion: A Study in the Psychology of Pictorial Representation*. New York: Princeton University Press, 1969.

Greer, Mary K. *Women of the Golden Dawn: Rebels and Priestesses*. Rochester, Vt.: Park Street Press, 1995.

Guiley, Rosemary Ellen. *The Mystical Tarot*. New York: Signet, 1991.

Gundersheimer, Werner L. *The Dance of Death by Hans Holbein the Younger*. New York: Dover Publications, 1971.

Hall, James. *Dictionary of Subjects and Symbols in Art*. London: John Murray, 1974.

———. *A History of Ideas and Images in Italian Art.* New York: Harper & Row, 1983.

Honderich, Ted, ed. *The Oxford Companion to Philosophy.* New York: Oxford University Press, 1995.

Hopper, Vincent Foster. *Medieval Number Symbolism: Its Sources, Meaning, and Influence on Thought and Expression.* New York: Dover Publications, 2000.

Hornblower, Simon, and Anthony Spawforth, eds. *The Oxford Classical Dictionary,* 3rd ed. New York: Oxford University Press, 1996.

Jung, C. G. *Psychological Types.* Bollingen Series XX. Princeton: Princeton University Press, 1971.

Kaplan, Stuart R. *The Encyclopedia of the Tarot.* Vol. 1. New York: U.S. Games, 1978.

———. *The Encyclopedia of the Tarot,* Vol. 2. New York: U.S. Games, 1986.

———. *The Encyclopedia of the Tarot,* Vol. 3. Stamford, Conn.: U.S. Games, 1990.

———. *Tarot Classic.* Stamford, Conn.: U.S. Games, 1972.

Kingsley, Peter. *In the Dark Places of Wisdom.* Inverness, Calif.: The Golden Sufi Center, 1999.

Klein, Arthur H. *Graphic Works of Peter Brueghel the Elder.* New York: Dover Publications, 1963.

Klossowski de Rola, Stanislas. *The Golden Game: Alchemical Engravings of the Seventeenth Century.* New York: George Braziller, 1988.

Lener, Ernst, and Johanna Lerner. *Devils, Demons, Death, and Damnation.* New York: Dover Publications, 1971.

Levi, Eliphas, translated by A. E. Waite. *Transcendental Magic: Its Doctrine and Ritual.* New York: Samuel Weiser, 1970.

Lull, Ramon. *Blanquerna.* London: Dedalus/Hippocrene Books, 1997.

Menestrier, C. F. *Bibliothèque Curieuse et Instructive de Divers Ouvrages, Anciens et Modernes, de Litterature et des Arts.* 2 vols. Trevoux, 1704.

Moakley, Gertrude. *The Tarot Cards Painted by Bonifacio Bembo.* New York: New York Public Library, 1966.

O'Neill, Robert. *Tarot Symbolism*. Lima, Ohio: Fairway Press, 1986.

Panofsky, Erwin. *Studies in Iconology: Humanistic Themes in the Art of the Renaissance*. New York: Harper & Row, 1972.

Pegis, Anton C., ed. *Introduction to Saint Thomas Aquinas*. New York: The Modern Library, 1948.

Regardie, Israel. *The Golden Dawn*. St. Paul, Minn.: Llewellyn, 1995.

Scott, Walter. *Hermetica,* Boston: Shambala, 1985.

Shakespeare, William. *Four Tragedies by William Shakespeare*. New York: Washington Square Press, 1961.

Thompson, Leslie. *Fortune: All Is But Fortune*. Washington, D.C.: The Folger Shakespeare Library, 2000.

van den Broek, Roelof, and Wouter J. Hanegraaff, eds. *Gnosis and Hermeticism: From Antiquity to Modern Times*. Albany: State University of New York Press, 1998.

Waite, Arthur Edward. *The Pictorial Key to the Tarot*. New York: Harper & Row, 1971.

———. *Shadows of Life and Thought*. Kila, Mont.: Kessinger Publishing, 1938.

Yates, Frances A., *The Art of Memory.* London: Pimlico, 1999.

INDEX

ABOUT THE AUTHOR

Robert M. Place is an author, artist, and Tarot expert. He is the designer, illustrator, and co-author, with Rosemary Ellen Guiley, of *The Alchemical Tarot* and *The Angels Tarot,* both of which have received international acclaim. He is the designer, illustrator, and author of *The Tarot of the Saints,* which was awarded 1st runner-up in the Sideline/Interactive category at the 2002 International New Age Trade Show. He has designed, illustrated, and authored a fourth deck and companion book, *The Buddha Tarot* and *The Buddha Tarot Companion: A Mandala of Cards.*

Place is not only an internationally acclaimed illustrator, but also an award-winning sculptor and jeweler who has worked at his craft for over twenty-five years. His sculpture has been exhibited on the White House Christmas tree, in The New York State Museum, The Delaware Art Museum, and The Irish American Heritage Museum. Place's jewelry has been exhibited in The American Craft Museum, The Philadelphia Museum of Art, The Montclair Art Museum, the International Wilhelm Muller Competition (which toured museums in Germany), Birmingham (England) Institute of Art & Design, and in numerous galleries in the United States, Ireland, Britain, and Japan. He has been awarded a New Jersey State Council on the Arts Fellowship and has twice been honored with the Niche Magazine Award for outstanding achievement in metal sculpture.

Place is a recognized expert on the Tarot and the Western mystical tradition. He has lectured regularly at the New York Open Center since 1996. He has spoken on numerous occasions at The International Tarot Congress in Chicago, the Southeast Tarot Conference in Florida, the Omega Institute, the New York Theosophical Society, and the New York Tarot Festival. He and his work have appeared on Discovery, the Learning Channel, and A&E.